Trinitarian Ontology and Israel in
Robert W. Jenson's Theology

Trinitarian Ontology and Israel in Robert W. Jenson's Theology

Sang Hoon Lee

☙PICKWICK *Publications* · Eugene, Oregon

TRINITARIAN ONTOLOGY AND ISRAEL IN ROBERT W. JENSON'S THEOLOGY

Copyright © 2016 Sang Hoon Lee. All rights reserved. Except for brief quotations in critical publications or reviews, no part of this book may be reproduced in any manner without prior written permission from the publisher. Write: Permissions, Wipf and Stock Publishers, 199 W. 8th Ave., Suite 3, Eugene, OR 97401.

Pickwick Publications
An Imprint of Wipf and Stock Publishers
199 W. 8th Ave., Suite 3
Eugene, OR 97401

www.wipfandstock.com

PAPERBACK ISBN: 978-1-4982-9464-5
HARDCOVER ISBN: 978-1-4982-9466-9
EBOOK ISBN: 978-1-4982-9465-2

Cataloguing-in-Publication data:

Names: Lee, Sang Hoon.

Title: Trinitarian ontology and Israel in Robert W. Jenson's theology | Sang Hoon Lee.

Description: Eugene, OR: Pickwick Publications, 2016 | Includes bibliographical references and index.

Identifiers: ISBN 978-1-4982-9464-5 (paperback) | ISBN 978-1-4982-9466-9 (hardcover) | ISBN 978-1-4982-9465-2 (ebook)

Subjects: LCSH: Jenson, Robert W. | Trinity | Christianity and other religions—Judaism | Theology

Classification: BT111.3 L22 2016 (print) | BT111.3 (ebook)

Manufactured in the U.S.A.   OCTOBER 31, 2016

Contents

Acknowledgments | vii
Abbreviations | ix

Introduction | 1

1. God's Decision upon His Being: Temporal Actualistic Ontology toward Post-supersessionistic Theology | 13
2. God's Bodily Being: Body Ontology toward Post-supersessionistic Theology | 33
3. God in the Jewish Flesh: Michael Wyschogrod's Theology of Israel | 59
4. The Two in the One Israelite Body: Jenson's Response to Wyschogrod | 89
5. God's Being in the Word-Torah: Hermeneutical Ontology | 119
6. God's Spirit: Eschato-pneumatological Ontology | 146

Conclusion | 173

Bibliography | 179
Author Index | 187
Subject Index | 189

Acknowledgement

Whenever I went up to Aberdeen along the Scottish east coast on the train, Dr. Donald Wood always welcomed me and offered a nice cup of coffee or tea, sometimes in a lovely refuge, *Kilau*. He allowed me to pursue my interest and encouraged me throughout, being exceedingly generous with his time. His insightful and probing interaction has been a constant inspiration. I also offer my thanks to Prof. Robert Jenson. Even though I could not have a chance to fly to Princeton to have "mutual objectification" with him, he always graciously replied to my emails and checked if my interpretation of his thinking was on the right track. Prof. Jenson is indeed a great inspiration to me. My special thanks are due to Prof. Kendall Soulen, Dr. Philip Ziegler, and Dr. Justin Stratis for their encouragement and support, and to Dr. Robin Parry for his editorial work.

My particular thank should go to Andrew Drybrough, Rev. Inki Kim, Yongjoo Kim, Jaekeun Lee, Jungwoo Lee, Sijong Lee, Heesun Park, and "This Mokjang" for their prayerful support, and to my parents, my parents-in-law, my brother Sangyoon, and my siblings-in-law for their sacrifice, love, and support beyond words. And my huge blessings, Seyoung and Hayoung, have understood and loved their daddy even when daddy had to hide himself away for work and study, and you never fail to infuse my life with joy and laughter. Finally, my deepest thanks are reserved for my wife, Moon Joung. She herself has been my tremendous comfort and help at every turn of my life. Without her encouragement and devoted companionship, I could have not come this far. She also generously listened to my talk about Jenson's theology.

Abbreviations

Works by Robert W. Jenson

AO — *Alpha and Omega: A Study in the Theology of Karl Barth.* New York: Nelson, 1963.

CC — *Canon and Creed.* Interpretation: Resources for the Use of Scripture in the Church. Louisville: Westminster John Knox, 2010.

ChrD — *Christian Dogmatics.* 2 vols. Edited by Carl E. Braaten and Robert W. Jenson. Philadelphia: Fortress, 1984.

GAG — *God After God: The God of the Past and the God of the Future, Seen in the Work of Karl Barth.* New York: Bobbs-Merrill, 1969.

KTHF — *The Knowledge of Things Hoped For: The Sense of Theological Discourse.* New York: Oxford University Press, 1969.

SP — *Story and Promise: A Brief Theology of the Gospel about Jesus.* Philadelphia: Fortress, 1973.

ST — *Systematic Theology.* 2 vols. Oxford: Oxford University Press, 1997–99.

TI — *Triune Identity.* Philadelphia: Fortress, 1982.

VW — *Visible Words: The Interpretation and Practice of Christian Sacraments.* Philadelphia: Fortress, 1978.

Works by Karl Barth

CD — Karl Barth, *Church Dogmatics.* 14 vols. Edited by Geoffrey W. Bromily and T. F. Torrance. Edinburgh: T. & T. Clark, 1936–69.

Introduction

SHOULD CHRISTIAN THEOLOGY ACKNOWLEDGE the significance of the continuing Jewish existence in the economy of God? If it ought to, what would be the biblical and theological rationale? And can it do so without diluting its christological-trinitarian faith? If Christian trinitarian theology has its own ontology, can it make room for the Jewish observance of Torah and their existence?

A towering ecumenical trinitarian theologian, Robert W. Jenson, developed a post-supersessionistic theology of Judaism in his later career, without losing his commitment to trinitarian faith. He holds that Christian trinitarian theology can ignore the covenantal significance of the Jewish existence only by putting itself in danger. Jenson's voice in modern post-supersessionism is unique and original in that his Christian faith and his trinitarian ontological formulation are not downplayed in his approach to Judaism and in that his reflection on the Jews is deeply ontological. For Jenson, doing trinitarian theology is learning to formulate a unique Christian *ontology*. His daring trinitarian ontological insights have carried forward into his ecumenical and post-supersessionistic thinking of Judaism, without blunting its force, even though it is not always explicit on the surface of his texts. Here I will attempt to make explicit the crucial links between post-supersessionism and trinitarian (onto-)theology in Jenson's theology even though these two have been considered at odd with each other for a long time.

This requires us to distinguish two ways of misreading Jenson: one seeks to explicate and analyze Jenson's trinitarian theology without reference to his recent work on the Christian theological understanding of the continuing existence of the Jews; the other seeks to reckon with his writing on Judaism without reference to its trinitarian coordinates. Thus, this book will see how Jenson advances his Christian trinitarian theo-ontology in a post-supersessionistic direction and how a post-supersessionism can be thus secured and anchored into the doctrine of the Trinity.

Readings and Studies of Jenson's Theology

As Jenson's theology is multi-layered and multi-faceted, his theology has been characterized with many epithets and labels—often unfairly.

A trinitarian theologian after Barth. Jenson's theology is legitimately regarded as a trinitarian theology after Barth, since Jenson advances Barth's decisive achievement that roots the doctrine of the incarnation in the doctrine of God.[1] For instance, Scott Swain sees Jenson as a post-Barthian, though Swain does not believe that "the way beyond Barth lies in further metaphysical revision of the church's traditional teaching about God"[2] like Jenson's project, but that it lies in retrieval of the riches from the church's tradition, which includes the doctrines of divine simplicity, immutability, and impassibility. Yet it seems that Swain's prior commitment to those doctrines already prevents him from immersing himself deeper into Jenson's thought. So, as Brad East indicates, Swain's "analyses [still] leave open the door for a defense of Jenson's metaphysical modulations."[3] In my observation, while many consider Jenson rightly as "a post-Barthian trinitarian theologian," a crucial Barthian aspect often goes unnoticed: how the Barthian insight is carried forward into Jenson's doctrine of the resurrection, as Jenson reconfigures Barth's doctrine of eternal election.[4]

Jenson is considered, among Barthian scholars, as a perceptive commentator on Barth. George Hunsinger comments on Jenson's reading of Barth as follows: Jenson captures "the real pulse of what Barth actually had to say," and "puts his finger on the true significance of Barth's particularism."[5] Yet, Hunsinger sees Jenson's interpretation as an example of how *not* to read Karl Barth since Jenson "finally misses the full import

---

1. Webster, "Systematic Theology after Barth," 256.
2. Swain, *The God of the Gospel*, 27.
3. East, "Review of Scott Swain's *The God of the Gospel: Robert Jenson's Trinitarian Theology*," 474.
4. We will see this in chapter 1.
5. Hunsinger, *How to Read Karl Barth*, 15.

of what he himself has seen."[6] In Hunsinger's analysis, Jenson's reading of Barth is "perhaps the most provocative, incisive and wrong-headed reading of Barth available in English."[7] However, recent years have seen that Bruce McCormack's reading of Barth allies with Jenson's in that both theologians read Barth as claiming that God's act of election constitutes his triune being,[8] as we will see this in chapter 1.

A Hegelian? Jenson is often awarded an epithet "Hegelian"—in my view, unfairly. Hunsinger, a major critic, says, "It is Hegel, more than any other, who determines Jenson's view of the trinity. . . . Jenson develops his trinitarian proposal within the confines of a broadly 'Hegelian' metaphysics."[9] In the same line, Francesca Murphy argues that Jenson's narrative articulation of the Trinity is inevitably Hegelian, even though, she sees, Jenson's reflection does not rise from the German idealism.[10] Even "an admirer" of Jenson, David Hart, worries that "[t]he collapse of the analogical interval between the immanent and economic Trinity"[11] is the Hegelian nature of Jenson's theology. A recent author of an expositional monograph on Jenson, Russell Rook, confirms such readings: "Jenson's position within the tradition and his subsequent treatment of time"[12] is Hegelian, even though he is aware of that Jenson is not amused by that appellation: "For Jenson, Hegel is a heretic!"[13] Against this tide, however, Stephen Wright endeavors to do justice to Jenson's own voice and sees an "anti-historical drive" in Hegel which Jenson cannot align himself with. The Hegelian "Spirit" is after all "the cancellation of all finite things in infinity."[14] Hegel is regrettably Parmenidean for Jenson.[15]

---

6. Ibid.

7. Ibid.

8. Couenhoven, "Karl Barth's Conception(s) of Human and Divine Freedom(s)," 243. For Jenson's recent commentary essay on Barth's theology, see Jenson, "Karl Barth on the Being of God," 43–51. For Jenson's recent review on a study of Barth, see "On 'The Philosophy that Attends to Scripture': Commentary on 'Karl Barth on Theology and Philosophy.'"

9. Hunsinger, "Robert Jenson's Systematic Theology," 175.

10. Murphy, *God Is Not a Story*, 18.

11. Hart, *The Beauty of the Infinite*, 165.

12. Rook, *Rhyming Hope and History*, xv.

13. Ibid., 28.

14. Stephen, *Dogmatic Aesthetics*, 116.

15. Ibid., 114.

Labeling Jenson as a Hegelian often functions to denigrate his achievement and makes it irretrievable. Such hasty readings of Jenson tend to ignore Jenson's own voice and rationale and the significant un-Hegelian features of his theology. Especially, Jenson's revisionary conception of time and eternity may appear to bear resemblance to the German philosopher. However, as I argue in chapter 6, Jenson's revisionary conception of time is the very point where he decisively diverges from the German idealism.

An apocalyptic/futuristic theologian. Jenson's theology is also deemed a "Theology of Hope," along with those of Wolfhart Pannenberg and Jürgen Moltmann, since they lay great stress on the eschatological nature of the gospel. But Jenson's futuristic ontology has been another major target of some critics,[16] even though, as Shults indicates, this controversial or tantalizing ontology seems still obscure to many readers.[17]

In Jenson's theology, this revisionary and eschatological conception of time is particularly operative in his account of the preexistence of the Son. Most critics[18] complain that in Jenson there is no personal and individual existence of the Son prior to his birth, as they fail to see Jenson's underlying thinking in that account. Jenson is still to be read with more patience and more generosity,[19] particularly, on this issue.[20]

An ecumenical theologian. Jenson is also an ecumenical theologian, as he have actively involved in Lutheran-Catholic, Lutheran-Anglican, and Lutheran-Eastern Orthodox dialogues. Recently, Jeffrey Cary devotes a chapter to Jenson's ecumenism where he notes that Jenson greatly emphasizes the visible and embodied unity of the church for a christological reason: the incarnation of Christ must be considered with full ontological seriousness and so must not be over-spiritualized.[21] We will follow this

---

16. For example, Crisp, "Robert Jenson on the Pre-Existence of Christ," 27–45; Gathercole, "Pre-existence, and the Freedom of the Son," 38–51.

17. Shults, *Reforming the Doctrine of God*, 183–85.

18. Crisp, "Robert Jenson on the Pre-Existence of Christ," 27–45; Gathercole, "Pre-existence, and the Freedom of the Son," 38–51.

19. I hope that Jenson is read with charity as Hunsinger asks others to do so with Barth's text: "The principle of charity seeks to understand a point of view in its strongest form before subjecting it to criticism" (Hunsinger, *Reading Barth with Charity*, xii).

20. Chapter 6.

21. Cary, *Free Churches and the Body of Christ*, 95.

line of Jenson's incarnational thinking as it constitutes one of the layers of his account of the church's relation to Judaism in chapters 2 and 4.

A theologian of culture. Jenson has also developed interest in culture. Russell Rook has explored appreciatively the multiple facets of Jenson's cultural theology: the body, language, music, and architecture.[22] Here I note that the first three themes are not just of culture or external to the being God in Jenson's account. So, maintaining a different perspective on those subjects, I will try to offer a more ontological account of Jenson's theology on the body (chapter 2) and language (chapter 5).

A theologian of beauty. A recent fine theologian, Stephen Wright, pursues the ascetic strand of Jenson's thinking, offering a reliable expository account of Jenson's theology. Wright perceptively puts it, "In Jenson's theology, the future is irreducibly aesthetic. Poetic language is the proper mode of eschatological discourse."[23]

A postliberal theologian. Jenson can be viewed a postliberal theologian as well.[24] A preeminent Jewish theologian, Peter Ochs, places Jenson's theology on the postliberal trajectory. Ochs considers postliberalism as "another reformation" on the part of Protestant ecumenical movement, which makes "an effort for the unity of the church, the body of Christ" by reading the Scriptures and "uncovering sources of the church's inability to repair its disunity."[25] This Jewish theologian particularly emphasizes that "[n]onsupersessionism is a corollary of this postliberalism,"[26] which he considers is given impetus or made possible through recent hermeneutics of the Gospels and Pauline epistles.

A post-supersessionistic theologian. Ochs's brief historiography of non- or post-supersessionism in Christian theology deserves extensive attention here, as this would help us to locate Jenson's recent move in modern post-supersessionistic context. Ochs starts his historiographical sketch on the modern Christian post-supersessionism, by noting Barth's theological account of Israel. Even though Ochs is not pleased to see Barth's view of the synagogue as "the disobedient, idolatrous Israel of every age,"[27] he regards Barth as "the single most significant contributor to

---

22. Rook, *Rhyming Hope and History.*

23. Wright, *Dogmatic Aesthetics,* 237.

24. Cf. Murphy also sees Jenson as a Hegelian and so problematic (Murphy, *God Is Not a Story,* 18).

25. Ochs, *Another Reformation,* 259.

26. Ibid.

27. *CD* II/2, 234 quoted in Ochs, "Judaism and Christian Theology," 648.

postliberal Christianity's reaffirmation of Israel's enduring Covenant."[28] Ochs notes Barth's remarks: "Without any doubt, the Jews are to this very day the chosen people of God in the same sense as they have been from the beginning, according to the Old and New Testaments."[29] Crucially, Barth also holds that a "church that becomes anti-Semitic or even only a-Semitic sooner or later suffers the loss of its faith by losing the object of it."[30]

On this line, Ochs names two German theologians who offer "a Barthian-yet-post-Barthian doctrine of non-supersessionism":[31] Friedrich Marquardt and Peter von der Osten Sacken. Marquardt's contribution is his construal of Israel as "formal Christology . . . to display the continuities of Christian theology with the biblical history of Israel."[32] For Marquardt, "incarnation is itself a Jewish notion, display[ing] God's indwelling in the people Israel."[33] Von der Osten Sacke argues for God's tenacious faithfulness to Israel's covenant: God adheres to his election of Israel even if Israel says no to Jesus Christ. In his account, "Jesus is Messiah . . . bringing Gentiles into fellowship with God and thereby bringing Jews into fellowship with Gentiles—but 'without becoming Christians.'"[34]

Further, Ochs mentions such postliberal non-supersessionistic theologians as George Lindbeck, R. Kendall Soulen, and Bruce Marshall. In Ochs's account, Lindbeck's postliberalism entails non-supersessionism: a fresh reading of the biblical text leads to a recognition of "the enduring place of the people Israel in the gospel narrative."[35] In *The God of Israel and Christian Theology*, as Ochs notes, Soulen argues that "God's identity as the God of Israel is inconceivable apart from the election of the Jewish people"[36] and that supersessionistic sentiment with Christianity tends to cause "a semi-gnostic distortion of Christian covenant history,"[37] denigrating the goodness of God's creation. Later, Soulen ex-

---

28. Ochs, "Judaism and Christian Theology," 648.

29. Barth, "the Jewish Problem and the Christian Answer," 200 quoted in ibid.

30. *CD* II/2, 234 quoted in ibid.

31. Ibid.

32. Wyschogrod, "Review of Friedrich-Wilhelm Marquardt, *Das Christliche Bekenntnis zu Jesus, dem Juden Ein Christologie*," 275–76, quoted in ibid., 649.

33. Ibid.

34. Von der Osten Sacken, *Christian-Jewish Dialogue*, 58, quoted in ibid.

35. Ibid.

36. Ibid., 650.

37. Ibid., 651.

tends his argument against supersessionistic disregard of the holy name of God, YHWH: even though Christian theology has always affirmed in some fashion that YHWH is the Triune God, in practice it has considered the Tetragrammaton as left in the *past* and so outmoded. Soulen holds that replacing the Tetragrammaton with the trinitarian name, "Father, Son, and Spirit" is a serious supersessionistic distortion of Christian theology.[38]

Another postliberal non-supersessionistic theologian, Bruce Marshall, is introduced, and yet he is distinguished in that he employs the tools of analytic philosophy to clarify the post-supersessionistic argument. In Marshall's argument, the God of Israel and the Trinity refers to the same divine entity, but have different senses. Accordingly, "when Israel fails to recognize the Triune God as the God of Israel, [it does not mean] it then fails fully to worship the God of Israel."[39] Along with these figures, Bader-Saye, Yoder, Cartwright, and Hauerwas, Hardy, and Ford are briefly mentioned in Ochs's account of Christian (post-liberal) post-supersessionism.

Alongside with Ochs's sketch of the Protestant movement, it is noteworthy that a *Catholic* theologian, Matthew Levering, has developed his post-supersessionistic theology, arising from the Thomistic tradition. Responding to Soulen's postliberal critique of the traditional concept of God's essence, Levering argues that, in Aquinas, God's being does not replace the God of Israel and the Tetragrammaton, revealed through Moses to Israel: "Aquinas avoids in his treatment of God's essence the form of supersessionism that Soulen ascribes to the classical account."[40] This Catholic theologian recently authored a monograph on a prominent Jewish theologian: *Jewish-Christian Dialogue and the Life of Wisdom: Engagements with the Theology of David Novak*. There, Levering argues not only that his conversations with the Novak are mutually constructive

---

38. In his recent monograph, *The Divine Name(s) and the Holy Trinity*, Soulen examines the place of the Tetragrammaton within trinitarian theology from early Christian creeds to medieval, Reformation, and modern theologies, and proposes a trinitarian way of naming of God. Soulen holds that there are theological/patrological, christological, and pneumatological ways of naming of God. In this work, the Tetragrammaton as a theological/patrological name of God is not disregarded but upheld with the other two, christological and pneumatological namings.

39. Ochs, "Judaism and Christian Theology," 651.

40. Levering, *Scripture and Metaphysics*, 74.

but also that the two covenant communities make a theological voice together, "contributing to true human flourishing"[41] in this secularized age.

Now we are ready to see Jenson on this post-supersessionistic trajectory. Ochs states that postliberal Jewish theologians have learned a lesson from the Shoah: an exclusivist formulation of the Trinity could "lead Christians to exclude not only Jewish beliefs but also the people Israel's right to exist."[42] But this does not mean that Christians should "overcome their Trinitarianism in order to make room for Jewish monotheism" since such an alternative "weakens that witness to God in the world that is displayed in the Old Testament (or Jewish Bible) as well as in the New."[43] For Ochs, "the postliberal Christian reading of Nicea is . . . doubly good for the Jews, because it strengthens Christian witness to the God of Israel at the same time that it respects the validity of God's Covenant with Israel."[44] For Ochs, the doctrine of the Trinity is no longer a stumbling block, as he envisages the possibility that "Jews and Christian may discuss the Christian doctrine of the Trinity."[45] In Ochs's observation, "Robert Jenson has offered one of the most comprehensive postliberal arguments of this kind,"[46] rightly grounding it on the historical revelation of God of Israel.

In his recent doctoral thesis, "The God of Israel in Robert W. Jenson's Theology," Andrew Nicol has pursued this post-supersessionistic line of thinking in the fabric of Jenson's theology, tracing in detail Jenson's rich explication of God's triune life with Israel.[47] Yet, like other critics, Nicol expresses concern about Jenson's "conflation" of God's being and the economy, and argues that "the abiding significance of the God of Israel's identity is . . . undermined by his tendency to conflate the being of God with the divine economy, and by promoting futurity at the expense of protology."[48]

A number of Nicol's findings converge with mine. Yet, my approach differs from Nicol's in two fundamental respects: Firstly, I have attempted

---

41. Levering, *Jewish-Christian Dialogue and the Life of Wisdom*, 11.
42. Ochs, "Trinity and Judaism," 439.
43. Ibid.
44. Ibid.
45. Ibid., 433.
46. Ibid., 437.
47. Nicol, "The God of Israel in Robert W. Jenson's Theology," 238.
48. Ibid., i.

to identify in some detail the leading intellectual influences on Jenson's theology, arguing that his theology of Judaism is developed through intensive engagement with a range of key figures and sources. In particular, I have focused on Jenson's appropriation of the work of Michael Wyschogrod, suggesting that it is only by appreciating Wyschogrod's influence that we fully grasp the character of Jenson's development of an explicitly post-supersessionistic theology of Israel. Secondly, I suggest that a more charitable reading of Jenson's metaphysical commitments is possible, and I argue that acceptance of Jenson's revisionary metaphysics allows for a stronger, more consistent construal of the triune God *as the God of Israel*.

Outline of Work

This book will argue that Jenson's revisionary trinitarian theology—which upholds the ontological import of the temporal, bodily, hermeneutical, and eschatological life and being of Jesus within the inner being of God—can accommodate a post-supersessionistic view of the Jews, by recognizing the significance of Israel's irrevocable covenant in Jesus Christ. Conversely, a post-supersessionistic doctrine of the Jews can be secured when it is anchored in the doctrine of the Trinity which centers upon the ontological significance of the time and body of Jesus Christ, who is also the (hermeneutical) Word and the Eschatos, in the eternal being of God.

Jenson's post-supersessionistic theology of Judaism and his trinitarian revisionary ontology are inextricably related, as his trinitarian reflection considerably moves in a post-supersessionistic direction in his later career. For Jenson, Christian trinitarian theology calls for an audacious revision of our inherited ontology. So this book will demonstrate how Jenson's trinitarian revisionary ontology sets out to embrace the existence of the Jews in his trinitarian reflection, tracing the developments of relevant ontological and trinitarian concepts: the Father's election of the Son, the body of the Son, the (hermeneutical) Word of God, and the eschatological power of the Spirit. This work will also suggest that Jenson's trinitarian theology deserves a more accurate and charitable reading than it often receives and that this requires reading a broad range of his works and also some of the major theologians he engaged with throughout his career.

Each chapter may be sketched as follows: chapter 1 centers on the effect of God's election upon his own being, as it follows through the strand of Barth's actualistic ontology, which Jenson studied and developed from early on for his own revisionary ontology, also seeing how Jenson's actualistic ontology would operate in his later developed theology of Judaism. In his doctoral research on Barth's doctrine of election, Jenson adopted a crucial line of doctrinal thinking from Barth, one that closely links the doctrine of eternal election and the doctrine of God. Boldly advancing Barth's insight, Jenson reconfigures the doctrine of God in the light of the doctrine of eternal election, weaving them with the doctrine of the resurrection. Consequently, the resurrection of the Son, Jesus, becomes operative with the doctrine of God and the doctrine of election, determining the shape of Jenson's onto-theological thinking. And these theological strands are carried forward into his later post-supersessionistic development.

Chapter 2 outlines Jenson's understanding of the body of the Son placed in the eternal being of God. Jenson's unremitting commitment to the Lutheran way of conceiving of the relation between the humanity of Jesus and the divinity of the Son, leads him to reject any attempt to separate the carnal existence of Jesus of Nazareth from the being of God. In this chapter, I show how Jenson's Lutheran christological-ontological commitments shape his ecclesial and ecumenical theology and lead him to embrace the doctrine of deification. After all, it is suggested that on this trajectory Jenson recognizes the divine presence and the salvific energy in the flesh of the Jews.

Chapter 3 looks at the most conspicuous Jewish source in Jenson's post-supersessionistic theology—the theology of Michael Wyschogrod—exploring the Jewishness of the body of the Son, Israel. Wyschogrod is the most visible Jewish interlocutor in Jenson's works, who bears striking similarities with Jenson, as he brings together insights on the election of Israel, the body (of Israel), and the identity of Israel's God, arguing that election and the body of the elect are *not* external to the being of God. Wyschogrod displays his congenial and kindred interest in the Christian doctrine of the incarnation for his own theology of the Jews, in which the Jews/Israel are construed as the dilute incarnation of God of Israel. Wyschogrod also envisages the "new" relation between the Jewish community and the Christian church, by perceptively reading the Gospels and the Pauline epistles, even though he is aware of some dangers, carried over from the long history of Christian supersessionism.

Chapter 4 explores how Jenson as a Christian theologian favorably responds to Wyschogrod's theology, without losing his sight of the ontological significances of trinitarian theology. Jenson develops a Christian account of Judaism, increasingly recognizing the irrevocability of God's covenant with the (old) Israel, the significance of their Torah observance in the Jewish community, and most importantly the ontological significance of Jewish existence in relation to the identity of God. And Jenson proposes a paralleling relation between the two communities, suggesting that the ecclesial body of Christ cannot be established with the gentile church alone, without her union with the Jewish community, which still functions as the carnal abode of God.

Chapter 5 pursues another ontological strand developed into Jenson's theology of Judaism: hermeneutical ontology. This chapter focuses on the (hermeneutic) Word of God. For Jenson, God is Word, and the Word has the hermeneutical function to interpret all reality (including God's) in its own light. Therefore, the being of God is a hermeneutical event, which occurs as communication between the Father and the Son who embraces us in himself, in the economy. For Jenson, the hermeneutical Word-event occurs as a narrative in which all beings are and will be interpreted in the End. In this chapter, the Bultmann school (Gerhard Ebeling and Ernst Fuchs) and Gerhard von Rad are considered major sources with which Jenson engages for his hermeneutical-narrative ontology. Further, moving in a post-supersessionistic direction, Jenson's hermeneutical ontology comes to accommodate the codified aspect of the Word of God. For the Word of God is, after all, the Torah, which consists of the narrative *and* the law. Neither aspect must supersede the other.

In chapter 6, we will explore the eschato-pneumatological strand of Jenson's thinking, developed into his account of the role of the Holy Spirit in the relation between the Jews and Christians. Jenson's eschatological or futuristic ontology has developed, as he engages with Pannenberg, Barth, Bultmann, and von Rad. Also Jenson's daring reconfiguration of the doctrines of the eternal election of the Son and of the resurrection (as seen in chapter 1) comes into play in his eschatological ontology. And this develops with Jenson's pneumatology. For Jenson, the Spirit is the power of the future. In Jenson's post-supersessionistic account, the Spirit is construed as the eschatological agent who blows upon the two covenant communities so that they may be the *totus Christus* in the final eschaton, the communal self of the Son (Israel) offered to the Father by the power of the Spirit. Here we will also see how the power of the Spirit functions as a retro-active futural power, which constitutes a major strand of Jenson's revisionary metaphysics of time.

My work may be read as displaying a chiastic structure. At the center, chapter 3 and chapter 4 are coupled with each other, devoting respectively to the Jewish voice and the Christian voice, recognizing each's own calling and role in the economy of God of Israel and endeavoring to remove obstacles for theological companionship and collaboration. Chapter 2 and chapter 5 discuss the Word of God, devoting respectively to the visibility/embodiment of the Word and to audibility of the Word. Chapter 1 and chapter 6 are also closely related, as the centrality of the resurrection (chapter 1) decisively shapes Jenson's futuristic ontology (chapter 6).

Admittedly, this work focuses considerably on the christological motifs of Jenson's theo-ontology—election, the body, the Torah, and the Word—devoting only one chapter to the pneumatological motif. But this is not entirely illegitimate since the Jewish-Christian conversations often center upon those issues: the election of Israel, the significance of Jesus, the Torah, and so on. Yet, the role of the Holy Spirit is always presupposed in reflections of those matters: the Spirit works as the eschatological agent of the hypostatic oneness between God and his people in election, between the Word-Torah and his chosen people, and between the Jews and Christians in the age to come.

In sum, Jenson's theology of the Jews cannot be adequately understood without addressing his trinitarian ontology, which works out the implications of the effect of God's election upon his being, the Son's accommodative Jewish body, the hermeneutical Word of God, and the eschatological power of the Spirit. For Jenson's trinitarian theology moves considerably in a post-supersessionistic direction. This also entails that Jenson's trinitarian (onto-)theology cannot be exposited or evaluated adequately without delving into his theology of Judaism. The two *loci* are intricately related in Jenson. For Jenson's trinitarian theology accommodates non-supersessionism as it recognizes the irrevocability of Israel's covenant and works out the ontological implications of the time and the body of Jesus Christ, who has Israel in himself, and of the eschatological work of the Holy Spirit for the two communities, to the glory of the Father.

1

God's Decision upon His Being

Temporal Actualistic Ontology
toward Post-supersessionistic Theology

JENSON'S THEOLOGY OF ISRAEL is not merely an ecclesial consideration, but a deeply ontological reflection, conceptually closely related to his trinitarian theology. For Jenson, Christian trinitarian faith requires radical revision of the ontology inherited from the Greek philosophy. Christian post-supersessionistic theology of Israel/the Jews can be secured only when it is anchored into the trinitarian theo-ontology that requires rigorous and audacious recognition of the ontological significance of the *time* and the *body* of the incarnate Son, Jesus of Nazareth, who is placed at the heart of the being of God, as the second hypostasis of the Trinity. Jenson's revisionist trinitarian ontology, informing his post-supersessionism, is best understood when we explore his actualistic ontology, as the first step, which developed through his critical and creative reception of Barth's doctrine of election. In this actualistic ontology, the time and the body of Jesus Christ function as major determinants of the being of God, as God elects his Son Jesus in his "eternity" and in his eternal being.

So this first chapter will center upon Jenson's reading and reception of Barth's doctrine of election. In tracing this line, we will see that Jenson closely follows Barth's actualistic ontology, but makes a *temporalistic* turn. Focusing on his earliest works, *Alpha and Omega* (1963) and *God after God* (1969), in which the temporalistic turn is already visible, this chapter will proceed in four sections: 1) Jenson's reading of Barth,

2) Jenson's criticism of Barth, 3) Jenson's innovation, 4) Jenson's post-supersessionistic development.

Jenson's Reading of Barth

No Hidden Decree

On Jenson's reading of Barth's doctrine of election it is best understood as an extended attempt to overcome the problematic of the Reformation doctrine of the hidden decree. On this doctrine, even John Calvin himself felt the problem:[1] "[W]hence does it happen that Adam's fall irremediably involved so many peoples, together with their infant offspring, in eternal death unless because it so pleased God? The decree is *dreadful indeed, I confess*."[2] Luther also experienced deep anxiety about such an understanding of the divine decree: "who would not take offence? I have taken offence myself more than once, down to the depths and the abyss of despair, so that I wished I had never been made a man."[3] And precisely in this condition, Luther claimed, "This is the highest degree of faith to believe that he is merciful who saves so few and damns so many."[4] But it was indeed a "concealed and dreadful will of God,"[5] curiously in opposition to God's preceptive will, that is, his will to save all.

Perceiving the *Anfechtung* concealed in the doctrine of the double decree, Barth holds that the reformers' understanding of God's election cannot be the gospel. For Barth, "the truth of the doctrine of predestination, is first and last and in all circumstances the sum of the Gospel, no matter how it may be understood in detail, no matter what apparently contradictory aspects or moments it may present to us."[6] The doctrine of predestination should be "to us a proclamation of joy. It is not a mixed message of joy and terror, salvation and damnation. . . . The No is said for the sake of the Yes and not for its own sake. In substance, therefore, the first and last word is Yes and not No."[7] If in his hidden will God divided

---

1. McNeill, "Introduction," in John Calvin, *Institutes*, lix.
2. Ibid., 955. Emphasis mine.
3. Gerrish, "'To the Unknown God,'" 274.
4. Luther, *W. A.*, 18.633.15 quoted in ibid.
5. Luther, *W. A.*, 685.19 quoted in ibid., 276.
6. *CD* II/2, 13.
7. Ibid., 14.

humanity into right and left even from eternity, then "we cannot possibly be required or advised to entrust ourselves"[8] into God's hand. Barth is aware that Calvin's double predestination may be considered "extremely fitting and useful for piety,"[9] and that as Calvin believed it "rightly builds up faith and teaches us humility, [lifting] us to admiration of the immeasurable goodness of God to us and awakens us to celebrate it."[10] However, Barth cannot just gloss over the horror of the double decree and of God's hidden will as formulated in Calvin's theology.

So Barth jettisons the hidden or absolute will from his doctrine of election and upholds Jesus as the only will of God for us. Barth states, "There is no such thing as a *decretum absolutum*. There is no such thing as a will of God apart from the will of Jesus Christ."[11] The distinction between the perceptive will and decretive will is accordingly discarded: God's will is not divided, but one and unified will.[12] Jesus Christ who has borne the condemnation for us is God's one and only will for us. Thus, the conceptual cause of *Anfechtung* hidden in the reformers' doctrine has been removed in Barth's reformulation: "The doctrine of election is the sum of the Gospel."[13] Accordingly, there is only "Yes" in Jesus Christ for humans; God's "No" is borne by God himself. Jesus Christ as God's only will is God's Yes for us. For "[t]he wrath of God, the judgment and the penalty, fall, then, upon Him. And this means upon His own Son, *upon Himself*."[14]

Jenson closely follows Barth's reconfiguration of the double decree, sharing Barth's concern about Calvin's predestination. Jenson says in agreement, "One must not make election and reprobation equal partners. . . . [R]ather one must always speak of acceptance and rejection in such a way that acceptance is always the real content of God's decision. (II/2,

---

8. Ibid., 107.

9. Calvin, *De aeterna Dei praedestinatione*, 1552, C.R. 8, 260, quoted in ibid., 14. Here Barth cites Calvin's *De aeterna Dei preadestinatione* of 1552 as C.R. 8, but it seems appropriate to cite it as CO (*Calvini Opera*). Usually *Corpus Reformatorum* is cited as C.R.. In fact, C.R. 8 is Philip Melanchthon's work.

10. Calvin, *De aeterna Dei praedestinatione*, 1552, C.R. 8, 260, quoted in ibid.

11. Ibid., 115.

12. "It has as its content one name and one person. This decree is Jesus Christ, and for this very reason it cannot be a *decretum absolutum*" (ibid., 158).

13. Ibid., 107.

14. Ibid., 124. Emphasis added.

13–5; 13–6)."¹⁵ God's No or his reprobation exists in the service of God's Yes. Jenson says, "Reprobation is the mere presupposition of election, the unavoidable *condition* of God's will to show mercy. In God himself 'there is no "and," no duality,' but only the transcending of reprobation by election."¹⁶ God's No is pronounced only to be overcome by his Yes; death "exists" to be defeated by life. Thus, Jenson accepts Barth's reconfigured supralapsarianism: "something like Barth's teaching must be true: . . . sin and evil belong to God's intent precisely—but *only*—as they do appear in Christ's victory over them."¹⁷ After all, the whole creation exists for the victory of Jesus Christ and his redemption of all things. "God created us just in order to redeem us."¹⁸ Jesus is the reason and goal of the whole creation. Thus, the priority of Jesus Christ, the triumph of God's Yes over his No, emerges as Jenson's theological axiom.

No Hidden God

In Barth's diagnosis, the hidden decree becomes problematic also in its conceptual relation to the doctrine of God. The God who issues his decree remains a God hidden behind Jesus, who is God's love for us. Calvin's electing God is "a *Deus nudus absconditus*, . . . not the *Deus revelatus*."¹⁹ As the decretive will as the hidden and dreadful will is considered hardly reconcilable with God's loving will revealed on the cross of Jesus Christ, the *Deus absconditus* is not obviously congruous with Jesus. The issue of two contrasting wills becomes the issue of the (dis)unity within God himself, between God (the Father) and Jesus the Son. Seeing the dangerous implication of the traditional doctrine of predestination for the doctrine of the Trinity,²⁰ Barth expunges this seed of the danger from his theological construction, as he states, "In no depth of the Godhead shall we encounter any other but [Jesus]. There is no such thing as Godhead in itself."²¹

---

15. *AO*, 170.
16. *GAG*, 28–29. Emphasis added.
17. *ST*, 1:73.
18. Luther, *Grosser Katechismus*, 64 quoted in ibid.
19. *CD* II/2, 111.
20. *CD* IV/1, 54–66.
21. *CD* II/2, 115.

Jenson follows this move and comments on it approvingly: "There is no other God of election behind God-in-Jesus Christ. Therefore the old Calvinist doctrine which called Christ the mirror of election is not adequate. For if God's original decision about us is distinct from what happens in Jesus Christ, if it is only mirrored in Jesus Christ, then this decision and not what is decided in Christ will be decisive. Our relation to God will not in the last analysis by a relation in and through Christ. And the mirror will be impossible to trust completely."[22] In his later work, in this vein, Jenson sets forth his theological axiom: "To identify the gospel's God, we must identify Jesus. In this sense we may first say that God 'is' Jesus."[23]

No Logos *Asarkos*

Along with the hidden deity and the hidden decree, the concept of the Logos *asarkos* is also jettisoned in Barth's theology. Regarding the idea of the Logos *asarkos*, Barth says, "'Logos in itself' . . . does not have this content and form, [and] is the eternal Word of God without this form and content. . . . Like Godhead abstracted from its revelation and acts, it would necessarily be an empty concept which we would then, of course, feel obliged to fill with all kinds of contents of our own arbitrary invention. Under the title of a λόγος ἄσαρκος we pay homage to a *Deus absconditus* and therefore to some image of God which we have made for ourselves."[24] Such a concept of the Logos would only trigger dangerous speculation about God and the Son. Alternatively, the "divine essence could be defined on some other basis than in and from the perception of [Jesus'] presence and action as incarnate Word."[25] The eternal Logos, that is, the second person of the Trinity, must be conceived as *Jesus*, even in eternity before the creation.

Jenson also endorses Barth's rejection of the idea of the *Logos asarkos*, as he says, "we need posit no . . . antecedent extra entities—*Logos*

---

22. *AO*, 144.

23. *ChrD*, 1:100. Cf. For Jenson, "the primal systematic function of trinitarian teaching is to *identify the theos* in 'theology'" (*ST*, 1:60), and that is the one of the great achievements of Barth; in Barth's words, "the question who God is, which it is the business of the doctrine of the Trinity answer" (*CD*, I/1, 301).

24. *CD* IV/1, 52.

25. Ibid., 181.

asarkos."²⁶ For Jenson shares Barth's concern about speculative theology that would launch off God's concrete and particular historical revelation, Jesus Christ.²⁷ Following Barth in this regard, Jenson's theological construction will center upon the person of Jesus Christ.

Actualistic Ontology: God is the Event and the Decision.

In connection with this rejection of the *Logos asarkos*, we need to note in Jenson's reading of Barth that God *is* the event of (the enactment of) his decision. Here Jenson brings together closely Barth's doctrine of election and his doctrine of God's self-repetition in *Church Dogmatics* Volume 1. Jenson notes Barth's statement: "The name of Father, Son and Spirit means that God is the one God in *threefold repetition*."²⁸ For Barth, God the Trinity is "thrice of the one divine I."²⁹ Jenson takes this as an *act* of God which constitutes God's being as the Trinity. Put differently, God's triune being is his *action*. Jenson comments on Barth's idea: "God *is* in that he repeats himself. Just so he is an event."³⁰ Again, "God's act of possessing his one deity is the same act as his act of distinguishing himself from himself as Father and Son in the Spirit."³¹ God is triune in the act of the threefold repetition of his being.

More precisely, "God is a *particular* event."³² Barth says, "[W]hen we know God as event, act and life, He is definitely something different to be distinguished from what we are accustomed to understand by these

---

26. *TI*, 140.
27. Ibid., 137.
28. *CD* I/1, 350.

29. Ibid., 351. Cf. According to Alan Torrance, this account of the Trinity overcomes Arianism in that it is God himself that is repeated and differentiated. Also it overcomes modalism since the repetition is *differentiation* of himself in which the second and the third "mode" of his being is *new* to the first mode of God self. For this, see Torrance, *Persons in Communion*, 110. But Torrance's criticism is that Barth's understanding of the Trinity does not account for the communion of persons of the Trinity. However, Hunsinger's reading differs: the act of God's self-differentiation is the act of positing the other within his being: "In the trinitarian communion of God's love, the otherness of the other is not lost but enhanced" (Hunsinger, "Mysterium Trinitatis," 192).

30. *GAG*, 125. Emphasis added.
31. Ibid., 109.
32. Ibid., 126. Emphasis original.

views and concepts."³³ When we construe God as event, we need to think of "[t]he particularity of the divine event, act and life."³⁴ The question is: *which* event? "Barth's answer would be: what happens with *Jesus*."³⁵ At this point, as Jenson analyzes Barth's portrayal of the eternal event of God's self-differentiation *as* the particular event of Jesus, he draws together the event of God's self-differentiation and the eternal event of election and claims that *the two are one and the same event* in which he exists as this particular God. God's act of self-repetition to be triune occurs in and as his act of having Jesus as the second person of the Trinity. "That there are three identities in God means that this God's deed of being the one God is three times repeated, and so that each repetition is a being of God, and so that only in this precise self-repetition is God the *particular* God that he in fact is."³⁶

God's triunity is *constituted in* the enactment of his decision to be the particular God, that is, for Jenson, in the enactment of his decision to elect Jesus Christ as his Son. Or rather, as God is event, God *is* the event of the election, that is, of the decision to be the particular God. Jenson says, "God does God, and over again, and yet over again—and only so does the event and *decision* that is this God occur."³⁷ Jenson admits that one *may* read Barth to mean that "a decision [that is, election] occurs in the life lived between *antecedently* given triune hypostases."³⁸ But Jenson reads Barth to mean that "the threefold being of God itself [is] given in the event that is a decision."³⁹ In Jenson's reading of Barth, there is no such thing as the Trinity antecedent to the particular history. God's election of Jesus and his being as the Trinity has occurred in their inextricable relation.⁴⁰

---

33. *CD* II/1, 264.
34. Ibid., 267.
35. *GAG*, 126. Emphasis added.
36. *TI*, 111. Emphasis added.
37. Ibid. Emphasis added.
38. Jenson, "Karl Barth on the Being of God," 49. Emphasis added.
39. Ibid.
40. At this point, one can see the unmistakable similarity between Jenson's reading and McCormack's. Like Jenson, McCormack sees in Barth "the triunity of God logically as a function of divine election" (McCormack, "Grace and Being," 103). Again, we may recall, Jenson considers it one of the greatest Barth's achievements: the primal function of the doctrine of the Trinity is to identify God by his divine action (in the economy) (*ST*, 1:60).

Jenson's Criticism of Barth

The Pre-existent Jesus and the Temporal Jesus

Yet, Jenson goes beyond Barth—even the Barth in Jenson's interpretation—when he finds Barth's Jesus still an ambiguous reality. Barth famously states that Jesus is the electing God.[41] In his exposition of Barth's doctrine, Jenson notes that Jesus as the electing God is the *third* reality in Barth, a reality "between the eternal being of the Second Person of the Trinity and the temporal existence of the man Jesus," or "the reality of the choice in which the Son chooses to be *and is* one with man. (II/2, 114ff.; 106ff.)"[42] Jenson's observation is based on the following words of Barth: "Between the eternal Godhead of Christ which needs no election and His elected humanity, there is a third [reality] which was overlooked by Thomas. And that is the being of Christ in the beginning with God."[43] In Barth's account, Jesus the electing God is neither "the Son who planned to become one with man"[44] nor the fully incarnate one, Jesus in human history. The *Jesus* who exists before the foundation of the world as the electing God exists in pretemporal eternity *as if* he is *already* Jesus.[45] Jenson subjects this talk of an already-not-yet Jesus to critical scrutiny.

---

41. *CD* II/2, 103.

42. *AO*, 67. Emphasis original.

43. *CD* II/2, 107; *KD* II/2, 114: "Es gibt ein von Thomas übersehenes Drittes zwischen der ewigen, keiner Erwählung bedürftigen Gottheit Christi und seiner erwählten Menschheit, und das ist eben jenes Sein Jesu am Anfang bei Gott." Jenson translate Barth's Drittes as "the third reality"; Torrance and Bromiley translate it as "the third possibility." Since Barth speaks here of the *existence* of Jesus in the pre-temporal eternity, Jenson's translation seems more appropriate.

44. "[T]his does not mean only as the Son who planned to become one with man. Jesus Christ, the God-man, not just the eternal Son as such, is the one who in all eternity decides on grace. (II/2, 112f.; 104ff.)" (*AO*, 67).

45. Cf. McCormack views the pretemporal Jesus as the Son who exists by way of anticipation. "God is already in pre-temporal eternity—by way of anticipation—that which he would become in time" (McCormack, "Grace and Being," 100). Further, McCormack points out the seventeen-century term Logos *incarnandus* would not convey what Barth means about the pretemporal Jesus: "So, if precedent means anything at all, seventeenth-century terminology would allow Barth to speak of the *Logos incarnandus* prior to historical 'enfleshment' as One whose being was 'determined' by the eternal divine decision for incarnation in time. And yet, there remains an important difference between this traditional usage and Barth's claim. For seventeenth-century theologians, the Logos appeared in the eternal plan of God as *incarnandus* only insofar as he was the object of election. In this view, the *Logos* is determined to be *incarnandus* in the eternal plan of God as a consequence of a prior decision made by the triune

Jenson asks, "What is the relation between Jesus Christ's preexistence and His life in our time?"[46] What is the relation between the third reality and the fully incarnate temporal Jesus? Here Jenson notes the *language* that Barth uses to name the relation between the two modes: revelation, sign, analogy, and reproduction, etc. Barth writes, "In His revelation, in Jesus Christ, the hidden God has indeed made Himself apprehensible. Not directly, but *indirectly*. Not to sight, but to faith. Not in His being, but in *sign*. The Word was made flesh: this is the first, original and controlling *sign* of all signs."[47] In Jenson's reading, Barth's Jesus in human history functions only as the *sign* of the eternal history of the preexistent Jesus.[48]

Jenson traces this pattern of thought which also appeared in the later volumes of *Church Dogmatics*, as Barth says:

> The giving of the Son by the Father indicates a mystery, a hidden movement in the inner life of the Godhead. But in the self-sacrifice of the man Jesus for His friends, this intra-divine movement is no longer hidden but revealed. For what the man Jesus does . . . is . . . to actualize the human and therefore the visible and knowable . . . aspect of this portion of the divine history. . . . What would the man Jesus be apart . . . from the fact that He is the Revealer of this mystery? He lives and moves . . . as its Revealer, in the necessary decision and achievement here below of what is decided and achieved by God Himself up above . . . .[49]

There is a parallel in the act of God's self-giving between his act in the pretemporal eternity and his act in time. In eternity, on the one hand, God gave his only Son. This occurred as a hidden event in the inner life of the Godhead. In time, on the other hand, the man Jesus gave his life to his friends. It is not a hidden but revealed event of the inner life of the Godhead. Here the temporal reveals the eternal and functions as a *sign* or a *copy* of the eternal event.

Another passage from Barth is noted by Jenson: "The royal man . . . is created 'after God' (*kata theon*). This means that as a man He exists *analogously* to the mode of existence of God. In what He thinks and wills and does, in His attitude, there is a *correspondence*, a *parallel*

God" (McCormack, "Grace and Being," 94).

46. *AO*, 84.

47. *CD* II/1, 199.

48. "The humanity of Jesus Christ is the primary sign of this sort. (II/1, 223, 199)" (*AO*, 87).

49. *KD* III/2, 77; *CD* III/2, 66 quoted in ibid., 85–86.

in the creaturely world, to the plan and purpose and work and attitude of God. (IV/2, 185f.;166.)"[50] The exalted Jesus in human history exists in the analogous, corresponding, and paralleling relation to God's plan made in pretemporal eternity, which can be considered the pre-existent Jesus. For, in Barth, "the eternal purpose of the good-pleasure of God which precedes all created reality is identical with the reality of the divine-human person of Jesus Christ...."[51] Also in his humiliation the Son of man in his temporal existence "*copies* the humiliation of the Son of God; He exists in *conformity* with God's poverty in this world. (IV/2, 186–91; 167–71.) His life for man *mirrors* and *reproduces* God's solidarity with man. (IV/2, 200ff.; 179ff.)"[52] Once the existence of "Jesus" is posited in pretemporal eternity, the relation between the pretemporal Jesus and the temporal Jesus is conceived to be as the relation between reality and sign.[53] So construed, Jenson cannot avoid the impression that, in Barth, the temporal life of Jesus is regarded to be the analogy, the correspondence, the copy, the mirror, and the reproduction of the pretemporal Jesus, the third reality.

Urgeschichte and Human History

Along this line, Jenson claims that we may read Barth to mean that, before the creation of the world, the history of salvation *already* happened. For Barth, there was a *history* before the creation. The same pattern of Barth's language is observed in his account of the relation between the primal history (*Urgeschichte*) and human temporal history. Before the creation of the world, there was the covenant between God and man. The eternal covenant is the *Urgeschichte*. In that pretemporal history, God's humiliation and his self-giving already occurred: "God's election as the beginning of all things is God's self-surrender in his eternal decree. His self-surrender: for God gave—and this is not something that has just now happened, it is eternal divine *fore*-ordination—His own Son, He spoke His Word. And therewith He surrendered Himself, He gave Himself up ... for the good ... of the man whom He created and who had fallen away

---

50. *KD* IV/2, 185–86; *CD* IV/2, 166 quoted in ibid., 87.
51. *CD* II/2, 108.
52. *AO*, 87. Emphasis mine.
53. For more, see *AO* and *GAG*.

from him."⁵⁴ Jenson exposits: "the eternal covenant is *already* a covenant with man the sinner and requires God's substitutionary involvement with evil. In His eternal act of choice God then and there opens Himself to the attack of evil in order to be in covenant with man. Indeed, He then and there makes Himself the object of His own condemnation (II/2, 177ff.; 162ff.)"⁵⁵ And, in parallel to this, as God descends and bears the sin of man, man is elevated to the bosom of God in the pretemporal eternity. Jenson notes Barth's words: "He has taken the creature to himself even before it was, namely, in His own Son, who willed to live and die as a man for all men, as a creature for all creatures. He thus took it to Himself even in its very contradiction."⁵⁶ Thus, the humiliation of God and the exaltation of man have *already* happened in pretemporal covenantal history. "To put the matter in extreme form," Jenson says, "everything that happened in Jesus Christ's history on earth happened in eternity, and in God's pretemporal eternity."⁵⁷ And "[t]his [primal] history is the *basis* of all other history between God and man (II/2, 7; 8),"⁵⁸ the "*principle* and *essence* of all happening (II/2, 201; 183)."⁵⁹ "Barth," Jenson stresses, "is not being rhetorical. [Rather, he] means that in a particular but very real sense the Incarnation [the Jesus event] *happened* in eternity before all time (II/2, 157, 172, IV/I, 70; 145,158, 66)."⁶⁰

In sum, Jenson underlines two features of Barth's theology: first, in pretemporal eternity, there was Jesus, and the events of humiliation of God and of exaltation of man occurred (already); second, the temporal Jesus and the salvific history are considered the sign, the representation, and the mirror of those pretemporal events. When these two ideas are brought together, Jenson argues, the weight of reality falls on pretemporal eternity: the pretemporal Jesus and his events become a center of gravity and absorb the ontological weight of the temporal Jesus and the temporal history into the pretemporality. The temporal Jesus and his events are relativized, treated as mirrors and signs to some absolute eternal reality.

---

54. *KD* II/2, 176; *CD* II/2, 161 quoted in *AO*, 81–82. Jenson's emphasis.
55. *AO*, 79. Emphasis added.
56. *CD* III/1, 380–81; *KD* III/1, 436 quoted in *AO*, 80.
57. *AO*, 78–79.
58. Ibid., 78; *CD* II/2, 157.
59. *AO*, 78.
60. Ibid., 67–68.

And so the significance of time and creation are jeopardized. This is the substance of Jenson's critique of Barth's theology.

Hunsinger evaluates Jenson's interpretation as "the most provocative, incisive and wrong-headed reading of Barth available in English."[61] Jenson himself is aware that his interpretation leads to a conclusion that "is the opposite of what Barth intends,"[62] and indeed that "when we read his theology so we are reading it wrongly."[63] Yet, he insists, "[B]ut there is something that *compels* us to read it wrongly in this way."[64] For the incarnate Jesus is merely reduced to a sign and a mirror, and the body and the time (firstly of Jesus and secondly of all others) are endangered to be stripped of its ontological weight and so to be merely an illusion.

Jesus' Time

In Jenson's reading, the basic problem lies in Barth's conception of Jesus' time. In Barth, as Jenson puts it, "Jesus' time is 'eternal' because it is 'authentic, fulfilled time,' that is, it is time with a genuine past and future, genuine because his past is not lost or his future merely dreamed of, and therefore also time with a genuine present"[65] while human time is lost in the past and unknown in the darkness of the future. In human time only the present should be knowable. But even the present cannot be pinned down. The "now" always slips into the past. The present only "exists" between the forgetfulness of the past and the darkness of the future, between "no longer" and "not yet", that is, between nothingness and nothingness. Thus human time exists in contrast to God's time and to Jesus' time.

Further, in Barth, Jesus' Easter time is construed as *pure presentness*. Jenson sees this notion of the divine time as pure presentness problematic. For Barth, as Jenson indicates, "the Easter-narratives speak . . . 'of a present without future, of an eternal presentness of God in time.' Here is a time 'which just as it is can never become past and needs no future—a time of pure presentness . . .' [Barth, *KD* I/2, 126]."[66] The idea of eternity as the pure presentness reminds Jenson only of Plato's concept of eternity:

61. Hunsinger, *How to Read Karl Barth*, 15.
62. *GAG*, 152.
63. Ibid.
64. Ibid. Emphasis added.
65. Ibid.
66. Ibid., 153. Note Barth also says, "[I]t cannot become the past and has no future

"Was" and "will be" are aspects of time, and we are wrong in carelessly applying them to eternal Being. We say "it was," "it will be"; but "it is" alone may properly be applied to Being, while "it was" and "it will be" are properly said of the process in time; for these are motions, whereas that which is forever immovably the same cannot become either older or younger with time. For we say that "it was" and "is" and "shall be," but in verity "is" alone belongs to it: and "was" and "shall be" it is meet should be applied only to Becoming which moves in time.[67]

In Jenson's diagnosis, Barth's idea of Jesus' Easter time as eternity and as pure presentness suggests that Barth's concept still remains in the shadow of Plato, and this prevents Barth's great insight and emphasis on Jesus from fully coming through in his theology. "Barth may have banished the Cheshire cat of timeless eternity from his theology, but the grin decidedly lingers on."[68] Moreover, the tenacious patterns of language observed above features also in Barth's account on eternity and time: "Our time . . . stands under the *sign* and *shadow*, of this quite different time. This time is God's time."[69] Jenson remarks, "This sort of language is rather too close for comfort to *Plato's* talk of time as the moving image of timeless eternity."[70]

In Jenson's analysis, Barth's theology is unfortunately still tethered to the Platonic notion of eternity as timelessness or simultaneity. For Jenson, the critical task is then to purge such a Platonic spirit and to develop an account of God's eternity beyond inherited tale of timelessness or simultaneity. This means that the identity of the Son can no longer be anchored in pretemporal eternity as if he somehow existed in some timeless place or in some eternal present. Jesus must be identified in

---

at all before it . . ." (*KD* I/2, 127). Cf. Along this line, Barth suggests the idea of eternity and of Jesus' time as *simultaneity* without succession. "[The eternal God] is supremely temporal. For His eternity is authentic temporality, and therefore the source of all time. But in His eternity, . . . present, past and future, yesterday, to-day and to-morrow, are not successive, but simultaneous" (*CD* III/2, 437). Like this divine eternity, Jesus' time is also simultaneous. For Barth, Jesus' words that "I am the Alpha and the Omega . . . which is, and which was, and which is to come, the Almighty" (Rev. 1:8) means that "I am all this simultaneously. I, the same, am; I was as the same; and I will come again as the same. My time is always simultaneously present, past and future" (*CD* III/2, 465).

67. Plato, *Timaeus*, 37d–38a. Translation modified.
68. *GAG*, 153.
69. *CD* I/2, 66.
70. *GAG*, 152. Emphasis mine. Note Plato said, "[Creator] decided to make a kind of moving image of eternity . . . namely that which we call time." Plato, *Timaeus*, 37d.

thoroughly temporal terms, and any talk of a pretemporal Jesus (and of the *Logos asarkos*) must be abandoned. Jenson flatly rejects any form of pretemporal reality. Consequently, for Jenson, the temporal Jesus must be thought of not as a copy or mirror of the pretemporal Son, but simply as the Son. Only so can the reality of the incarnate Son (temporal Jesus) be fully maintained, and the significance of time and creation fully recognized. Jenson, in short, seeks to hold onto the concrete and particular reality of Jesus Christ as the axis of his constructive reflection.

Jenson's Innovation

The Eternal Double Election on the Horizon of Time

In deconstructing the Platonic notion of eternity that has informed Christian thinking for many centuries, and more generally in seeking to mitigate the corrosive effects of Greek philosophy on Christian theology, Jenson lays the groundwork for a radically innovative account of Christian doctrine.[71] In developing his system, Jenson has to reconstruct the concept of eternity, revolving around the concrete and temporal reality of Jesus of Nazareth. As in Barth's account of eternity, Jesus and his time should be placed at the bosom of God's eternity.[72] This particular person, Jesus Christ, is the *arche* and the *telos* of creation, and the constituent of divine eternity. Jesus of Nazareth, the man who lived in the first century in Palestine, died under Pontius Pilate, and resurrected in three days—this one *is* the *eternal* Jesus. *Just so* he is eternal.

In other words, eternal election is located in the time of the Nazarene. To grasp the meaning of God's eternal decree, we must not look back to the time of beginning or to some point of eternity "before" the beginning of the creation but direct our attention to the life time of Jesus

---

71. Cf. In a recent occasional statement, Jenson remarks, "[I]n volume II/2 of the *Church Dogmatics*, Barth teaches a drastically innovative doctrine of election that is often regarded—also by me—as the pivot of his mature theology. Crudely stated: the event of election is God's decision to be God-for-us as the man Jesus. Since with God his choice of himself cannot be separate from his eternal being as that self, this entails that the God-man Jesus Christ is somehow actual in the beginning of all reality. I will not here further develop this truly radical claim. . . . [I]f it is true then the relation of eternity to time is very different than we have thought in any tradition. And that must surely impact the relation of philosophy to theology" (Jenson, "On 'The Philosophy that Attends to Scripture'" lines 58–66).

72. *CD* II/2, 191.

God's Decision upon His Being

Nazareth. The Calvinistic doctrine of the double decree was reconfigured by Barth, and now Barth's "double decree" by Jenson: the doubleness of God's *eternal* election, God's Yes and No, is to be placed on the temporal *horizon* of the life of Jesus Christ, that is, in his reprobation and his election—his death and resurrection. In Jenson's analysis, Barth's Jesus occupies the place of the double decree of Calvinism all too literally. So, contra Barth and yet by prosecuting Barthian concept of God's eternity as Jesus' time, Jenson states, "we must seek to describe God's will—its eternity undiminished—as an event in history, as the chronologically and geographically fixable event of the life of Jesus of Nazareth, the Christ.... In *our* history God makes His *eternal* decision."[73]

So God's double will occur in the life of Jesus. Following Barth, Jenson affirms that God's No exists in the service of his Yes: God's Yes overcomes and transcends his No to us. But the locus of God's eternal will for creation is not pretemporal eternity but the temporal event of Jesus Christ. God's eternal decision—reprobation and election—occurs as the crucifixion and resurrection of Jesus Christ. The resurrection of Jesus Christ *is* God's eternal decree for us. God's decree is concomitant to the resurrection of Jesus over his death. The unity of God's double will, that is, the transcendence of reprobation by election, is not just found but "*constituted* . . . in the succession of the Crucifixion and the Resurrection."[74] The unity of God's wrath and mercy is "the unity of the Crucifixion with the Resurrection, . . . an *historical* unity."[75] There is no antecedent or underlying reality in the resurrection of Jesus Christ. The resurrection *is* the *eternal event*. "[W]hat happens between the human Jesus and his Father . . . *is* eternity."[76] Thus, in Jenson's theology, God's eternal election of the Son is located *on the horizon of time*. For Jenson, then, the doctrine of God's eternal double will and the doctrine of the resurrection of Jesus are inextricably related.

---

73. *AO*, 163.
74. Ibid., 165.
75. Ibid., 164.
76. *TI*, 141. Cf. "[T]o assert the Son's eternity, we have had to say [traditionally] that Jesus is the dwelling and manifestation of his own preexistent Double and with that all the impossibilities we have trudged through present themselves. It is the need for the 'pre-' that causes them; that is, it is the interpretation of eternity as Persistence of the first past that causes them" (*TI*, 141).

The Resurrection as the Locus of Eternal Generation and Eternal Election

The doctrine of the eternal generation also is woven into the doctrine of the resurrection and the eternal decree.[77] As seen above, in Jenson's reading of Barth, the eternal election of the Son and the eternal generation of the Son are not two separate events in eternity; these two are one and the same event. Jenson maintains this identity of the two. And this identification is observable in the following speculation: "The Crucifixion put it up to the Father: Would he stand to *this alleged* Son? To *this candidate* to be his own self-identifying Word? Would he be a God who, for example, hosts publicans and sinners, who justifies the ungodly? The resurrection was the Father's Yes."[78] For Jenson, God's declaration of Jesus as the Son by the resurrection is the moment that God accepts him into his own divine life and so posits a "you" within the life and the being of God. In the resurrection, Jesus is elected to be the Son of God in the resurrection and so declared to be the Son of God in the same event (Rom 1:4).[79] Jenson claims: "Christ's Sonship comes 'from' his Resurrection...."[80] For Jenson, the eternal generation occurred in the economy, precisely, in the resurrection.

Thus, the divine unity between the Father and the Son Jesus is achieved in the resurrection: "The Resurrection was the *executing* of the triune God's unity with himself."[81] God is the Trinity by electing Jesus, that is, by raising him from the dead.[82] Put it into more generic terms: "to be is *to rise from the dead*. Such is the description of reality that coheres with trinitarian doctrine of God."[83] In other words, God is triune *by* the resurrection. But would this mean that the God could have not had the Son without the resurrection? God could have been other than triune? Jenson says, "The Father can have his Son and us with him into the bar-

---

77. "The Father can have his Son and us with him into the bargain, or he can abolish us and have no Son, for there is no Son but the one who said, 'Father, forgive them.'" (*ST*, 1:191).

78. Ibid., 189.

79. Ibid., 142.

80. Ibid., 143.

81. Jenson, *Unbaptized God*, 140.

82. Hart states regarding Jenson's theology, "[God] is himself by determining and finding and becoming himself" (Hart, *The Beauty of the Infinite*, 161).

83. *TI*, 182. Emphasis added.

gain, or he can abolish us and have no Son, for there is no Son but the one who said, 'Father, forgive them.'"[84] For Jenson, God's triune being is constituted in God's *will or choice*. But should we think of the reality of God underlying or antecedent to his decision? Jenson would say: Never.

In Jenson's theology, the role of the Holy Spirit in the eternal generation is not forgotten. The tri-unity is achieved by virtue of the Holy Spirit who enables the overcoming of this impasse between infinity and finitude.[85] The infinite God and the finite Jewish man could have never been in unity. Or the infinity could have not embraced the finitude into itself and so could have been a kind of infinity that stands against and in sheer opposition to finitude and delimited by the boundary of finitude.[86] But by the Spirit, who overcomes every boundary, the impasse between the two is transcended, and the unity of God has been accomplished.[87] The role of the Spirit will be discussed in the last chapter.

Jenson's reconstruction of God's eternal decree and his eternal procession in close connection with the resurrection of Jesus also requires a reconfiguration of the doctrine of creation, especially the notion of *time*. If the resurrection of Jesus Christ functions *as the locus of God's eternal decree and his eternal procession*, then the resurrection must be construed as the *arche* of all things, somehow antecedent to all the creation. And at this conceptual juncture, Jenson's revisionary metaphysics of time comes into view. For Jenson, put briefly, time is not linear but recursive. Or more precisely, "Time is more like a helix, and what it spirals around is the risen Christ."[88] How this idiosyncratic notion operates with Jenson's emphasis on the role of the future will be discussed later. For now, it suffices to note that, due to this reconfigured notion of time, major christological charges leveled against Jenson are made off-target.

Does Jenson's Christology fall into arianism or adoptionism? If the resurrection is the locus of the eternal generation, was there time when the Son of God was not? Or, was Jesus the Son of God before the resurrection? These christological questions are to be settled in view of

---

84. *ST*, 1:191.

85. Ibid., 120.

86. Cf. "The Infinite is truly infinite only when it transcends its own antithesis to the finite" (Pannenberg, *Systematic Theology*, 1:400).

87. One may see here the dialectic movement: thesis, anti-thesis, and synthesis. But Jenson would not see himself as a Hegelian, as his philosophy is not quite eschatological after all (chapter 6).

88. Jenson, "Scripture's Authority in the Church," 35.

Jenson's revisionary work of metaphysics of time as well as of his account of the Spirit. Much criticism of Jenson's Christology falls short through lack of serious engagement with and full appreciation of Jenson's revisionary metaphysics and the doctrine of the Holy Spirit.[89] For now, before fuller unpacking later, we may note briefly that, in Jenson's scheme, the Son of God, Jesus of Nazareth, was preexistent from the very beginning of time, when the universe was created by the Word. Also Jesus was the Son already somehow before the resurrection by the coming of the Spirit who will unite Jesus with God of Israel. He is the Son already when the Spirit rested upon him in his baptism and when he was conceived by the Spirit in the womb of Mary. Again the role of the Spirit comes into play.[90]

Now we may identify the axiom of Jenson's theology: what is the doctrinal conviction that drives Jenson in this unconventional direction? His axiomatic doctrinal conviction comes into view when we look back at the starting point of all this revisionary theological enterprise: Jenson's rejection of Barth's *pretemporal* Jesus *and* of the dualistic conception of time and eternity. The time-proof eternity and the pretemporal eternity are jettisoned already in his early constructive theology. Positively stated: Jenson's theology rigorously holds onto the *particular and concrete reality of Jesus Christ*. Jenson never allows any kind of gap between Jesus of Nazareth and the Son of God. Jenson's (broadly) Lutheran *christological* commitment drives him to make this innovative maneuver.

Jenson's Post-supersessionistic Development

The resurrection continues to function as the center of Jenson's *trinitarian* theology also in his later developed post-supersessionistic theology of Israel. The resurrection is the primordial enactment of God's being as the Trinity and the event which cannot be preceded by any thought or being. As Jenson has recently stated to a Jewish theological audience, the resurrection is "not the consequent apprehension of God's triunity,"[91]

---

89. Cf. Simon Gathercole, "Pre-existence and the freedom of the Son in Creation and Redemption," 38–51; Crisp, *God Incarnate: Explorations in Christology*, chapter 3; Hunsinger, "Robert Jenson's Systematic Theology," 161–200.

90. "Father and Son are one God even as the Father abandons the Son, in that the Spirit who will raise Jesus had come in advance—as Spirit, anticipation is his being—and 'rested' on him from the moment of his dedication to this death, to be the bond of triune love also in abandonment" (*ST*, 1:191).

91. Jenson, "What Kind of God Can Make a Covenant?" 14.

implying that the Trinity is constituted in the resurrection. Also in his post-supersessionistic account, Jenson reiterates often his central point that "the doctrine of the Trinity only explicates Israel's faith in a situation in which it is believed that the God of Israel has prior to the general resurrection raised one of his servants from the dead."[92]

In his mature two-volume *Systematic Theology* (1997 and 1999), Jenson accounts for why the resurrection of one Israelite had to precede the general resurrection—even though old Israel did not expect this.[93] This will be discussed in chapter 4 when we will see how Jenson develops his account of the deity of Jesus as the enactment of the resurrection and how the resurrection of the one Israelite resolves the antinomy of Israel's hope. For Jenson, this Christian faith in the resurrection and in the Trinity must not be a cause of mutual dissent between Judaism and Christianity, but a standing invitation to the Jewish theologian for the deeper constructive dialogue and recognition of theological convergences and parallels within the economy of the one God of Israel.[94]

For Jenson, the Christian God is the God of Israel—of Christians and the Jews. As the doctrine of election is incorporated into the doctrine of God, God is construed as the one who determines his *eternal* identity by his election. In Jenson's theology, as we have seen, God is the one who determines and even constitutes his being by the act of election of Jesus of Nazareth. Later, in his post-supersessionistic development, Jenson comes to recognize that God's election embraces his election of Israel and that this act of election functions as a determinative element on his own eternal being. This strand of Jenson's thought will be explored in more detail, as we see later Jenson's congenial conversations with a leading Jewish theologian, Michael Wyschogrod's "actualistic theology" (chapter 4), which is in striking parallel to the "Barthian" Jenson's (chapter 3).

One may feel that Jenson has gone too far as he relentlessly temporalizes God's eternal election and generation of the Son. The consequent revisionary conception of God's eternity might also be hardly acceptable for many. I would not here precipitate my judgment on Jenson's revisionary trinitarian theology. However, believing that we can still appreciate his effort and identify his crucial insights from his post-supersessionistic theology, I will continue to explore the subterranean layers of or

---

92. *ST*, 1:63. Cf. Jenson, "What Kind of God," 14.

93. Ibid., 63–89.

94. Jenson, "What Kind of God," 15.

developing trajectories to his post-supersessionistic theology, following his daring theological enterprise which perdures in his unwavering conviction in Jesus of Nazareth as the Alpha and Omega.

Conclusion

Jenson's theology can be characterized as *temporal* actualistic ontology. For, in Jenson, God determines his eternal being by his act of election. God's acts of election and eternal generation of the Son are one and the same event, in Jenson's reading of Barth and also in his own constructive theology. Yet, diverging from Barth and rejecting the antithetical conception of eternity and time and the notion of pretemporal eternity, Jenson relocates God's eternal election and the eternal generation on the horizon of time, that is, in the resurrection of Jesus Christ. Thus, the resurrection becomes the locus of the eternal election and generation, and so of the enactment of God's being as the Trinity. Thus, Jenson temporalizes the Barthian actualistic ontology.

Also we have only briefly seen how Jenson's revisionary trinitarian theology, centering upon the resurrection, would develop in a post-supersessionistic direction. We will see in the following chapters (especially in chapter 4): Jenson offers an account on how the Christian doctrine of the Trinity is nothing but an explication of Israel's faith and hope that God of Israel will raise one of the Israelite as anticipation of the whole Israel. Further, we will see how Jenson construes the Christian God is God of Israel who determines his eternal identity by his election of Israel, as he deeply engages with Jewish theologians, especially Michael Wyschogrod (chapter 3).

2

God's Bodily Being

Body Ontology toward Post-supersessionistic Theology

THAT GOD HAS A body is not a traditionally accepted theological claim, but for Jenson it is a veridical ontological claim. Indeed, for Jenson, God *is* bodily existent insofar as Jesus Christ is regarded to be the body of God. Even after the resurrection and ascension, Jesus is present bodily to us, and just so is present as God. He is bodily present to us as the eucharistic elements of which Jesus said, "This is my body," and "This is my blood." So the bread and wine *is* his body. The church is his body as the eucharistic body of Jesus Christ is given and shared to those around it. The divine body of Jesus (as the church) is accommodative of other human bodily beings, so that the humans may enter into the life and being of the Trinity. In other words, Jenson's conception of the body of God develops through christology, sacramentology, and ecclesiology. For Jenson, the church comes to carry the weight of God's being, through Christ. In this chapter, I will attempt to trace this conceptual strand in Jenson, which will be woven into his post-supersessionistic theology of Judaism. In this chapter, this exposition develops in five sections: 1) God as the bodily being, 2) the christological body, 3) the eucharistic body, 4) the ecclesial body, and lastly 5) the body within the Trinitarian communion.

God as the Bodily Being

In his account of the body of God or of God as bodily being, Jenson begins with a generic analysis of the materiality of religious culture. In his analysis, any religion has material or bodily aspects and needs objects and rituals for their belief to be shared with and communicated to other people. All communications are mediated by material objects and bodily gestures. Given such characteristics of communication, any religious revelation requires "an *embodied* revelation, a grant of divine objectivity."[1]

However, "[i]f religious longing for God *himself* comes alive, it must leave such revelatory objectifications behind."[2] At the higher stages, religions seek to enter into atemporal or ineffable realm, leaving revelatory material objects behind. In religions, a material "revelation is a mere starting point and impetus."[3] Their god is atemporal, immaterial, and disembodied, after all. To enter into the divine, all objectifications and revelations must be a ladder only to be discarded in the end.

According to Jenson, some branches of Christian theology also—regrettably—have developed a synthetic account of divine revelation, according to which God has to submit to some physical additions[4] in order to come to us. In such a theology, God is regarded permanently disembodied. The disembodied Son of God had to assume a human body to come to us. In that sort of theology, "the Son can involve himself with embodiment, while the Father remains pure."[5] In such a "spiritualized" version of Christianity, the bread and cup on the eucharistic table are regarded merely symbols of God's presence.

In Jenson's account, the gospel prohibits such a religious attempt of immaterialization. When the revelation of God is given to us, our reflection must not transcend the revelation. And if the revelation is fully human as a bodily being—obviously Jesus Christ, then God's being must not be abstracted from that revelatory object. Any such abstraction will trigger a human enterprise to search for God in darkness—contrary to the gospel, according to which it is God that searches for us and comes to us. And when such an abstract and transcendental enterprise "succeeds,"

---

1. Jenson, "The Body of God's Presence: A Trinitarian Theory," 85. Emphasis added.
2. Ibid.
3. Ibid., 86.
4. Ibid., 87.
5. Ibid.

and so when the human soul reaches what it identifies as the atemporal, immaterial, and ineffable being, the revelation of God in and as Jesus Christ is relativized, and human projection of their individual or communal good or desire onto the screen of eternity is more or less necessitated. For Jenson, any attempt to transcend divine revelation through some intellectual-mystical ascent presumes and trades upon separation of God's being from his revelation. That is merely a form of idolatry.[6]

The Christological Body

That God is bodily in and of himself is a christological claim, for Jenson, since Jesus is the body of God. Jenson's notion of the body of God is worked out exegetically and theologically as well as philosophically. In "The Body of God's Presence" and *Visible Word*, Jenson presents a generic account of the body *first and then* moves onto the account of the body of God. So it seems that Jenson confers an antecedently conceptualized notion of the body on the God of the gospel.[7] However, in my reading, his presentational order seems to work as a communicative strategy, for the sake of many readers whose thinking generally moves from a universal to a particular and concrete, while the deeper trajectory of Jenson's argument runs in the other way around. Hence, it would be helpful here to reverse Jenson's presentational order in order to understand his particularistic notion of the body of God.

Jenson starts his account of the body of God by noting that "God is Word eternal in himself."[8] God does not speak a word or "merely have a word, [but] he *is* his Word."[9] For Jenson, this striking claim is derived from a trinitarian belief that the Word is (*homoousios*) with the Father.[10]

---

6. Ibid., 86. One may hear the resonance of Barth in Jenson's identification of the revelation and God's being.

7. Following Webster's observation that Jenson "begins from observations about embodiment rather from the identity of who the metaphor is predicated," Swain raises concern about Jenson's methodology with regard to his conception of the body of God and poses a question, "Is such a starting point legitimate, given the unique identity of this agent and the unique nature of this agent's relationship to the community that is his body?" (Swain, *The God of the Gospel*, 119). See also John Webster, "'In the Society of God,'" 200–222.

8. Jenson, "The Body of God's Presence," 88.

9. Ibid., 87. Emphasis added.

10. *ChrD*, 1:175.

Or it may be said that the Word spoken by God captures the reality of God so well and profoundly that there is no epistemological or even ontological gap between the Word and the reality of God himself. If God's Word is true, then the Word cannot fail to capture the reality, in this case, God himself.[11] God's revelation is God himself. Or, God *is* his Word.[12]

The Word that is one being with God himself is also the object of God's self-knowledge. "God does not know himself by seeing himself in a sort of metaphysical mirror. . . . God *speaks* himself, and so, in what he says, knows himself. . . . [In the beginning there was] the Word by which God knows himself."[13] For Jenson, God's self-knowledge is linguistically mediated. As God listens to his self-speech, God knows himself. By listening to this Word that is uttered by himself about himself, God knows himself. Thus, the Word is the *object* of God's *listening* for his self-knowledge. In short, the Word is the (auditory) self-object of God.

God's self-speech is directed not only to himself but also to us. It is revelation of God himself to us. Here for the revelation to be true, God's self-speech must be given to us. The Word that God has and listens to for his self-knowledge must be given to us for the sake of the verity of God's revelation. According to the gospel, it is the very Word that captures the reality of God precisely, that is, the auditory object of God himself, which has been given to us in history. In Jenson's reading, the apostle John's point is: "The word we hear from God—the story John is about to tell about Christ and the words of Christ he will report—this word is none other than the Word in the beginning, the Word by which God knows himself."[14] The Word, the auditory self-object of God, is a historical figure that the apostle John is going to tell us about in his gospel, Jesus of Nazareth. This bodily being is the Word, the self-object of God. By listening to Jesus of Nazareth, God listens to himself and knows himself, and we know God. So "[a]s God turns to himself, to what he knows and wills for and of himself, he turns to Jesus, the man from Nazareth."[15] Jesus of

---

11. Here it is notable that Jenson states that God is his Word rather than that the Word is God. The latter is usually taken to be about the deity of the Word. But that is not Jenson's concern here. Rather, his concern is the veracity of God's revelation.

12. Here it seems that Jenson depends on Luther who argues in his Christmas sermon on John 1 that God is Word, not changing the order of the Johannine original language. See chapter 5 for Jenson's notion that God is Word.

13. Jenson, "Joining the Eternal Conversation," lines 133-40.

14. Ibid., line 136.

15. *VW*, 34. Similarly, Jenson says, "The truth of its knowledge of God occurs in

Nazareth is the audible and visible self-object. In this sense, in Jenson, Jesus is the body of God. Thus, in Jenson's account, the notion of the body as *objectivity* comes into view.[16]

Here what could have been said is that the immaterial Word has become incarnate in the first century. But Jenson has not said that. For Jenson, there is no such thing as the *Logos asarkos* even before the creation. Consequently, there is no duality within the person of Jesus between Logos *asarkos* in the upper level and the human nature or Jesus in the lower level. It would be only the *extra Calvinisticum* which posits some entity beyond Jesus of Nazareth. Moreover, there is *no Barthian "distinction"* either, the distinction of the pretemporal Jesus and the temporal Jesus, in which for Jenson the latter is taken to be a repetition or a copy of the former, as seen in the first chapter. Jesus of Nazareth the fully temporal and bodily figure is the object that God has for his self-understanding. In Jenson's theology, any form of atemporal or pretemporal Logos/Jesus has to be expunged in order to give due ontological weight to Jesus Christ, the revelation of God. Jesus, the revelation and God himself, must not be transcended in tantalizing hope for the knowledge of God behind or beyond the concrete reality of Jesus. Jenson fears that Jesus Christ as the true Word would become relativized or discarded in prioritization of a human search for the atemporal God via a mystical ascent.

This is obviously a *theological* exegesis of John 1, in which Jenson's radical commitment to Lutheran theology is in operation. Jenson deeply shares Luther's rejection of any notion of the divinity abstracted from the humanity of Jesus—the rejection famously captured in Luther's dictum:

---

that God freely identifies himself in the same way that he lets us identify him. The fact of revelation is the fact of freely granted coincidence of the way we pick God out and the way he picks himself out" (*VW*, 38).

16. In Jenson's reading of John's Gospel, the moment of creation and the moment of the utterance of God's Word are inherently related. In the beginning, God spoke the Word by which this particular world was created. There is no Word as such apart from the creation. The moment of the utterance of the Word is the moment that the creation came into being. The Word does not exist apart from the creation. But the primacy of the Word over the creation is indeed emphasized in Jenson, as it is by the Word that all things were created. And the Word has the particular content, which the apostle John is going to speak of: Jesus of Nazareth. Put differently, because the Word has the particular content (the life of Jesus) in eternity or from the beginning, when the Word (the person of Jesus) was uttered, the universe came into being. Further, in Jenson's theological exegesis, the Word is not inner idea in God's mind, contra the classical theology. But it is *spoken* Word not only internally to God himself but also externally. When this Word was uttered, the creation came into being.

"Don't give me any of that God."[17] A 'naked' deity—a God not clothed in Jesus—"has nothing to do with us."[18] Moreover, for Jenson, even the Barthian pretemporal preincarnate Jesus has no place in the gospel. A sheer deity abstracted from his body only terrifies Luther and the Lutheran Jenson. Thus, Jenson's notion of the body of God is a theological and exegetical conception. So far, the body of God is characterized in terms of objectivity.

In the next step, the body of God is characterized in terms of *availability*, as Jenson develops the concept of the body in the context of *conversation*. In normal conversations, mutual objectification of the other's body occurs. I can see you and touch you (your body). Your body becomes the object of my seeing, speech, and touch. So you are available to me in our conversation. In turn, you objectify me for your seeing, speech, and touch. Thus, mutual objectification occurs in conversation. But if one's objectification of the other's body occurs only in one way, that is, if I evade being available for you, by withholding my bodily presence from you, our relationship will turn to be a "lordship-and-slavery" relation.[19] Jenson explains this plainly in his Lecture at Princeton: "Suppose that I were disembodied before you. What would happen? Let us suppose that the thoughts that constitute this lecture continued to emerge in your head. . . . You would not be able to get at me. Supposing that what emerged in your head was so offensive that you wanted to throw me out of the room, where would you find me? Or suppose that what emerged in your head was so great that you wanted to kiss me, how would you manage that? You see, the 'existential' reality of a body is its availability. My body is simply me insofar as I am available to you."[20] If I refuse to be an object for your subject, our relationship becomes destructive. "A disembodied personal presence to me could only mean my bondage, no matter how benevolent in intention; and were the person in question God, the bondage would be absolute."[21]

However, such a destructive relationship does not occur between God and us, according to Jenson, since God allows mutual objectification in his communication with us. God does not withhold his bodily

---

17. "Mir aber des Gottes nicht!" (Luther, *Vom Abendmahl Christi, Bekenntnis*, WA 26, 332, quoted in *ST*, 2:214).

18. *ST*, 2:214.

19. *VW*, 21–22.

20. Jenson, *A Theology in Outlines*, 38.

21. *ST*, 2:214.

presence from us. God allows our subjectivity to stand before him to objectify him as he has made himself an object before us. He does not destroy our subjectivity before his Subjectivity. God graciously allows his relationship with us to be reciprocal. Our existence is allowed before him as genuine "thou," not being reduced to a merely pure object. Jenson writes, "Were Christ not embodied in his community, were his presence there merely to and in thought and feeling, he would be the community's destruction, however fond the thoughts and feelings; and were he not embodied for the world in his community, his presence in the world would be the world's damnation."[22]

Here it is noteworthy: underlying Jenson's notion of the body is the idea that God's speech to us awaits our speech to him. That one should be bodily available to another for mutual objectification means that one should be an object for another's *speech* to him. In other words, one's bodily availability is an invitation for others' speech to himself. Theologically speaking, that God is bodily present to us and available to us means that God is ready to be spoken to by us and that by his bodily presence, God invites us to speak to him. Moreover, for Jenson, speech to each other is an ontologically weighty act: to share one world with each other[23] or even to be interpenetrative to each other. Accordingly, when God invites us to speak to him by his bodily presence, we are invited to share and even become one reality with him and so we enter into God's being, by and through his body Jesus. Thus, this communicative notion of the body plays out as an ontological and soteriological concept. Already it is noticeable that his concept entails the soteriological doctrine of *theosis*. This will be discussed further later. For now, it seems suffice to note that Jenson would never separate communication from the mutual bodily presence.

Jenson makes yet another step: "God *identifies* himself by Jesus."[24] The body of God is his identifiability. As God's body is Jesus, God can be identified when we point out to the locality of Jesus' body or narrate what he has done in the past with his body. We can identify God because God has a body. That is the object by and with which *God* identifies himself, as said in the first point. God's body is identifiability in that by the body

---

22. Ibid.

23. "It is in speech about the world, in whatever kinds of signs, that we inhabit a world that is not my world only or yours only but precisely ours, so that we can come together in it" (*ChD*, 1:175–76).

24. *VW*, 37.

God identifies himself and we identify him. Jenson's notion of the body as identifiability is explicated with his conviction of the irreplaceability of God's choice. Jesus as the body of God cannot be replaced with any other persons or with any other objects once God's decision is made eternally. Jesus is the only God's irreplaceable self-object precisely because he is eternally *chosen*.

As the last step, Jenson states: "[T]o say that God has a body is to say that God transcends himself, that he has history."[25] The body is one's self-object to be transcended. But transcending one's body can be "either to be deathless disembodied spirit, to have fully *escaped* from the body, or it is to *rise* from the dead."[26] For Jenson, God has transcended his body not by being disembodied but by way of resurrection. God's body has been transcended to be the resurrected body. Now his body is transcending, as his body becomes available at different places (eucharistic tables) and in different times still as the one body, and as his body is given to embrace and accommodate other human beings into his (ecclesial) body.

In sum, the body of God is the object that God has for himself, for his self-understanding, that is, the object that God takes *as* himself. And it is the very object given to us so that we may objectify him in our address to him and so that mutual objectification may be possible in communications between God and us. Here mutual objectification is made possible *graciously* in our relationship with God since God has given us the very object of God himself. In this sense, the body of God is his availability to us, for our speech to him. Also by this object, God is identified and yet transcends it so that it may be given and it may embrace others for salvation. Finally, an ontological implication of Jenson's notion of the body of God is to be noted: in Jenson, the body is not a husk or a gift-wrap that wraps around something more important within it. His body is an essential constituent of his eternal being, of course, by his gracious act of choice.

The Eucharistic Body

Jesus is resurrected and taken up into heaven. Then questions are raised: how is God embodied for us now, after the ascension? Does God cease to be bodily present to us? Has the mutual objectification involved in

---

25. Ibid., 35.
26. Ibid., 36. Emphasis original.

our conversation with God been made impossible by the ascension of Jesus so that our relationship with God lapses into the horror of Hegel's master-slave dialectic? In Jenson's theology, "[t]he object-problem about Jesus' presence is the problem of prayer: when we respond to the gospel-address, at what do we speak? Where do we look when praying? In what direction do we speak?"[27] In this section, we will examine this complex of questions by exploring Jenson's account of the bodily presence of God to the church in the Eucharist.

The Eucharistic Body of Jesus Christ

In Jenson's theology, Jesus is still bodily and objectively present even after his resurrection and ascension, *as* the bread and cup. It is not quite satisfactory for Jenson to state merely that Jesus is presence "in, with, and under" the elements. In expressing his discomfort with this traditional formulation of the eucharistic mode of Christ's presence, Jenson is aware that he is breaking with the language of the Lutheran confessions. But he denies that he thereby is rejecting their central doctrinal tenet. Jenson says, "The Lutheran confessions' discussions of these matters have a complicated background, and are done in an Aristotelian conceptual framework which sometimes obscures their point."[28] But their aim is simply to secure in their theology the real presence of Jesus Christ at the Eucharist table and therefore to affirm that "the Lord is present . . . *as* the objects bread and wine."[29]

"But if the Lord is present persistently as the objects bread and wine, what is to prevent our misusing this availability?"[30] Jenson is unflinching here: as the eucharistic objects are vulnerable to misuse, so is the very body of Jesus. As Jesus was vulnerable on the cross, so is his body at the table. At the Eucharist, "we *can* steal Jesus and try to use him as a charm; we *can* carry him about in procession, and the practices of the procession *can* very well be the practices of self-justification. . . . [I]t is that they are violations of the present Lord. The violators at Corinth did not by their

---

27. *SP*, 163. Cf. "We are to turn neither to shrines and idols nor to nowhere. . . . When we gather, we gather around the bread and cup" (*VW*, 46).
28. Jenson and Gritsch, *Lutheranism*, 85.
29. Jenson, *Unbaptized God*, 32. Emphasis added.
30. Ibid. Emphasis added.

unsisterly use of the bread make it not be the body of Christ; they made themselves guilty over against the body of Christ."[31]

Now in light of the discussion in the previous section, let us consider the meaning of the statement that the eucharistic elements are the body of Jesus Christ. First, the bread and wine is the *object* that Jesus takes as himself. Now "[a]s [Jesus] turns to himself, he turns to the shared loaf and cup, to the bath, to our sheer visible and tangible presence to one another, and in general to all our community's objectivity in the gospel. In all this, he sees himself. That he does so, is our salvation."[32] Further, as the object is taken to be himself by Jesus himself, now we turn to the bread and wine when we want to turn to him. "[W]hen we turn to the object loaf and cup or bath or gathered community, we have precisely the body of God for our object."[33] Just so the bread and wine is the *availability* of Jesus to us. And for this reason, as Jesus is available to us, and of course as we are to him, the mutual objectification is still possible in the communication between us and him.

The particular eucharistic elements are the body of Jesus *irreplaceably*. Jenson speculates: "If the church had begun in a northern climate, doubtless its sacramental drink, if it had one, would be beer. . . . God might not have chosen Israel from the nations, or Jesus from among the Israelites, or washing instead of incensing, or bread instead of potato chips."[34] Here it is his decision that makes certain objects his own body. The actualistic ontology discussed in the first chapter is at work here. God's contingent and free decision determines which object is his body and so determines his being. It is true also of the relation of Jesus and the bread and wine. Jesus has chosen them to *be* his body when he says "This is my body." "[J]ust this contingency is what binds us."[35]

---

31. Ibid., 33. Emphasis added.
32. *VW*, 35.
33. *ST*, 1:229.
34. *VW*, 9.

35. Ibid. In connection with this, it must be noted that Jenson's notion of the body is not "elastic." Burgess argues that Jenson's notion of the body is so elastic and *ad hoc*, interpreting Jenson to mean, for example, that "the pen with which I write, or the computer into which I type might become my body in that I utilize them in communicating stretches the notion of body rather a long way" (Burgess, "A Community of Love?" 294). Only the *chosen* objects such as the bread and the wine are God's body because Jesus said of them, "*This* is my body." Burgess misses how the actualistic ontology and the power the Word of God play out in Jenson's account of the body.

In this regard, Jenson upholds the power of the word of God in his understanding of the Eucharist. One of the differences between God and us is the power of his word. When God says so, it *is* so. Manifestly in creation: when God said, "Let there be . . . ," it *was* so. Likewise, when Jesus says, "this is my body," the loaf *is* his body. Solely because of the power of his divine word, the bread and cup *is* his body and blood.

Pertinent to the second point in our previous discussion on the body of God: the bread and wine is the identifiability of Jesus Christ. If we point to the bread and wine on the eucharistic table, we are referring to where Jesus is now, in Jenson's account, as Jesus has identifies himself with the elements. Lastly, the bread and wine as the body of Jesus Christ is to be transcended. It does not remain as it was but will be what it will be. It is true that the eucharistic elements are the body, but his body must be more than that. The bread and wine is broken and poured out and taken into the mouths of the people who gather around the table. The body is broken but living in those who share the body around the table and even *as* those partakers.

The Lutheran Characteristics

In consideration of these three points on the eucharistic body, we can perceive a prevailing Lutheran cast to Jenson's account. Jenson distances from the Zwinglian statement that "Christ's body is not everywhere, even if his divinity fills all things; and nor then is he bodily present where there is faith in Christ."[36] At its root, the issue is christological. Zwingli's Christology appears to Jenson inadequate, falling short of a crucial insight that the humanity and the divinity of Jesus should never be torn apart: where Jesus is present in divine manner, he is also humanly and bodily present. In the Eucharist Jesus is present not only in his spirit but also bodily. Jenson writes, "It is perhaps the chief strictly theological achievement of the Lutheran wing of the Reformation, in the conceptual turmoil of the time, to have seen how [Zwingli's sacramental statement] were provoked by inadequate Christology."[37]

So Jenson claims that Zwingli cannot do full justice to the force and veracity of Jesus' word, "This is my body." Per contra, the Lutherans made an effort to uphold the authority of the words of the Lord in their

36. *ST*, 2:256.
37. Ibid.

sacramentology: "Luther stuck to the authority of the word that Christ is really present in the Lord's Supper."[38] Accordingly, Luther claimed that "[t]he 'real presence' is neither dependent upon human faith [as the Reformed theologians argue] nor on the laws of physics [as the Roman Catholic theology seems to assume]."[39] So centered upon the authority and veracity of the words, the Lutherans revise the inherited ontology.

This leads us to the Lutheran formula: *finitum est capax infiniti*. In the Lutheran theology, the body of Jesus Christ is capable of using the infinite powers of God. His body or the man Jesus is transcendent over space. Jenson states, "The man Jesus, also as man, participates in the divine transcendence of time and space."[40] And this man's transcendence over space is exactly God's transcendence over space. Jenson pointedly puts it, "[Without Jesus,] God would neither create space nor transcend it. Thus the risen man Jesus not only transcends space but is constitutive of God's transcendence of it."[41] God's transcendence over space and time is therefore always characterized by this man and so by his body.

Clearly the Lutheran eucharistic Christology calls for revision of the inherited metaphysics: the Lutheran "Christology cannot be worked without damage to the metaphysical tradition."[42] Jenson recalls his days in Luther Seminary when he was in his twenties (in 1950s): one of the faculty members, Herman Preus, "led me to read the Lutheran scholastics, and reading led me to revere them. I remain in awe of the old Lutherans' intellectual power and daring christologically driven ontological revisions, and have hoped to follow in their steps. Insofar as I am still a recognizably Lutheran theologian, it is the hyper-Cyrillian Christology/sacramentology of Johannes Brenz—shortly adopted by Luther himself—that is the chief bond."[43] The Lutheran metaphysics militates against any view that the body cannot transcend space and time or that a plurality of objects in different locations and times cannot be one body. Since the Lutheran theology upholds that the eucharistic bread and wine *is* the body of Jesus *and* that Jesus is also at the right hand of the Father in heaven, it must be that the human body of Jesus is transcendent of space and time.

---

38. Jenson, *Lutheranism*, 77.
39. Ibid.
40. Jenson, "Christ in the Trinity," 66.
41. *ST*, 2:254.
42. Jenson, *Lutheranism*, 104.
43. Jenson, "A Theological Autobiography, to Date," 47.

If this sacramentological and christological metaphysics collides with any inherited ontology, then that must be deconstructed.[44]

In the Lutheran revisionary metaphysics, the body of Jesus Christ is transcendent of space and time: the breads and wines at different locations and times are one body of Jesus Christ who is also seated at the right hand of the Father. Yet, that conception seems to imply that the transcendence of Jesus is only where the eucharistic elements and the churches are and so still *within* the ecclesial boundary.

Then, how is Jesus bodily present where the objects such as the bread and the church are absent? To grasp Jenson's position on this issue, we need to recast the question in *temporal* terms. For, in Jenson's work, the bodily presence of Jesus Christ is considered in the *temporal* relation between the present space and the future space. On Jenson's account, the "heaven" to which Jesus ascends and from which he is present to the church is conceived to be the future in which God dwells.[45] The whole of time and space is related to the final time, the *eschaton*, in which Jesus takes up his proper space. The whole creation is present to God and Jesus in the eschaton; creation thus is present to the future. In other words, Jesus is present to the whole of time and space, spiritually and bodily, from the eschatological future. We will return to this in the final chapter.

At this point, our prime concern is with Jenson's implicit claim that the presence of Jesus Christ is *not* exhausted in or as the bread and wine. Given Jenson's strong language about the identification of the risen Jesus with the eucharistic elements and community, it is understandable that some readers have claimed that Jenson's Jesus is risen almost onto the table and so into the church.[46] Jenson clearly says that the risen Christ "needs no other body to be a risen man. . . . There is and needs to be no other place than [the bread and cup] for him to be embodied."[47] However,

---

44. Cf. Accordingly, the human body is not to be defined by such a worldview: "if a human can share in God's omnipresence, etc., even as so interpreted, then the embodied character of human creaturehood is not primarily to be defined by 'materiality' as the label of a land of substance and so by Newtonian rules about where and when such substances can be" (Jenson, *Lutheranism*, 109).

45. "[H]eaven is . . . the created space God takes, from which to be present to his other creatures" (*ST*, 2:121).

46. Cf. "In so far as Christ is risen, he is for [Jenson] risen into, almost as, the church" (Gunton, *Father, Son, and Holy Spirit*, 219).

47. *ST*, 1:206. I think it is legitimate to replace "the church" for "the bread and cup" in our context. Cf. "the only body of Christ to which Paul ever actually refers is not an entity in this heaven but the Eucharist's loaf and cup and the church assembled

this claim must be interpreted in view of Jenson's eschatological understanding of the presence of Jesus; it certainly does not signal a sheer collapse of the resurrected Christ into self-sustaining Christian rituals. It is to be noted that Jenson emphasizes that the body is to *be transcended* in the anticipation of the future. As indicated just above, Jenson affirms that Jesus "can be *both* 'seated at the right hand of the Father' (as the creed asserts) and in the bread and wine."[48] The bodily presence of Jesus is present to us as certain eucharistic elements and to the whole of creation as the *eschatos*. The two temporal modes of his presence will be abolished when our time arrives at the eschaton, that is, when the unity of his body will be achieved in an unprecedented way. Until then, the futural aspect of the bodily presence of Jesus is not to be disregarded.

Now how does the Lutheran Jenson's understanding of the Eucharist differ from that of the Roman Catholic church? According to Aquinas, the real, substantial presence of the body and blood of Christ under the form of the bread and wine "can happen only by a miracle, a new miracle at each Mass."[49] "It must be a predictable miracle; we must know where to find it. This is guaranteed by the existence of the church. Summarizing Aquinas' position: God grants to the church, through its own sacramental structure, the authority to invoke the miracle, to say 'This is my body' and have it become true."[50] For Jenson, however, such a miracle is unnecessary.[51]

A miracle of transubstantiation of the bread and wine is not required, "once the miracle of the resurrection and the ascension is posited."[52] If the resurrected Jesus has a transcendental character, then he can be bodily available and present (from heaven) at the eucharistic table as the bread and wine. How then the consecration of the bread and wine occur according to Jenson's Lutheran theology? It is neither by the act or faith of a priest nor by the faith of a receiver. The consecration does occur in a linguistic context, and it "need not be one single act."[53] "There are many

---

around them" (Ibid., 204).

48. Jenson, *Lutheranism*, 77. Emphasis added.
49. *ChrD*, 2:356.
50. Ibid.
51. Ibid., 358.
52. Ibid., 359.
53. Ibid., 360.

verbal contexts that can in this sense consecrate; the recitation of the narrative of institution is but one possibility, though an obvious one."[54]

In Jenson's account, the Eucharist is a memorial offering of thanksgiving. "When we give thanks and share the bread and wine, we do it for the sake of Christ's 'remembrance'"[55] since Jesus said, "Do this *for my remembrance.*" In Jenson's account, it is God who is to be reminded in our eucharistic petitionary prayer, as

> [i]n the Old Testament, God's being reminded and remembering are pivotal theological concepts. For the central example: "And God heard [Israel's] groaning [in Egypt] and God remembered his covenant with Abraham." It is a standard beginning of Israel's prayer: "Remember your mercy, O God, and your steadfast love from of old." This divine "remembering" is not an act enclosed within divine subjectivity; it occurs precisely as his hearing of Israel's cries and as his answering intervention.[56]

Such a petitionary prayer is offered to God in the context of the Eucharist. And God's answer makes the elements what it should be. *Just so* the bread and wine is consecrated in the visible *linguistic* context of our prayer offered in our bodily gestures and God's answer. "When it is God who remembers, his answer creates what it mentions, as do all his addresses."[57]

This construal of the Eucharist, Jenson holds, "offers a way beyond the ancient ecumenical impasses."[58] For it recognizes the concerns that lie behind the doctrine of the transubstantiation, "honor[ing] the reality and efficacy of the church's eucharistic act [of the consecration],"[59] and so avoiding the individualization of faith that Roman Catholics perceive in the Reformed understanding of the Eucharist. In the Lutheran view that Jenson creatively appropriates, the consecration of the elements occurs when the gathered people communally perform the Lord's Supper and thus offer a petitionary prayer and when God answers their prayer. In this

---

54. Ibid.

55. *ST*, 2:258.

56. Ibid. The language of Old Testament could be understood to suggest supersessionism, with the new replacing the old. However, Jenson himself uses "Old Testament." He says, "When in the following I speak of the 'Old Testament,' it is with the stipulation that 'old' is to mean simply 'older' or even 'senior,' and not 'antiquated' or 'superseded'" (*Canon and Creed*, 20).

57. Ibid.

58. *ChrD*, 2:361.

59. Ibid.

Lutheran view, moreover, the efficacy of the Eucharist does not depend on "the kind of church-controlled miracle the Reformed has protested [against the Roman Catholics tradition]."[60] Thus, this Lutheran proposal is presented as a middle way and offered for consideration in an effort for ecumenical unity.

The Ecclesial Body

As the bread and wine as the body of Jesus Christ is shared with and taken to those around the table in the church, the church is the body of Christ. Here, as we follow Jenson's account, we will be able to see also his *ecumenical* effort to recognize the legitimate concerns in other denominations of the church. Later on, this ecumenical trajectory, Jenson's theology of Judaism will be construed.

The church is the body of Christ. Here we see the notion of the body consistently worked out in Jenson's ecclesiology. The church is the object that Jesus turns to when he turns to himself. The church is "*truly* Christ's body for us, because Christ himself takes [it] for the object as which he is available to himself."[61] The church is the body of Jesus Christ also in that she is the *availability* of Jesus *for others*. "There is where creatures can locate him, to respond to his word to them."[62] She is the object-body that the creatures can and should turn to when they want to turn to and speak to Jesus in reply. If I am in the church, "[i]n the assembly of believers, where am I to direct my intention, in order to be intending my Lord? The first answer is: I am to look around me, at the assembly itself."[63] What about the world? "Where can the world find him? The world can find Christ as the assembly of his faithful around his sacraments. The church is the body as which Christ confronts his world."[64] So the church is the body or even the objective self of Jesus Christ, available to all human creatures.

---

60. Ibid.

61. "Sacrament and church are *truly* Christ's body for us, because Christ himself takes these same things for the object as which he is available to himself. For the proposition that the church is a human body of the risen Jesus to be ontically and straightforwardly true, all that is required is that Jesus indeed be the Logos of God, so that his self-understanding determines what is real" (*ST*, 1:206). Emphasis added.

62. Ibid., 205.

63. Jenson, "The Church and the Sacraments," 210.

64. Ibid.

At this point, Protestant anxieties may arise: if the church is too closely identified with the body of Christ, it seems to entail a sort of ecclesial triumphalism, which Protestant theology traditionally disavows. On the other hand, the Roman Catholics has conceived the church as the subject of salvation.[65] In their view, Christ has entrusted to the church "an active ministry, that is, a ministry that is not a sheer announcing or attesting . . . but that involves the doing of concrete saving acts."[66] Over against this Catholic view, Protestants have conceived the church as the object to be open to reform: "The church is always the object of grace, never its subject."[67]

In Jenson's judgment, both concerns are legitimate and biblically right. In his analysis, "the issue may be grasped in terms of the meeting of Christ and believers and of believers among themselves."[68] Christ and the church are two, rather than one, in that they can confront one another. In the Eucharist, Christ meets the church as the gathering stands at a distance from the eucharistic elements. There "Christ is salvifically active and the church receptive,"[69] as the Reformation theologians would say. Moreover, it can be legitimately argued in favor of the Roman Catholics that it is the church that mediates the salvific presence of Christ to the world. For, in the Eucharist, Christ is bodily present within the church by the prayerful act of consecration.

In this context, Jenson makes an ecumenical proposal to construe the church as an association and a community at once, employing Max Weber's sociological terminology. For Jenson, the church is identified with Jesus Christ as the body of Christ *and* is also an "other" to him. This dialectical identification and distinction between the two are played out in the context of the Eucharist. The church as an *association (Gesellschaft)* of people gathers around the eucharistic table, standing at a distance from the body of Christ. So construed, the church is still an "other" to Jesus Christ. The sacramental elements that Jesus takes as his body are in the assembly as "other than us." So the church is an association "in that the church gathers around objects *distinct* from herself, the bread and cup."[70]

---

65. Jenson, *Unbaptized God*, 61.
66. Ibid., 92.
67. Ibid., 91.
68. Ibid., 95.
69. Ibid.
70. *ST*, 2:214. Emphasis added.

The church is also a community (*Gemeinshaft*), as those around the Eucharist take the bread and wine and by so doing are the one body of Christ. In this sense, the church is more than an aggregate of people but a community. "In the Supper . . . we all receive one and the same Body of Christ. . . . And because in this way the members of the church are joined together to one Body of Christ, they are also joined with one another and become one Body whose head is Christ."[71] The partakers of the body of Christ are the body of Christ, jointly with other partakers and also with all the saints in history who have already partaken of it. Thus, the church is a community, the body of Christ overcoming the distance or otherness between the people around the table and the eucharistic objects that Jesus takes to be himself. "[T]he body of Christ received in the Eucharist is . . . itself identical with the community it creates."[72] So construed, the church is the availability of Christ to the world. It can find him when it turns to the church. As a community, the church is identified with Jesus Christ to the world.

Again, has Jenson identified the church too closely with Christ? Susan Wood worries about Jenson's conception of the church as the objective self of Jesus and proposes a Catholic alternative: the church is to be regarded as a sign or a sacrament distinguished from the risen Lord while identified with him. Wood writes, "The concept of sacrament is able to express the unity between the sign and the referent of that sign at the same time that it maintains the distinction between sign and referent. . . . Too close an identification between Christ and the church ignores the fact that the church has not fully arrived at the eschaton."[73] However, for the very idea of the church's *distinction* from and its unity with Jesus, Jenson has offered the concept of the church as an association and a community, also highlighting that the church is still to arrive at the eschaton. Moreover, Wood stresses that the Christ-church relation is like the subject-subject relation rather than the subject-object relation. However, such a relation is entailed in Jenson's conception of the church as the body of Christ, as *mutual objectification* characterizes any personal relationships. In my judgment, the two theologians' ecclesiologies are considerably closer than Wood thinks.

71. Chemnitz, *Fundamenta sanae doctrinae de vera et substantial praesentia . . . corporis et sanguinis Domini in Coena*, ix, quoted in ibid., 221.

72. Ibid., 222.

73. Wood, "Robert Jenson's Ecclesiology from a Roman Catholic Perspective," 183.

On Jenson's account, the church is not only an association and a community but also a *communion* because the church is invited and embraced into the life of the triune God. "She is to be a communion within the communion that is the life of the triune God."[74] When the church is drawn into the life of the Trinity, she is united with her Head, Jesus Christ, and so exists as a communion. As the church is taken into the divine communion, the church is the *totus Christus*, the Ego of Christ, or even the eschatological second person of the Trinity. In the triune communion, the church in identification with Jesus Christ speaks to the Father, as the Son, in the Spirit. This is the inner communication and life of the Trinity. That is the life of the eschatological Trinity, anticipated by God and the church. Even though the church in this age only tastes vaguely her eschatological destiny, it will be an intensely visible and palpable reality of her and her Head together. In that eschatological life of the Trinity, the church will be a communion within Communion, in which "[t]he risen Christ now offers himself and his church, the totus Christus, to the Father. This offering anticipates his eschatological self-offering, when he will bring the church and all creation to the Father that God may be 'all in all.'"[75]

Underlying Jenson's account of the church as a communion is the Eastern Orthodox concept of *theosis*. Jenson is aware of the Western classical anxiety over against the Orthodox doctrine of deification. To many Western ears, it sounds like a residue of paganism: if men could become gods, then there would be many gods or more than three hypostases in the Godhead; and that would entail polytheism or some heresy. Per contra, Jenson indicates that the early church fathers freely taught that "we will partake of God's own deity, and that will be our blessedness."[76] "In the classic comprehensive formula of Athanasius: 'He (the Word) became human that we might become God.'"[77] Jenson claims that the classical Western theology diverges from Eastern Orthodoxy on this issue of deification because it operates with a different ontological paradigm: in the Augustinian substance ontology, Jenson argues, the doctrine of deification is inevitably misunderstood as compromising the unity and uniqueness of God. However, in the ontological scheme underlying Cap-

---

74. Jenson, "The Church and the Sacraments," 216.
75. *ST*, 2:253.
76. Jenson, "Theosis," 108.
77. Ibid.

padocian trinitarian theology, the being of the one God is construed not in substantialistic term but as "the coherence of the *one life* or one history lived between the Father and the Son in the Spirit."[78] In Eastern Orthodoxy, since the being of God is the life of the communion, God can open up his being to embrace others into his communion. "Thus as Cappadocian trinitarianism understands God, we can become God . . . without becoming additional instances of that nature."[79]

Jenson comes to accept the Orthodox doctrine of *theosis*, without a much conceptual stretch, in my view, as his Lutheran Christology is conceptually related to it. His theology upholds the Lutheran doctrine of *communicatio idiomatum* in which the divinity is communicated to the humanity in the person of Jesus Christ, and so his humanity is capable of exercising infinite power (*finitum capax infiniti*). Accordingly, the body of Jesus Christ is understood to be transcendent of time and space, as mentioned earlier. Thus, Jesus' humanity is elevated into the divine being. Here the soteriological implication of this Christology is this: those who are united with Christ and so in Christ are elevated into the divine being and so *deified*. In Jesus Christ, God is incarnate, and the church becomes

---

78. Ibid., 110.

79. Ibid. Cf. Recent decades have seen a wave of the patristic studies that reconsider the Eastern-Western paradigm in trinitarian theology, along with reexamination of Augustine's Trinity. Lewis Ayres argues that in Augustine God's unity or essence is not essentialistic but that God's essence is nothing other than the Trinity itself. Ayres quotes Augustine: "[the persons] are only one God; not that the divinity, which they have in common, is a sort of fourth person" (Ayres, "Remember That You Are Catholic," 71). He says, "Augustine does not use the language of God's essence or substance to talk of an essence in any way distinct from the *communion* of the three persons" (ibid., 68; emphasis mine). Jenson is aware of the recent patristic studies but adamant in his interpretation of Augustine: "What is not done by those who bash us Augustine-bashers is to face up to the truly disastrous propositions Augustine did in fact emphatically and insistently lay down, propositions that became maxims of subsequent Western theology. He did in fact say that the Cappadocian distinction of ousia/hypostasis—the very distinction that enabled the creedal doctrine of the Trinity—could be no more than a purely linguistic device, that it could tell us nothing about the reality of God. . . . He did say that it is absurd, as violating divine simplicity, to think that the Father could not be what he is apart from the Son, and vice versa—thereby rejecting a foundational proposition of Trinitarian thought and worship from Tertullian on" (Jenson, "A Decision Tree of Colin Gunton's Thinking," 11–12). Indeed, the two theologians' interpretations of Augustine diverge, but they are in significant agreement that the unity of God is *not* essentialistic but the *communion* of the three hypostases.

deified. Jenson's Christology can be in rapprochement with the Orthodox doctrine of *theosis*.[80]

Further, later in his theological career, Jenson's ecumenical sweep reaches to Judaism, stressing the notion of the church as a *detour* to the kingdom of God. The church has not arrived at the End yet. The church is a community, and yet "not purely a community."[81] She church is a communion, and yet in this age, "this great *communio* cannot yet assemble."[82] She is the body of Jesus Christ, but she "cannot meet as one body."[83] Being one body of Christ will be completed only in the End, and yet, Jenson argues, this gentile gathering alone cannot complete the body of Christ. Jenson holds that the Jewish community is another detour alongside with the church to the End, when the two covenant communities will be one body of Christ. Later we will see in detail how this notion of the church as a detour plays out in Jenson's post-supersessionistic understanding of the relation between the church and the Jewish people.

The Body as the Gate to the Trinitarian Communion

This section explores what type of trinitarian theology is tacitly at work in Jenson's account of the embodiment of God and considers the trinitarian implications of the body of God.

As Jenson indicates, the Western conception of the personhood is much indebted to Augustine's trinitarian theology. Jenson remarks, "[Augustine] perceived a *personal*, in the modern sense, God, whose being is constituted in the inner dialectics of consciousness: in the place of—now we will use the language of [modern] time—immediate self-consciousness (Augustine's 'memory'), objective knowledge of self, and freedom that unites them."[84] In Augustine, God is personal: God is "Mind and Knowledge and Love that joins them."[85] To put this in trinitarian terms,

---

80. This conception plays out along with Jenson's endorsement of the new Finnish interpretation of Luther on justification and deification. According to the leading proponent of this interpretation, Mannermaa, God gives himself to us, and we receive God himself, and so we are made *capax Dei* (Jenson, "Why is Luther so Fascinating?" 10).

81. *ST*, 2:347.

82. Jenson, "The Church and the Sacraments," 218.

83. *ST*, 2:226.

84. *TI*, 134–35. More on Augustine's trinitarian theology, see *ST*, 1:110–14.

85. *TI*, 136.

"the Father is being, the Son knowledge, and the Spirit will; the Father is mind, the Son knowledge, and the Spirit love; the Father is memory, the Son knowledge, and the Spirit will. The Trinity is here indeed understood as a person, and Father, Son, and Spirit as the poles of the inner life that makes him personal."[86]

Jenson sees this concept of the divine personhood developed in Hegel, who "made the Augustinian Western version of the doctrine the center of his philosophy, the West's last universal and perhaps last great system of thought."[87] As Augustine does, Hegel conceives God as the mind or the subject: "the rational subject posits the object, that is, that which is not itself . . . then the rational subject achieves itself as the process, the act, of rediscovering itself in the object, that is, of finding meaning in what is not merely as such meaningful; this event of reconciliation between reason-as-subject, and object-made-reasonable is living reason, spirit."[88] God is the Subject, the Object that the Subject posits and finds itself within, and the Act of finding itself within the object. "Just and only so, God is personal."[89] Put differently, God is the subject; God is the object; God is the love, i.e., the reconciliation or the act of unifying the two. However, Jenson finds Hegel's conception theologically inadequate, as for Hegel the divine self-object is the world, "rather than Jesus."[90]

---

86. *ST*, 1:123. Cf. According to Ayres, "Augustine's argument in *De trinitate* 9–10 initially revolves around a distinction between a self-knowing necessary to the mind but constantly distorted by our attachment to the material world, and an eschatological, perfected self-knowing that would most fully image the Trinity" (Ayres, *Augustine and the Trinity*, 276).

87. *TI*, 134.

88. Ibid., 135.

89. Ibid., 144. Cf. Nevertheless, "[t]he great failure of this insight is that the dynamic dialectic of personhood is understood as entirely contained in God, who 'toward what is outside' is still a pure monad, only giving hints of his internal liveliness by analogues in creation. Just so, the Hellenistic interpretation of eternity as timelessness is not ultimately abandoned. The self-achievement of consciousness whether in God or in us—is still understood as the realization of possibilities in there from the beginning. And consciousness can be absolute in God, and be the analogue of absolute consciousness in us, in that it is self-consciousness, in that it is lining, that is, in that it is consciousness-as-substance" (ibid.). Here in Jenson's opposition to the view that God is self-contained, we see Jenson's pneumatology comes into view: the Holy Spirit is the one who holds God's self open to the future. This insight will be treated more fully in the last chapter.

90. Ibid., 135–36. Cf. As opposed to Jenson's reading of Hegel, we can see a christological reading is possible in Powel, *The Trinity in German Thought*, 131–34.

Jenson considers Barth's trinitarian theology on this Augustinian-Hegelian trajectory. "Karl Barth has reachieved an authentic doctrine of tri-unity by what amounts to a christological inversion of Hegel's. Only put Jesus in place of Hegel's 'world.'"[91] Now in Barth, the divine self-object is Jesus of Nazareth, in whom God finds himself and with whom he identifies himself. In Barth's own term, God is in triple repetition: God is God-after-God-after-God. The Subject is God, the Object is God, and the third is also God. "The name of Father, Son, and Spirit says that God is the one God in a triple repetition, and in such a way that this repetition itself is grounded in his deity, that is, in such a way that . . . only in this repetition is he the one God."[92]

In this context of the "psychological" understanding of God, Jenson's notion of the God's body has been developed and offered: God's body is considered to be the objective self of God's consciousness. However, Jenson's trinitarian theology goes beyond this psychological model. According to Jenson, such an understanding of God would not do full justice to the biblical depiction of God the Trinity. Even though that description shows us how the one God is a *person*, that alone does not offer the full description of the *communal* life and being of God. For Jenson, to be a person is to find himself in communal relation with an other. Jenson states, "[S]urely it is just from trinitarian doctrine itself that we should learn that a personal self is not a monad, that its 'internal' dynamic structure is inseparable from its relations to other selves, that personhood is intrinsically a *communal phenomenon*."[93]

In Jenson's doctrine of the Trinity, the second hypostasis is not just conceived to be an objective self but a speaking other. Within the Trinity, there are speaking, hearing, replying, and so on. There is an *eternal* conversation. The second hypostasis is not only as the object of the God-self but also "you" to the first hypostasis. There is communication in eternity and so "I" and "You" in eternity. *So* God is personal, that is, personal because they can converse. Moreover, in the communication, "I" do not remain untouched or aloof from "You," but "You" enter into the life of "I" and vice versa. So and just so "I" and "You" share a common reality and even are one being. God is one in and by conversation. "I—and God!—am the person that I am precisely in that *you* intrude into my life,

---

91. *TI*, 136.
92. Ibid., 138.
93. Ibid., 144–45. Emphasis added.

opening me to be what I am not yet in what would be myself were I not personal. It is the communality of God's and our personhood that we have yet to grasp."[94]

God is personal in that his inner life (and his being) is communication, in that the first enters into the second and the second into the first in communication and so they are mutually penetrative. The first hypostasis calls an other "my Son"; the other calls him back "my Father"; the ontological oneness is achieved by the Spirit. The mutual addresses determine their personal identities and make the two one reality, as this constitution of the being of God in conversation is enabled in the Spirit. Thus, God's being is conversation. God is personal in and by communication.

So God's self-consciousness or his being is socially and communicatively mediated. Jenson says, "traditional accounts that omit your role in my personhood and posit 'immediate self-consciousness' seem to have no other reason than the advance conviction that also personal beings must be substances, constituted in themselves."[95] The role of "you" and "your words to me" must be taken into account. It is as if a mom calls her baby "my girl," the baby accepts the mother's apprehension of her and determines her identity by her mom's address to her. It is primally true of God's triune being. So God's self-knowledge or consciousness is communally and communicatively constituted. For Jenson, God of the gospel is not a closed individualistic monad which finds himself only in his objective self, excluding the role of an other; God is personal in that one is opened up for an other and so constitutes oneself by having an other into himself in mutual address and conversation. "Personal presence and so personal knowledge occur always as address, always as the word-event by which one person enters the reality of another."[96]

What is amazing about God's triune being and his inner conversation is that the conversational being is open for us and invites us into his inner life. As Jesus intrudes into the first hypostasis by mutual address, so we "intrude" into God's life as we are allowed to address God as "our Father," and as graciously God accepts our objectification of him, that is, our address to him. Moreover, thereby he determines his eternal identity. Our address to God is ontologically determinative for both God and us.

94. Ibid., 145. Cf. Jenson quotes his *Doktorvater* Peter Brunner, "The wonder of God's inner trinitarian life is that the numerically single personal 'I' of the one being that God is... has his being only in the true community of a personal 'we'" (ibid., 147).

95. Ibid., 146.

96. Ibid., 145.

"[T]here indeed is no reason to deny that also *God* is constituted as personal in his community with us."[97] "That [God] *is* personal is established by our ability to address him, however little we may often have made of this conceptually."[98]

Now let us consider the trinitarian implications of Jenson's notion of the body of God in view of the communal understanding of God. As said earlier, in Jenson, God's body is defined as his objective availability to himself *and to us*. Again, this is a *communicative* concept. God is available to us as an object for communication so that we may *speak to* him as we turn to the object—it can be Jesus himself (his biological body) or his eucharistic body. His body is an invitation to communion with him insofar as there is some distance between our body and his body. Put differently, the divine body is "the gate" as Jenson has spoken so of the eucharistic body and the church.[99] It is the gate through which we enter into the divine inner conversation as we are united with the body of Christ. Through the gate, we participate in the conversation as the totus Christus, that is, as the Son. Thus, we participate in the communion of the Trinity through the heavenly gate, the body of Jesus Christ.

Conclusion

For Jenson, Jesus is regarded to be the body of God, and therefore, God is the bodily being. Even after the resurrection and the ascension, Jesus Christ is still bodily present, and so is God. For Jesus said of eucharistic bread and wine: "This is my body" and "This is my blood." By the divine power of his word and his free decision, when Jesus says so, the objects are truly so. Further, the church is the body of God, as those around the eucharistic table partake the bread and wine, the body of Jesus Christ. In a sense, the gathering is an other to Christ and so an object of God's salvation, as reformational theology emphasizes. For those around the table are distinct from the eucharistic body of Jesus Christ. In another sense, the church is one with Christ as the gathering partake the bread and wine. In that sense, the church is the bodily availability of Christ to the world. The Christ's presence is mediated through the church to the world, as the Roman Catholic theology stresses. Further, as the church is united with

---

97. Ibid., 146.

98. *ST*, 1:160.

99. Jenson, "For us . . . He was made Man," 80–81.

her Head, the church is going to be a communion and will have the place in God's being as the *totus Christus*, as the Eastern Orthodox doctrine of *theosis* emphasizes. The church is deified and so taken into the divine trinitarian communion, without increasing the number of the hypostases within the being of God. Jenson's ecclesiology is ontologically weighty at this point. On the whole, Jenson's notion of the body is an *ecumenical* conception, yet worked out on Lutheran doctrinal basis: the Lutheran *communicatio idiomatum* is operative, bent to the doctrine of the *theosis*. God has become a human being so that humans may become God. God comes to us as the incarnate one and yet embraces our bodily beings into his bodily being so that we may enter into his divine life and *being*. Further, a linguistic turn has been visible in Jenson's conception: the body is one's availability to others for and in *communication*. God's body is his availability in his revelation-communication to us; our body is our communicative availability to God (in distinction from the eucharistic body), but embraced into the body of the Son for the divine communication, the eternal conversation between the Father and the Son in the Spirit.

On this body-ontology trajectory, Jenson's gesture toward Judaism must be understood. For the Lutheran Jenson, God's being is not antithetical to the human body; God is inextricably related to the body, the body of his chosen one.

3

God in the Jewish Flesh

Michael Wyschogrod's Theology of Israel

IN THE 1990S, JENSON became intensively engaged with a question that had thus far not received sustained treatment in his work: what is the significance of the Jewish people in and for Christian theology? Jenson's theological reflection on the Jewish existence began when he was invited into "fantastically networked colloquia on dogmatics and social ethics. There [he] was in conversation with a range of Christians and Jews at a level matched only by [his] coming experience at the Center of Theological Inquiry. . . . [His] great profit from those sessions was that [he] came to see that discourse with such Jews as David Novak was not so much a matter of exchanging views as of joint theological work."[1] Later he met another Jewish theologian, Peter Ochs, "amazingly at home in Christian theology."[2] Then, in 1997 and 1999, the two volumes of Jenson's *Systematic Theology* came out, in which a number of Jewish interlocutors proved crucial in Jenson's articulation of an explicitly ecumenical theology. In later years, Jenson "began to lecture and write on Christian theology of Judaism, in a way that would have been unthinkable—not just for [himself] but for the church—even a few years earlier."[3] Among the Jewish theologians with whom Jenson engaged in reflection on Christian understanding of Judaism, Michael Wyschogrod is particularly notable. Jenson recalls: "When I first heard Michael Wyschogrod many years ago,

1. Jenson, "A Theological Autobiography, to Date," 52–53.
2. Ibid., 53.
3. Ibid.

I knew that here is a Jewish theologian whom Christian theology needs for its own sake."[4]

Born in 1928 in Berlin and educated in New York, Wyschogrod has pursued a career as a philosopher and theologian at leading academic institutions in the USA, establishing himself as a key figure in Jewish-Christian dialogue.[5] Wyschogrod served as Director of the Institute for Jewish-Christian Relations of the American Jewish Congress, working closely with the Vatican, the World Council of Churches, and various Christian bodies in the US and Europe.[6] Though his active theological conversations with Christianity was considered to be against the prevailing sentiment of the Jewish Orthodox community in the late 1980s,[7] his indefatigable theological engagement with Christians has inspired many Christian and Jewish scholars to recognize one another in an unprecedented conciliatory way.[8]

Throughout his career, Wyschogrod's work has been marked by a deep interest in the theology of Karl Barth.[9] Like Barth, Wyschogrod is unflinchingly and unapologetically committed to the authority of the Scripture and the historical revelation of God, refusing to subjugate his theology to foreign philosophical categories. As Shai Held says, his "readings of scripture are often striking in their daring and originality."[10] At the same time, however, Wyschogrod emphasizes, "Judaism is more Barthian than Barth"[11] in that it more consistently seeks to draw out the metaphysical significance of the irrevocability of the divine covenant with Abraham and his descendants. Wyschogrod strives to expunge the Greek philosophical influence from Jewish theology in order to uphold

---

4. Wyschogrod, *Abraham's Promise*, back cover endorsement.

5. Soulen, "The Achievement of Michael Wyschogrod," 677.

6. Soulen, "A Biographical Sketch of Michael Wyschogrod," xiii.

7. Goldman, "Kosher by Design," line 66.

8. "We [Jews] live in a world where, for the first time in many centuries, there are Christians who believe that participating in God's love for the Jewish people is demanded by the divine in Hebrew Bible" (Soloveichik, "God's First Love" lines, 299–301).

9. Wyschogrod recalls, "On a sunny morning in August 1966 I visited Barth in his modest home on the Bruderholzallee in Basel. He had been told that I was a 'Jewish Barthian,' and this amused him to no end" (Wyschogrod, "A Jewish Perspective on Karl Barth," 161).

10. Held, "The Promise and Peril of Jewish Barthianism," 319.

11. Wyschogrod, "Why is the Theology of Karl Barth of Interest to a Jewish Theologian?" 218.

the ontological significance of the bodily existence of the chosen people in close connection with God's being. In his theology proper, Wyschogrod rejects a priori accounts of divine incorporeality and seeks to depict the divine strictly in its covenantal relationship to the *bodily* existence of the people of Israel. It is at this point that Wyschogrod's work displays obvious convergence with Jenson's theology: for both theologians, God is the one who determines his eternal identity by his act of election; and for both, God's being is inextricably related to the carnal existence of the elect, whether Jesus or Israel.

It is important to note that Wyschogrod engages with Christian theologians in *theological* conversation. In this regard, Wyschogrod differs from his teacher Rabbi Joseph B. Soloveitchik (1903-93), who "argued that Jews can engage in fruitful dialogue with Christians and others on matters of common secular concern, but not on matters of faith."[12] Directly concerning central matters of Jewish-Christian teaching, Wyschogrod's conversations with Christians are boldly theological.

The claim pursued in this chapter is that Jenson's post-supersessionistic theology may be seen as instigated primarily by his conversations with Jewish theologians, especially with Wyschogrod, who is particularly visible in Jenson's trinitarian reflections on Judaism and God of Israel. Jenson's post-supersessionistic theology, in other words, may be seen as an extended conversation with Jewish theology as represented especially by Wyschogrod. We will explore Jenson's constructive claims about Israel in the next chapter, seeing how Jenson's theology moves in a post-supersessionistic direction; but first in this chapter, we attend directly to Wyschogrod's theology, focusing on the aspects of his work that stipulate Jenson's thinking.

The primary purpose of this chapter is not just to seek theological convergences between the two theologians, even though it would be significant in its own right. More importantly, it is to see how Wyschogrod himself articulates the theological or covenantal identity of his Jewish community in relation to the Christian community and through conversations with it. In conversations between the two communities, Wyschogrod warns, the participants are not to water down their distinctive identities in order to find a middle ground, compromising the distinctive features of both communities or subjugating their faiths to external philosophical categories of universal reason and morality. Rather,

---

12. Soulen, "The Achievement of Michael Wyschogrod," 677.

theologians are to seek to uphold and articulate the unique identity of their own community in relation to the other community. So Wyschogrod himself seeks to uphold the identity of Judaism, especially through his reflection on the Christian doctrine of the incarnation and the (early) Christian teaching of the Torah, as he understands Christianity as the covenant community cooperative in God's one redemptive history. In doing so, he has also opened a fresh way for Christians to rethink the supersessionistic tendency within Christian theology and to rediscover Christianity in relation to Judaism.

So, before we explore Jenson's non-supersessionistic theological response, we will see here Wyschogrod's theological formulation of Judaism in relation to Christianity. In this chapter, we will proceed in two sections, asking 1) how Wyschogrod seeks to rediscover the self-identity of the Jewish community, a) through engagement with the Christian doctrine of the incarnation and b) the New Testament teaching of the Torah, and 2) how he offers a new Jewish perspective on Christianity in relation to Judaism, seeking mutual acknowledgement of the other community's distinctive role in God's one redemptive history.

Rediscovering the Jewish Identity in Relation to Christianity

Toward an Incarnational Understanding of God and His People

"The divinity of Jesus has been unanimously rejected by all Jewish (and Muslim) authors as incompatible with true monotheism and possibly idolatrous. For Jews, once this issue is raised, it is no longer necessary to examine seriously any teachings of Jesus. A human being who is also God loses all Jewish legitimacy from the outset. . . . I cannot dilute the severity of these words. To point to a human being and to say of him that he is God can only arouse terror in the Jewish soul."[13] This provocation of this passage lies not only in its stark recognition of the fundamental difference in Jewish and Christian evaluations of Jesus, but also particularly in Wyschogrod's insistence that this difference is not the final word; rather, "it is also necessary to remember what unites us. . . . [T]he deepest bond between Judaism and Christianity is a common text, the Hebrew Bible."[14]

---

13. Wyschogrod, "Incarnation and God's Indwelling in Israel," 166.
14. Ibid., 167.

God in the Jewish Flesh

Accordingly, he proposes that it is not a prior rejection of incarnation but exegesis of the Hebrew Bible that should lead the conversation between the two communities and will open a new way for the two.

The Bodily Description of God in the Bible

In Wyschogrod's reading, the Hebrew Bible does not disallow the incarnation; rather, the biblical descriptions of God move *toward* it. The God of the Hebrew Bible is "not totally anti-incarnational;"[15] the most direct contrast is not with the God of Christian theology but with the God of Maimonides, Wyschogrod claims.[16] This is the God introduced into Judaism by the distinguished medieval rabbi Moshesh ben Maimon, who on philosophical grounds claimed that "God has no body and that all expressions which seem to state or imply that he has a corporeal dimension cannot mean what they seem to assert. God and corporeality are totally incompatible and this, for Maimonides, is the essential message of Judaism."[17] While Wyschogrod recognizes that Maimonides's intention was to protect God from being the object of idolatry, he maintains that Maimonides's commitment to the incorporeality axiom led him to commit the greatest interpretive error in the history of Jewish thought.[18] For if the "anthropomorphic"[19] passages of the Hebrew Bible are interpreted only as phenomena or appearances, a gulf opens up between the manifestation of God and reality of God's being. Further, God is portrayed in terms directly contrastive to the human body. In Wyschogrod's view, it is Maimonides's hellenization, not the Christian doctrine of incarnation, which most profoundly distorted Jewish theology.

Wyschogrod reads the Hebrew Bible as teaching that "God . . . has two dwelling places or two addresses."[20] One of the addresses is the tabernacle/temple. "There [in the tent of meeting] I will meet with the people of Israel, and it shall be sanctified by my glory."[21] Wyschogrod also notes

15. Ibid.
16. Ibid.
17. Ibid., 168.
18. Ibid.
19. Probably the term "anthropomorphism" itself is problematic if it implies incorporeality as a superior reality of God. But my usage of this term here follows Wyschogrod's.
20. Ibid., 169.
21. Exodus 29:43 quoted in ibid., 168.

1 Kings 6:12–13 where God says to Solomon that he would "dwell among the children of Israel and will not forsake my people Israel"[22] when Solomon was building the temple for YHWH, and also 1 Kings 8:10–11 where "the glory of the Lord filled the house of the Lord," the newly built temple. Of course, even the highest heaven cannot contain God himself. Wyschogrod does not reject God's transcendence over the creation. Here what strikes him is God's sheer immanence: "the transcendence of God is not newsworthy. What is newsworthy is that God dwelled in the Tabernacle . . . and now dwells in the Temple built by Solomon. God has taken residence among the people Israel. That is what makes the space and its environs—Jerusalem and Israel—in which he dwells holy and it makes the people among whom he dwells holy."[23] God is the one who can and does take up some space and reside in a place, particularly, "Number One Har Habayit Street. Number One Temple Mount Street."[24]

Further, moving toward an incarnational understanding of the God of Israel, Wyschogrod notes a passage from midrash. It narrates the event when God created a man in his own image: "Said R. Hoshaiah, 'When the Holy One, blessed be he, came to create the first man, the ministering angels mistook him [for God, since man was in God's image] and wanted to say before him, "Holy [holy, holy is the Lord of hosts]." . . . [So] [w]hat did the Holy One, blessed be he, do? He put him to sleep, so everyone knew that he was a mere man.'"[25] In this midrashic account, the physical resemblance between God and a human being was so great that even the angels confused the first human being with God himself. Wyschogrod comments: "It is, of course, tempting to restrict man's resemblance to God to his rationality or some other non-corporeal aspects of the human person. But that would be neither biblical nor rabbinic. Man is created by God as a physical being and if there is a human resemblance to God then his body also resembles God. That is why the human corpse does not fully lose the divine image and must therefore be treated with great respect. And if the human body can resemble God, then *there must also be a physical aspect to God's being*."[26]

22. 1 Kgs 6:13 quoted in ibid., 169.
23. Ibid., 169.
24. Wyschogrod, "Incarnation," 210. This language is used in Jenson's article.
25. Gen. R. VIII:X quoted in quoted in "Incarnation and God's Indwelling in Israel," 170.
26. Ibid., 171. Emphasis added.

The willingness of earlier Jewish commentators to affirm something approaching divine corporeality is further illustrated with reference to the question posed by Rabbi Nahman bar Isaac to Rabbi Hiyya bar Abin: "As to the phylacteries of the Lord of the world, what is written in them?"[27] Wyschogrod sees in this question another evidence that, before it was influenced by the Greek philosophy, the ancient Jewish tradition was "certainly not as disturbed by anthropomorphism as Maimonides was later"[28] and spoke genuinely of "Hashem's limbs."[29]

"What then does he look like?"[30] This is indeed a provocative question, "given the strength of the conviction in later Judaism that Hashem has no body."[31] However, Wyschogrod says, the absence of descriptions of the physical appearance of God in the Bible is not "a calculated omission explainable by the biblical conviction that Hashem . . . has no body."[32] Like other ancient epic literature, since the Bible is primarily narrative rather than descriptive, the biblical authors do not focus, "as do modern novelists, on elaborate descriptions of the physical appearance of the characters or the decor of the environment."[33] The ancient record offers relatively few descriptions what God looks like but focus intensely on narratives of what God does: he speaks, sees, hears, throws, walks, ascends and descends, sits and rises, shows his back to someone, makes his face shine upon some people, even meets someone face-to-face, and so forth. To allow in the most straightforward way that God is the agent of these acts is to admit that God is not incorporeal.

If God may be understood in this way, then why does Scripture insist that we cannot see him? Indeed, the Scripture says that no one can see God and live. However, we should be careful, Wyschogrod suggests, in interpretation of such biblical statements: in context they do not affirm God's incorporeality but rather "intend to assert the *royalty* of Hashem, that he is an exalted king on whom no commoner, in this case created man, may gaze. The frightened commoner who longs for a glimpse of his monarch might steal such a glimpse of his back, since he thereby sees the

27. Ibid., 173.
28. Ibid.
29. Wyschogrod, *The Body of Faith*, 99.
30. Ibid.
31. Ibid.
32. Ibid., 100.
33. Ibid.

king but is not forced to come face to face with him, an encounter that is far too threatening."[34]

From this, it may appear that Wyschogrod is offering a positive account of divine embodiment, just as Jenson argues for the bodily aspect of God's being. However, we must recall that Wyschogrod at once distances himself from the traditional Christian doctrine of incarnation while insisting that the Hebrew Bible moves Jewish theology *toward* its own distinctive understanding of divine non-incorporeal presence. Confession of the deity of Jesus and the rigorous affirmation of the doctrine of the incarnation is *constitutive of* the gulf between the two communities. Wyschogrod only *nearly* affirms that God has a body. Wyschogrod holds the bodyliness in *close affinity* to God's being, but he does not seek to "carnalize" Judaism. In his view, such a carnalization occurs in Christian theology: "Curiously enough, it is Judaism that has often been characterized as a carnal religion and contrasted with Christianity. . . . And yet, when it came to the final unification of God with flesh, it was Christianity that took that leap and Judaism that rejected it."[35] On these lines, it must be noted that Wyschogrod does not use the term "corporeality" of God but only "non-incorporeality." Wyschogrod's theology is thus differentiated from the Hellenistic immaterialization *and* from the Christian "carnalization" of God.[36]

However, one may legitimately argue that Wyschogrod does not fully embrace the theological reliability and sufficiency of the Bible's descriptions of God; having displayed sustained exegetical and theological courage, he loses his nerve at the decisive juncture. For the descriptions of God in the Bible do strongly suggest that God not only acts in a bodily way but does so because he has his body. To prosecute this thought more consistently than Wyschogrod, it is necessary to hold that affirming the incarnation of God would not compromise one's Jewish identity.

---

34. Ibid. Emphasis added.

35. Wyschogrod, "Incarnation and God's Indwelling in Israel," 176.

36. Here to support Wyschogrod's theological stance, it may be helpful to appeal to Peter Ochs's philosophical criticism on the dyadic logics. "When the lived situation calls for a dichotomous logic—as in the case of suffering—I label the logic binary. When binary logics are employed inappropriately, I label them *dyadic*" (Ochs, "Christian Postliberalism and the Jews," 9). For a detailed discussion, see Ochs, "Response: Reflections on Binarism."

Alternatively, like Jenson, one may need to offer a christological reading of the biblical description of God's body.[37]

Nevertheless, as Wyschogrod emphasizes, on his own terms the Christian doctrine of the incarnation is not a "total separation" between Judaism and Christianity when we read the Hebrew Bible without the Maimonidean lenses. The gulf between the two communities is not unbridgeable. In Wyschogrod's view, the biblical vision of divine presence stands closer to the Christian doctrine of incarnation than to the teaching of Maimonides, who rides roughshod over the bodily description of God in the Bible.

God Deep in the Jewish Flesh:
The Significance of the Jewish Identity as the Dilute Incarnation of God

God's second "address" is his people Israel. That is his *permanent* residence. Here the significance of the Jewish existence comes into view. "God's affinity to the people is thus deeper than his affinity to the land [and to the temple]."[38] The God of Israel is the God of *Israel,* for he was with Israel even before the tabernacle/the temple was built. God could depart from the Har Habayit Street and managed to be "camping out" while remaining with his people.[39] God could leave the temple unprotected so that the gentiles could destroy the fabric of the building.[40] However, God has not or even could not leave his people Israel. As with the temple, "[w]hen the Temple is out of commission, God's presence on the Temple Mount is reduced though not absent. But then his presence in the people Israel is increased."[41] When Israel was displaced, he "moved into exile

---

37. As we will see later, Jenson offers a christological reading of those biblical descriptions of God's bodily engagement with his people. Those divine bodily appearances are construed as the pre-existence of Jesus Christ.

38. Wyschogrod, "Incarnation and God's Indwelling in Israel," 169.

39. Wyschogrod, "Incarnation," 211.

40. Wyschogrod, "Incarnation and God's Indwelling in Israel," 170.

41. Wyschogrod, Ibid., 174. It is intriguing to note in Wyschogrod's account that God did not depart from the Temple site completely but he is still present at a reduced level. "[M]any Jews report that they have this sense of the indwelling of God before the western wall. There are all kinds of stories about extremely assimilated, secular Jews arriving in Jerusalem and showing up at the western wall and being overcome by a deep emotional experience. . . . This, of course, also means that somehow his residence will be more comfortable for him when the temple is rebuilt. . . . [W]ith the rebuilding of the temple, he will have a home and he will dwell there in a more concentrated way

along with the people."⁴² With or without the land or the temple, God is still God *of Israel*. "The Jewish people is the dwelling place of Hashem. . . . Wherever three Jews gather the shechina ('divine presence') is present."⁴³

At this point, it must be emphasized that God dwells and resides in Israel because God has *freely* chosen to do so and faithfully does so. God's dwelling in Israel is not Israel's achievement but solely due to God's sovereign will and faithfulness. Israel's election and God's dwelling in Israel are not earned by herself or by her patriarchs. "The Bible does not portray the election of Abraham as a merited one."⁴⁴ And it is by God's own sovereign will and his faithfulness to the covenant alone that God tenaciously and irrevocably dwells in Israel.

This means, conversely and importantly, that the divine dwelling in Israel cannot be undone by Israel's infidelity or indeed by any human power. God's dwelling in Israel does not entail that Israel does not sin. Indeed, Israel does commit sin sometimes or often hideous and abhorrent to God. "At every crucial turn, as God displays his mercy and love for Israel, Israel responds by disobedience and ingratitude. And this vision of a sinful Israel has penetrated deeply into the consciousness of Christianity. It has of course, also penetrated deeply into the consciousness of Israel."⁴⁵ However, "[w]hile sin is a reality, the eternal election of Israel is a greater reality. However catastrophic the consequences of sin are—and they are frequently catastrophic—they do not . . . sever the bond between Hashem and Israel."⁴⁶ The covenantal bond cannot be canceled by any deed of Israel however grave it is. Further, Wyschogrod stresses, even their *unbelief* cannot undo God's faithful covenantal unity to her. "[A] descendant of Abraham, Isaac, and Jacob is a Jew irrespective of what he believes."⁴⁷ Even when Israel followed and worshiped other pagan deities, the covenantal presence of God is not revoked or removed from Israel. This entails that even their rejection of Jesus Christ would not revoke the covenant and God's covenantal presence in them. Whatever Israel makes

---

. . . [H]e will be more present when the temple is rebuilt" (Wyschogrod, "Incarnation," 211).

42. Wyschogrod, "Incarnation and God's Indwelling in Israel," 169.
43. Wyschogrod, *The Body of Faith*, 103.
44. Ibid., 213.
45. Ibid.
46. Ibid.
47. Ibid., 175–76.

of the divine presence in herself, God's faithful presence never ceases to dwell in them.

Thus, it is important to note in Wyschogrod that God dwells in Israel, not in their belief or virtue, but in their *fleshly existence* which has been irrevocably chosen by his grace. God's covenant is binding only on the very existence of Israel as the abode of God's dwelling, which is nothing but the fleshly existence. Wyschogrod says, "the *flesh* of Israel is the abode of the divine presence in the world. It is the *carnal* anchor that God has sunk into the soil of creation."[48]

This is the significance of the Jewish carnal existence derived from the God's sovereign election and his tenacious faithfulness to the covenant and promise that he will be among and in Israel. Israel (the Jewish people) carries the divine presence *in* their flesh, whether they accept their destiny or not. They sometimes resisted their election, feeling it burdensome and wanting to be free from it, by unbelief or disobedience to God. Judaism is not a religion of virtue or of belief but relentlessly "a carnal election"[49] for God's tenacious covenantal presence in their *bodily* existence.

It can be argued then that the divine presence is accessible only through the people of Israel. Wyschogrod puts it as follows: "There is no way to God except through the Jewish people. . . . To be *Judenfrei* ('free of Jews') is to be abandoned by God."[50] Wyschogrod argues that Hitler understood this: "sin does not drive Hashem out of the world completely. Only the destruction of the Jewish people does. . . . [Hitler] knew that it was insufficient to cancel the teachings of Jewish morality and to substitute for it the new moral order of the superman. It was not only Jewish values that needed to be eradicated but Jews had to be murdered. . . . [T]he most convincing intellectual refutation of Jewish values is worthless as long as the Jewish face is seen in the world."[51] The most effective way to evict God's presence from the earth would be to annihilate the Jews since God has seared his presence into the Jewish fleshly existence.

On this line of reasoning, Wyschogrod holds that there would be no Christianity without Judaism since Christianity is essentially a recognition of the divine presence in the Jewish flesh. Wyschogrod says, "To

---

48. Ibid., 256. Emphasis added.
49. Ibid., 175.
50. Ibid., 214.
51. Ibid., 223.

believe that God became incarnate in Jesus the Jew is to encounter the Divine Presence in the people Israel."[52] Wyschogrod claims that "the Christian teaching of the incarnation of God in Jesus is the intensification of the teaching of the dwelling of God in Israel by concentrating that indwelling in one Jew rather than leaving it diffused in the people of Jesus as a whole,"[53] even though he views Christian belief in the divinity of Jesus as a mistake.

Here a number of conceptual questions present themselves for consideration: how closely and deeply is God related to the bodily existence of Israel? Does God dwell *in* them? Wyschogrod suggests that this is best regarded as a matter of the shape of God's covenantal love. "The Hebrew *betochom* can be translated as 'among' them or 'in' them."[54] "Numbers 35:34: '. . . for I the Lord dwell among the Israelites'—perhaps a better translation should be *in* the Israelites."[55] Wyschogrod argues that this is not a philological or even philosophical issue but about covenantal love: "As this love intensifies, as lover and beloved draw closer together, a certain indwelling of God *in* his people results."[56] Does this mean that God is *incarnate* in Israel? For Wyschogrod, "that would be going too far."[57] In his account, the classical Christian doctrine of incarnation has no constitutive role in a Jewish theology of the divine presence. The Jewish people are not to be regarded as divine as Jesus is in the Nicene christology. The dwelling of God in the Jewish flesh is not incarnation; the human flesh does not get on the upper ontological plane. "To say that Hashem dwells in the Jewish people does not deify the Jewish people any more than to say that Hashem dwells in the Temple in Jerusalem is to deify the stones of the Temple."[58]

Nevertheless, the Christian doctrine of the incarnation, Wyschogrod insists, remains a helpful conceptual device to affirm and highlight the significance of the Jewish existence in God's redemptive history. Wyschogrod states, "The doctrine of the incarnation thus separates Jews and Christians but, properly understood, also sheds light on incarnational

---

52. Wyschogrod, "Incarnation and God's Indwelling in Israel," 178.
53. Ibid.
54. Ibid., 170.
55. Wyschogrod, "Incarnation," 212.
56. Wyschogrod, "Incarnation and God's Indwelling in Israel," 170.
57. Wyschogrod, *The Body of Faith*, 11.
58. Ibid., 212.

elements in Judaism which are more diffuse than the Christian version but nevertheless very real. If the Christian move was a mistake—and I believe it was—it was a mistake that has helped me better understand a dimension of Judaism—God's indwelling in the people of Israel—that I would probably not have understood as clearly without the Christian mistake."[59] By the help of the Christian doctrine of the incarnation, Wyschogrod could articulate the redemptive meaning of the Jewish existence as "the more diluted form of incarnation."[60]

In Wyschogrod, we still need to note, the act of God's election determines the being of God himself, as in Barth and Jenson. God's election of Israel—his covenantal relationship with Israel—determines not only the meaning of the Jewish existence but also the being of God himself.[61] For example, the oneness of God is best conceived in close relation to Israel's bodily existence. He appeals to *Babylonian Talmud, Tractate Berakhot* (b. Ber.): "'Hear O Israel, the Lord our God, the Lord is one' (Deut. 6:4). And I shall make you a singular entity in the world, as it is said, 'And who is like you people Israel, a singular nation on earth' (1 Chron. 17:21)."[62] Here, Wyschogrod says, oneness or singularity (*echad*) means exclusiveness: God alone is to be worshipped and loved. Wyschogrod takes one step further and holds that oneness is also attributed to Israel herself: "If *echad* attributed to God means that *only* he is to be worshiped, then *echad* attributed to Israel must mean something comparable. Among the nations, Israel is God's only betrothed. . . . Israel must have no other God and God will never have another people."[63] The oneness here is the mutual devotion and commitment between God and Israel. God is embedded deeply into Israel, and Israel into God.

Even the divine oneness would be compromised without Israel's existence, Wyschogrod argues. Since Israel is deeply seated into God's being, her sin is taken as "a very serious assault *on the presence of Hashem*."[64] "When Israel is separated from Hashem, God's *unity* is

---

59. Wyschogrod, "Incarnation and God's Indwelling in Israel," 178.

60. Wyschogrod, "Incarnation," 215.

61. The christological import of this point will be noted and appreciated by Jenson as we will see in the next chapter.

62. b. Ber. 6a–b quoted in Wyschogrod, "Incarnation and God's Indwelling in Israel," 173.

63. Ibid., 174. Emphasis added. Cf. "The key word is *echad* which is best translated in this context as 'unique'" (Ibid., 173).

64. Wyschogrod, *The Body of Faith*, 214.

impaired."[65] Israel's attempt to detach its existence from God is not only "always, directly or indirectly, the mutilation of Israel [herself]"[66] but also strikes directly on the oneness of God and the oneness of Israel herself. However, God cannot leave his divine unity in jeopardy. As Israel's sin is not only self-estrangement but also "a divine self-estrangement,"[67] "the estrangement cannot be permanent and final. Hashem returns to himself. He becomes *one*."[68] Even though Israel places the divine unity in peril, God will restore and achieve his oneness and thereby will restore the oneness of Israel, their full devotion to God. God will *heighten* his presence more powerfully within her and restore the relationship with her. God bears the pain and suffering in Israel's attempt to detach herself from God. Thus, God will be all to her, and she will be all to God. Just so, "God will be one."[69]

Some remarkable similarities can be observed here between the two approaches of Wyschogrod and Jenson. First, both share scruples against the Hellenistic elements inducted into their theological legacies, which find an expression particularly in the immaterialization of God's being in total antithesis to the body. Both readily acknowledge the *theological significance* of the bodily description of God in the Bible. Second, both deploy an "actualistic ontology" in giving expression to their "body ontologies." On their accounts, God's act of election determines the very being of God, and this ontological determination has *incarnational* elements. For Wyschogrod, the enactment of God's election of Israel results in the divine ontological affinity to the bodily existence of his people or the diffused incarnation of God in Israel; for Jenson, God's election of his Son is enacted not in the *asarkos Logos* but essentially in the carnal existence of Jesus. Having said that, it is not difficult to see that it would be hard for Jenson just to pass by "the Jewish Barth."

The Identity of the Jews

Who are the Jews? The question of Jewish identity has been implicit in our considerations thus far and must now be taken up directly. Election

65. Ibid.
66. Ibid.
67. Ibid.
68. Ibid. Emphasis added.
69. Zech 14:9.

is the integral motif by which the being of God is characterized *and* the identity of the Jewish people is defined in Wyschogrod's account. So Wyschogrod offers a theological articulation of Jewish identity, holding that recognition of the divine election of Israel can illuminate the abiding unity of the Jews without preventing full awareness of the complexities and dynamics of the identity of the Jewish people living in this age of "unprecedented Jewish fragmentation."[70] Conceptions of Jewish identity today, he says, "range from a relatively intact version of premodern Jewish self-understanding to a completely secular and almost non-national Yiddishist self-definition. In between are the varieties of Zionist definitions with all their religious and other complexities."[71] Even among the Orthodox Jews, there is a wide spectrum, ranging "from the most uncompromising to the modern branches of Orthodoxy."[72] A variety of beliefs and even non-beliefs and also of religious practices and non-practices within Jewish societies makes this issue more complicated. Further, "[w]ith all the many Jewish definitions in existence, they also all overlap each other so that a staggering number of permutations is both theoretically possible and actually realized in Jewish life."[73] While it is possible to render the Jewish identity in exclusively sociological or anthropological terms, Wyschogrod presents a *theological* portrayal of Jewish identity through the motif of the divine election: the Jews are the carnal descendants of Abraham and Sarah, the chosen ones. Even though it may be tempting for some Torah-observant Jews to exclude secularized Jews from their Jewish communal identity, Wyschogrod holds that such an aristocratic definition would be only damaging to themselves.[74] As mentioned above, by election and covenant, God dwells in the carnal descendants of Abraham and Sarah and through that lineage, regardless of their belief or non-belief, their obedience or disobedience, or even of their apostasy. The identity of the Jews is only defined by "the nature of Jewish election as seed of Abraham, Isaac, and Jacob. This is the unshakable foundation that unites all Jews, *irrespective of their beliefs*. . . . This is a destiny that encompasses all Jews."[75]

70. Wyschogrod, "Theology of Jewish Unity," 45.
71. Ibid.
72. Wyschogrod, *The Body of Faith*, 186.
73. Wyschogrod, "Theology of Jewish Unity," 45.
74. Ibid., 47.
75. Ibid., 51. Emphasis mine.

Thus, any perceived historical gap between the Israel in the canonical period and the modern Jews would not, for Wyschogrod, be finally determinative. Indeed, such a gap between the ancient and the modern cannot be overlooked. The way of reading and observing the Torah and their belief in God indeed differ even from those of the orthodox Jews today. Already in the first century, there was a variety of ways of being a Jew such as Pharisees, Sadducees, Essenes, Zealots, Christians, and so on. While this variety can be indicated, Wyschogrod stresses that what runs through all generations and every group of the Jews is not simply more or less their common belief or practice, but the divine energy of election. By their chosen bodily lineage, they are one, and they are what they are.

What of the purity of this lineage? Wyschogrod indicates the enduring marginalization of the Jews, arguing that their exclusion from mainstream society prevented the wholesale dilution of Jewish difference. The Jews has inhabited the margin and within the border hardly crossed over for many centuries. In the middle age, the Jewish people were excluded from the Christian European society mainly for religious reasons.[76] When the waves of modernity and secularization swept across the European culture, a religious way of identification of a people became considerably weakened, and many Jews took it as an opportunity to get into the mainstream of the European societies. However, "[a]s religion lost its altogether preeminent role, it was gradually replaced by [nationalism]."[77] As national demarcation now replaced the religious one, the Jews still had to remain marginalized. "Jews could not be Germans or Frenchmen because they already belonged to the Jewish nation."[78] It is only in recent history when religious and nationalistic ways of demarcation have much receded into the past, that the fence between the Jews and others nations has been considerably lowered. And people could cross over the ethnic fence more freely than ever, and its effect was conspicuous in Judaism. A number of the Jews became "gentilized," and so the very existence of the Jewish community faced a new and grave challenge. But the matter of the Jewish identity at its root, Wyschogrod insists, still depends solely on the fidelity of God to his covenant with Abraham. The question is: in spite of all social and historical flux, does God keep his covenant and continue to dwell in them? Does God keep the chosen lineage for his dwelling

---

76. Ibid., 44.
77. Ibid.
78. Ibid., 45.

and as his abode on the earth even while some gentiles are inducted into the Jewish lineage, through Torah observance, as before in the biblical history? The answer is a matter of faith in God's fidelity to the covenant of election.

While all the Jews are the Jews by virtue of their flesh, Wyschogrod argues, "the Orthodox Judaism cannot simply be considered one of the branches of Judaism"[79] even though they are a minority, according to Wyschogrod, only 10 to 20 percent of the Jews. The Orthodox Judaism is continuous with the historical rabbinic Judaism which survived and was practiced since the postexilic time. Moreover, it is the Orthodox Judaism that can explain the meaning of the Jewish existence and offer a platform for the Jewish unity, encompassing the wide spectrum of their practices and beliefs, on the basis of their theological understanding of *their bodily existence itself*. Further, one may legitimately think, it may call for the Jewish fidelity to their own God in this age of rapid secularization.

Thus, Wyschogrod consistently works out his account of the Jewish identity and the significance of the Jewish existence, centering upon the theological reflection of God's election and the irrevocable covenant.

However, one may consider Wyschogrod's unapologetic and unremitting theology of Israel's election "blatantly chauvinistic and inexcusably arrogant."[80] To this, Wyschogrod responds, "Indeed it would be, were [election conceived as] the self-election of a people. [But as] it is, it is a sign of God's absolute sovereignty which is not bound by human conceptions of fairness."[81] God's sovereign decision is only to be accepted in humility by the elect and the non-elect.

Moreover, Wyschogrod argues, God does not relate to humanity in sheer impartiality. Engaging with every individual with sheer equality and neutrality would be something that some neo-Platonic deities would do. Such deities would focus on humanity in general and remain aloof from all the personal relationships after all. "[I]t would then clearly not be a real encounter but a clever imitation of real relationship."[82] Perhaps, such an abstract relation would be possible only in the world of pure *ideas* where the self is somehow bodiless and not perspectival. It would be only a kind of Kantian concept: "Kant projects the non-centered space

---

79. Wyschogrod, *The Body of Faith*, 185.
80. Held, "Promise and Peril of Jewish Barthianism," 317.
81. Wyschogrod, "Divine Election and Commandments," 26.
82. Wyschogrod, *The Body of Faith*, 62.

of Newton and the mechanics resulting from it into the ethical domain."[83] Love or obligation for all humanity with sheer impartiality is after all inhumane. In our real life, we take up a certain location, from which we are perspectival and from which closeness and remoteness in relationship are actual. In reality, we need inner and outer circles; we need a father and a mother in a family, distinguished from the other members of a bigger society. A parent, as a particular individual, "devotes himself [or herself] to [another] person completely, listening with all of his being to the presence of the other."[84] In Wyschogrod's theology, "[e]thical space is not geometric, centerless space. The ethical is rooted in the human presence in the world and human presence is always perspectival, centered. The space of the world radiates outward from a natural center that is I."[85] That is how we are *personal*, according to Wyschogrod.

Given such a concept of personhood, Wyschogrod claims, the election exhibits God's personhood. "The election of Israel is . . . a sign of the humanity of God. . . . [H]e could have played a more godly role, refusing favorites and loving all his creatures impartially. His love would then have been a far less vulnerable one because impartiality signifies a certain remoteness, the absence of that consuming passion that is a sign of need of the other."[86] God's relationship with humanity does not occur in geometric and centerless space. However, there are remoteness and closeness from his perspectival center. God encounters some individuals and particular groups, and a particular nation in his proximity.

God displays his fatherhood in that way. "If Abraham was especially loved by God, it is because God is a father who does not stand in a legal relationship to his children, which by its nature requires impartiality and objectivity."[87] Even within a family, parents find hard or even impossible to love their children equally, even though "[t]here is usually great reluctance on the part of parents to admit this."[88] Such fatherhood is attributed to the God of Israel in Wyschogrod's account. So other siblings may take their father's love for one particular child intolerable and try "to substitute an impartial judge for a loving father . . . [to] eliminate the

---

83. Ibid., 216.
84. Ibid., 62.
85. Ibid., 216.
86. Ibid., 62.
87. Ibid., 64.
88. Ibid., 65.

preference for the specially favored, but [that] would also deprive all of them of a father."[89]

Wyschogrod notes that Christians frequently depict the God of the Old Testament as hot-tempered, easily provoked, and hardly placated and contrast it with that of the God of Jesus Christ in the New Testament. However, Wyschogrod argues, this is to forget that in dealing with Israel, God was dealing with his *natural* son. As human parents discipline their natural children harshly, when necessary—while they deal with their adopted children more carefully, so does God.[90] There is a kernel of truth to some Christians' impressions about the God of the Old Testament as the wrathful God: God is indeed harsh. Yet, God is so as he is the Father to Israel, his "natural" and first-born son. God's harsh discipline only proves that "there is a security that cannot be shaken"[91] between the two.

Wyschogrod does not forget to indicate that Israel's "election is for service"[92] and that it is not a sign of any inherent superiority of the people. He says to his Jewish audience that they must not forget the *purpose* of God's election: God has chosen Abraham and his descendants to be a blessing *for* all the nations. The nations are to be blessed through Israel. Israel should "accept [her] election . . . in humility, in fear and trembling."[93] Accordingly, it is incumbent upon Israel to be open to the nations and "to welcome the covenant of the nations with the God of Israel."[94]

The nations, in turn, must be aware that, Wyschogrod argues, "[s]urely non-election does not equal rejection."[95] "Ishmael and Esau, the sons of non-election, are suffused in the divine word with compassion in some respects more powerful than the love of the sons of election."[96] God shows Esau, the non-elect, compassion even when the chosen Jacob does not.[97] Wyschogrod remarks, "The very fact that the Bible does not

---

89. Ibid.

90. Wyschogrod, "Why was and is the Theology of Karl Barth of Interest to a Jewish Theologian?" 219. Again, Wyschogrod daringly describes God as if he is a human father, considering the divine fatherhood as his "humanity."

91. Ibid.

92. Wyschogrod, "Israel, the Church, and Election," 180.

93. Ibid., 185.

94. Ibid., 186.

95. Ibid.

96. Ibid.

97. Wyschogrod, *The Body of Faith*, 64.

begin with Abraham but rather with the creation and Adam, signifies the broader human significance of the story."[98] The election of Israel is "in a sense, the *means* chosen by Hashem for the redemption of humanity."[99] Further, Wyschogrod envisages that "[i]n the end of days, there will be a reconciliation of all the families of the earth."[100]

In sum, Wyschogrod's theology of election of Israel is not blatantly chauvinistic as God's election of Israel is not antithetical to non-election. The non-election does not mean God's rejection; Israel's election is in service of the gentile nations. Israel's election does not mean either that God's discipline and punishment of his chosen people are lenient; in fact, it is opposite. Also, Wyschogrod has highlighted that God's election of a people reveals the sovereignty and the personhood of God. God is not a principle of impartial ethics; God encounters some humans in his close fatherly embrace. Wyschogrod, after all, advises that people should accept their election and non-election in humility and anticipate the final redemption of all the nations through Israel's election.

Through his reading of the Hebrew Bible without the Hellenistic lenses, Wyschogrod could see the bodily description of God in the Bible (almost) as the portrayal of God himself—though he does not press it into his understanding of the reality of God himself or affirm the incarnational characteristics of God. Yet, Wyschogrod sees the relation between God and his people in terms of incarnation: God is present in the flesh of Israel; Israel is the diluted form of incarnation. Thus, Wyschogrod's bold commitment to the Bible makes his Orthodox Judaism move *toward* the doctrine of incarnation and so toward Christian theology. As we will see later, this incarnational understanding of the relation between God and Israel is recognized and appreciated in Jenson's Christology, ecclesiology, and soteriology.

The Jews as the Torah Community

In conversation with Christian theology, Wyschogrod characterizes the Jewish people as the Torah community. Another basic feature of Judaism

---

98. Ibid., 104. How can the redemption of the whole humanity be achieved? "The prophetic picture of the end of days envisages a reconciliation among the peoples of the world, so that the redemption of Israel is also the redemption of humanity" (ibid.). Or the nations can approach to God by approaching Israel.

99. Ibid. Emphasis added.

100. Wyschogrod, "Israel, the Church, and Election," 186–87.

is its observance of the Torah. Judaism is fundamentally a faith of election, *and therefore* of the Torah. The Torah is given to the Jewish people *because* they are elected. The single most definitive character is election, and yet the Torah comes with election. So "there is no Judaism without law.... [I]t is the most characteristic feature of Judaism."[101]

The Bearer of the Torah

The Torah is given to Israel only. It is not a universal law that all the nations are commanded to obey. The Noachide law is given to the nations; the Torah is given to Israel. In this connection, Wyschogrod relays an intriguing episode from midrash: "Hashem [was] attempting to bestow the Torah on various nations, all of who reject it because its provisions, such as the prohibition of theft and murder, are found unacceptable. Only Israel accepts the Torah as soon as it is offered, without inquiring into its provisions."[102]

Israel is called to obey the Torah, according to Wyschogrod, because they were elected to be the bearers of God's presence. This people chosen to be the bearer and the abode of God's presence on the earth should be holy by observance of the law of God. The Torah is to be obeyed by this nation so that it may be the proper and holy abode of YHWH, set apart from the nations. As Israel is called to be the abode of YHWH, she is also called to be the bearer of the Torah.

Wyschogrod goes so far as to claim that Israel is called to *incarnate* the Torah, the Word of God. Wyschgrod states: traditionally, "[a] talmid chacham ('rabbinic scholar') is considered a living Torah,"[103] while in a broader sense, "the Jewish people is the *incarnation* of Torah."[104] The Jewish people are to "flesh out" the teaching of the Torah, to be the incarnation of the Torah, and so the "diluted incarnation" of God's presence by election.

Wyschogrod readily admits that Israel unfortunately often failed to live up to the demands of the Torah and so resists to be the communal and diffused incarnation of the Torah: "the history of the Jewish people

---

101. Wyschogrod, "The Impact of the Dialogue with Christianity and My Self-understanding as a Jew," 230.

102. Wyschogrod, *The Body of Faith*, 211.

103. Ibid. Emphasis mine.

104. Ibid. Emphasis mine.

is a history of obduracy and unfaithfulness. It is a people that, time and again, has returned evil for God's good and has suffered grievously for it."[105] The Jews have often attempted to live without the Law, prying their blessing and responsibility from their covenanted flesh. Whenever the Torah was resisted by the Jews, however, the intensity of the covenantal unity of God and Israel was made manifest through God's discipline.

The Traditional Christian View of the Torah

Wyschogrod is well aware that Christian theology has often held a contemptuous view of the Torah and its observers. It has considered the law as cursing, condemning, and death-bestowing: no one can live up to the demands of the law, and therefore anyone under the law is under curse and death. Wyschogrod writes, "Instead of being a gift of love, then, the Torah is a trap, a Trojan horse which appears at first sight as a divine gift but which really turns out to be a potent poison that causes the painful death of those who place their trust in it."[106] In many Christian minds, those *still* under the law are under condemnation and deserve divine punishment, and they "paid dearly for their foolish confidence in the Torah"[107] particularly in the modern history. Holocaust, of course, is not a Christian teaching at all or encouraged by it, as Wyschogrod admits. "[N]evertheless, the Holocaust could probably not have occurred if not for the two thousand years of preparation that took place in the 'teaching of contempt.'"[108]

Wyschogrod finds a particularly impressive instance of Christian "contempt" in Aquinas' extensive reflection on the divine law. Wyschogrod indicates: in his reflection on the reasons why Christians do not keep the Mosaic law,[109] Aquinas divided the law into two categories—the moral law and the cultic law. The moral law is still binding on Christians, but the cultic law became obsolete when Christ came and fulfilled it. For this reason, in Aquinas's thinking, an act of keeping the cultic law after

---

105. Wyschogrod, "Why was and is the Theology of Karl Barth of Interest to a Jewish Theologian?" 223. Wyschogrod humbly confesses that this would have not been made clear as it should be, without his reading of Barth. "It might be surprising that this should require a reading of Barth when this point is so clear in the Bible" (ibid.).

106. Wyschogrod, "A Jewish View of Christianity," 161.

107. Ibid.

108. Wyschogrod, "Resurrection," 105.

109. Wyschogrod, "Christianity and Mosaic Law," 452.

the coming of Christ amounts to an act of rejecting his coming and his work. It follows in Aquinas that those who observe the Torah even after Christ's ministry is committing *a mortal sin*. Wyschogrod confesses, "I was not, until I read Thomas, aware that that was what I was doing."[110] Further, Wyschogrod holds that observance of the Torah and the coming of Messiah are "quite distinctive subjects."[111]

Wyschogrod holds this Christian bifurcation of the Torah (between cultic and moral elements) to be alien to the Tanakh; the Tanakh does not make such a distinction or know of any sort of it. The Jews accept the whole of Torah as divine simply because it is the Word of God.[112] Wyschogrod adds, "To the Jewish reader, it is difficult to escape the feeling that in Christianity there is a tendency toward the rationalization of the commandments, though the word 'rationalization' might not be the best possible."[113] Autonomous human reason plays a significant role in compartmentalization of what is ethical and what is not in Christian theology. According to Wyschogrod, Christian theology subjugates the Torah to the Kantian categorical imperative or something similar. The philosophy of Enlightenment could not accept some of the commandments in the Torah, for example, the call to pray for vengeance on God's enemies. For Wyschogrod, to put it in a Barthian term, it is merely "a form of *natural ethics* corresponding to that other error, natural theology."[114]

110. Ibid.

111. Ibid. Wyschogrod tells of a conversation with the then-Cardinal Ratzinger when he was the head of the Congregation for the Doctrine of the Faith. When they came to touch upon the relation between the Vatican and Israel, Wyschogrod indicated that there was a widespread impression among the Jews: the Vatican was not supportive to the establishment of the State of Israel for theological reasons. Cardinal Ratzinger denied it and said that it was a purely political issue: "It has to do with the welfare of the Catholics in Arab countries, and all the difficulties Christians in general and Catholics in particular are having in countries such as Lebanon.... It also has to do with the absence of borders and the settlement of the question of the Palestinians on the West Bank" (Wyschogrod, "Incarnation," 212). But he then added, "If the Jews rebuilt their temple and reinstituted the sacrifices, that would cause us some problems"(Ibid.).

112. "The Bible is first and foremost the word of God" (Wyschogrod, *The Body of Faith*, 59).

113. Wyschogrod, "Why was and is the Theology of Karl Barth of Interest to a Jewish Theologian?" 218.

114. Ibid., 217. Emphasis mine. In light of the autonomous reason, some commandments of the Torah are taken to be "universal" while the others are merely cultic and must be made obsolete. However, Wyschogrod questions the autonomous reason: do we really know why some moral laws are binding on every human being? Because

At this point, we may agree with Wyschogrod: it would be hard to say that Christian theology has been free of Hellenistic or rationalistic elements. However, it may be still argued that Christian theology has sought to observe the very distinction that Wyschogrod indicated, the distinction in the Bible between the Mosaic law given to the Jews only and the Noachide law given to the gentiles. If such a distinction can be legitimately made, Christian bifurcation of the Torah may not be considered necessarily as rationalization but as recognition of what is binding on non-Jews. So construed, both communities may agree that the laws given to each community do not overlap at every point.

Rediscovering the Jewish Identity as the Torah Community through the Early Christian View of the Torah

Another issue is whether the coming of Messiah has abolished the Jewish observance of the Torah. If it has, then, it seems justifiable that Christians hold onto a contemptuous view of the Mosaic law and the Jews. If not, Christianity needs to rethink the relation of the observance of the Torah and the coming of Messiah. Wyschogrod reexamines Paul in the book of Acts and Pauline epistles and says, "the complexity of the Christian position [on the Torah] is the source of hope for the future"[115] in Jewish-Christian relation. The apostle Paul traditionally was considered to have left behind Jewish roots. In Wyschogrod's view, however, Paul is noticeably Jewish precisely in his view of the Torah.

In his discussion on the Pauline view of the Torah, Wyschogrod often focuses on the Jerusalem council in Acts 15. The debate was about whether the gentile Christians should be circumcised in accordance with the Mosaic law, like the Jews. Here Wyschogrod makes a keen observation: "If anyone in Jerusalem had thought that with the coming of Christ the law, or the ceremonial law, was no longer obligatory for Jews, there certainly could not have arisen a debate about whether it's obligatory for Gentiles."[116] The issue was not the Jewish observance

---

we owe ethical obligations to "all human beings equally? Then why not to animals? If also to animals, then why not to plants? And why not to inanimate objects? If we owe ethical obligations equally to all human beings only, then do we owe such obligations equally to all human beings or is it permissible to prefer our own children?" (Wyschogrod, *The Body of Faith*, 215).

115. Wyschogrod, "A Jewish View of Christianity," 161.
116. Wyschogrod, "Christianity and Mosaic Law," 456.

but the *gentile* observance of the Torah. At that time, rather, there were thousands of Jews who converted into Christianity and were still zealous for the Torah.[117] Their Jewish observance was not questioned or challenged by the apostles. The tacit assumption of the Jerusalem council was then that the coming of Messiah and his work did not make the Torah obsolete for the Jews.

So construed, Wyschogrod argues, it becomes understandable why Paul's tone was so negative on the Mosaic law. "[Paul] emphasizes and even exaggerates all the disadvantages and dangers of living under the law. He carefully omits all the advantages of Israel's covenant under the Torah because he has a specific purpose in mind: to dissuade gentile Jesus-believers from placing themselves under the obligations of the Torah."[118] Paul painted "a pretty dark picture of the law. But that is a tactical maneuver. It is designed to achieve a certain purpose, namely to discourage the Gentile from conversion."[119] And this Pauline tactic is characteristically Jewish: "the Jewish rabbis of this time also were trying to discourage Gentiles from circumcision, quite apart from the issue of Jesus."[120]

Wyschogrod finds his reading of Paul aligned with that of a Catholic New Testament scholar Raymond Brown, who claims that if Paul had had a son, he would have had him circumcised for his son would be a Jew.[121] One may well also consider the so-called "New Perspective" on Paul, N. T. Wright, whose own construal of Paul's gospel "in no way commits Paul to being anti-Semitic, or even anti-Judaic. He does not wish to prevent the Jews from practicing their ancestral religion. Indeed, he himself continues to attend synagogue."[122] Thus, Wyschogrod stresses that

117. Acts 21:20. Cf. Wyschogrod, "Paul, Jews, and Gentiles," 197.
118. Wyschogrod, "A Jewish View of Christianity," 163.
119. Wyschogrod, "Christianity and Mosaic Law," 458.
120. Ibid.
121. Ibid., 456.
122. Wright, *The Climax of the Covenant*, 173. Of course, there are critics, running counter to the New Perspective: Carson, O'Brien, and Seifrid, *Justification and Variegated Nomism*; Westerholm, *Perspectives Old and New on Paul*; and Kim, *Paul and the New Perspective*. In this connection, it would be worth mentioning that even though the Jews are called to bear the Torah on their bodily existence, Judaism should not be caricatured as a legalistic religion. For the Jews do not seek their salvation by observing of the Torah. In Judaism, seeking justification by works would be equivalent to asking God to judge me in accordance with what I have done, instead of asking for his mercy. "It is unthinkable for Judaism or a Jew to strike such a pose before God. Judaism has always understood that if judged by the strict demands of the Law, no Jew

the Jewish community is essentially the community of the Torah, seeing it affirmed by Christian apostolic teaching. So he says, "The contact with Christianity has therefore strengthened—if it needed strengthening—my appreciation of the centrality of law in Judaism."[123]

Jewish Rediscovery of Christianity

Having seen Wyschogrod's outworking the self-identity of Judaism in relation to Christianity, now we will turn to see Wyschogrod's views Christianity and how an unprecedented mutual reconciliatory recognition of the other within Abrahamic family resemblance is cautiously envisaged.

Precisely because of God's call to Abraham to be a blessing to all the nations, Wyschogrod holds, his Jewish descendants must be interested in all the nations, particularly "Christianity, which mediated the vocabulary of Israel to all parts of the earth."[124] On every Sunday, the Jewish vocabularies are spoken out in the gentile gatherings: Passover, Pentecost, the Day of Atonement, the Tabernacle, and so on. The most figures in their speech are Jews: David, Solomon, Ezekiel, Jeremiah, Isaiah, Jesus, Paul, and so on. "How can a Jewish theologian not perceive that something wonderful is at work here, something that must in some way be connected with the love of God of Israel for all [the nations]?"[125] At this point, Wyschogrod could have affirmed that Jesus is the Messiah, for all the nations are gathering to worship of God of Israel through their belief in Jesus. However, without affirming the Messiahship of Jesus, Wyschogrod relies on Maimonides in this regard, who said, "[Jesus] only served to clear the way for King Messiah, to prepare the whole world to worship God with one accord, as it is written 'For then will I turn to the people a pure language, that they may all call upon the name of the Lord to serve him with one consent' (Zeph. 3:9)."[126] For Wyschogrod, Jesus plays a very crucial role in the gentile community to purify their languages and thus prepares the way for the Messiah.

---

can prevail" (Wyschogrod, "Paul, Jews, and Gentiles," 199).

123. Wyschogrod, "The Dialogue with Christianity and My Self-understanding as a Jew," 234.

124. Wyschogrod, "Why Was and Is the Theology of Karl Barth of Interest to a Jewish Theologian?" 213.

125. Ibid.

126 Maimonides, "Law of Kings" XI.4, quoted in Kellner, "How Ought a Jew View Christian Beliefs About Redemption?" 273.

In Wyschogrod's understanding, Christianity is regarded as "the gathering of peoples around the people of Israel, the entry of the adopted sons and daughters into the household of God."[127] Christianity does not replace the people of Israel as the people of God while "[t]hrough the Jew Jesus, when properly interpreted, the gentile enters into the covenant and becomes a member of the household."[128] And Wyschogrod is aware that there is such "a form of Christianity that does not intend to replace Israel as the people of God but join it as adopted sons and daughters in the house of God."[129] Such a "new" Christianity "sees, based on Romans 9–11, that the promises of God are irrevocable, that the election of Israel remains in full force, and around it the Gentiles have gathered in solidarity with the Jewish people, worshiping the common God of Israel and the gentiles."[130] The Christian solidarity with Judaism is possible, Wyschogrod suggests—and this is the way it should be—when Christians acknowledge the redemptive significance of the Jewish existence in light of God's irrevocable covenant with Abraham and his descendants. Otherwise, Christian supersessionism would be only self-destructive in the end. Wyschogrod states, "were Jews to disappear from the world, Christianity would disappear."[131] Without the Jews, Christianity would not be able to access the God of Israel. Conversely put, God of Israel would not access the nations without the channel of the Jewish bodily existence. For, as said above, the Jews are the carrier of God's presence and the channel through which God reaches the nations.

Wyschogrod's approach to Christianity is in general friendly. But Wyschogrod's concern about Christianity lingers with regard to Christian missional approach to the Jews since that poses a threat to the Jewish existence. When the Jews were admitted into and stayed in the early Christian community, which quickly became pervasively gentile, it was extremely difficult for the Jews to keep their Jewish identity among the gentile fellows. The Jews in the church were hardly able to keep the Torah and to resist marrying with other gentile believers. Their observance of the Torah and their effort to keep their lineage pure seemed not encouraged in the church. Particularly, intermarriage with a gentile partner was

127. Wyschogrod, "Incarnation," 215.

128. Ibid.

129. Wyschogrod, "The Dialogue with Christianity and My Self-Understanding as a Jew," 236.

130. Wyschogrod, "Incarnation," 215.

131. Ibid.

a great danger to the Jewish identity within the church. "Throughout the ages, the church . . . has invited Jews to enter the church and when they did, within one or two or three generations, they disappeared as Jews. They intermarried and within a couple of generations all traces of their Jewishness was lost."[132]

However, Wyschogrod still indicates that, in the very earliest time of the church, the Christian church had two segments, the Jews and the gentiles. The Jewish believers could remain as the Torah-observants, and the gentile believers respected them to keep their identity by their observance of the Mosaic law. It was the gentile believers in those early days that were often tempted to follow the Jewish observance of the Torah—not the way around. So the apostle Paul had to discourage the gentile believers from pursuing the Jewish way of life, as indicated above.

Can Jews now hope for a "new" Christianity that fully respects the Jewish observance of the Torah, and can they be free of the danger of intermarriage even within the church? We may find the following suggestive: Wyschogrod recalls, "About three years ago, I met Cardinal Lustiger,"[133] the Cardinal Archbishop of Paris, who is a Jewish Christian and proud to say that he is a Jew. Once Wyschogrod wrote to him, saying: "Your Eminence, isn't it time that you started fulfilling the Mitzvot?"[134] What can be noted here is that Wyschogrod does not only emphasized that even a Christian Jew is still accountable to the Law but also implies—even though Wyschogrod never draws this implication—that belief in the deity of Jesus (and in the Trinity) is compatible with the Jewish observance of the Torah. Then, if the Christianity, in turn, recognizes afresh the irrevocability of the Mosaic covenant and God's faithfulness to it, as Wyschogrod suggests, then Christianity can enter into a new phase in its relationship with Judaism.

Conclusion

In his reminiscence of "more than thirty years of involvement in Jewish-Christian dialogue,"[135] Wyschogrod admits that he has come to

---

132. Wyschogrod, "Christianity and Mosaic Law," 458.
133. Ibid., 459.
134. Ibid.
135. Wyschogrod, "The Impact of the Dialogue with Christianity and My Self-understanding as a Jew," 225.

articulate his Jewish identity more clearly in relation to Christian theology. Wyschogrod says, his Judaism is biblical.[136] Yet, his experience in Jewish-Christian dialogue has pushed him more in the biblical direction. "It is, after all, the Hebrew Bible, the Old Testament of Christians, that Jews and Christians have in common."[137]

As the influence of Maimonides or the Greek philosophy is on the wane, Wyschogrod's unapologetic commitment to the Hebrew Bible comes through and takes the biblical description of God as a genuine portrayal of God himself. So Wyschogrod's theology moves *toward* the doctrine of incarnation. The diffused form of incarnation of God is affirmed by the conceptual help of the Christian doctrine of incarnation, and that incarnation is construed to have been realized in the existence of the people of Israel. By this, Wyschogrod also upholds the redemptive meaning of the Jewish people in the history of humanity.

Moreover, through his sustained conversations with Christianity, Wyschogrod has affirmed the identity of the Jewish people as the community of the Torah. In his reading of the New Testament, Wyschogrod finds that the apostle Paul is noticeably Jewish: even though Paul's rhetoric towards the law is quite harsh, his intention becomes understandable for Wyschogrod. It is to discourage the *gentile* observance of the Torah as other Jewish rabbis did at that time. But Paul never dissuaded his Jewish fellows from keeping the Torah. Paul himself did undergo the ritual of purification in the temple so that everybody may know that "there is nothing to the things which they have been told about [him], but that Paul himself also walk orderly, keeping the Law."[138] Even for Paul himself, the Torah has enduring, eternal, and irrevocable meaning upon the Jewish people. Paul never impoverished Judaism; rather, that strongly suggests how the Torah is essential in Judaism. Thus, Wyschogrod finds that his reading of the New Testament as a Jew may strengthen the identity of the Jewish people as the Torah community. And he takes this as an opportunity to call Christians today to rethink their traditional contemptuous view of the Torah and of the Torah-observants, and also their Christian relation to the Jews.

136. Wyschogrod is not a Karaite, "the medieval Jewish sect that rejected rabbinic Judaism as inauthentic and placed all its faith in the Hebrew Bible" (Wyschogrod, "The Impact of the Dialogue with Christianity and My Self-understanding as a Jew," 226).

137. Ibid., 228.

138. Acts 21:24 (ESV); Wyschogrod, "The Impact of the Dialogue with Christianity and My Self-understanding as a Jew," 233.

Now it may be envisaged that listening to the other community or reading the Bible together can lead to recognition of the redemptive meaning of the other community within God's economy and shed new light on the relationship between the two communities. Now the two covenant communities seem cautiously entering into a new chapter of history—probably they have already, in which the two communities may overcome the long history of hostility and strengthen mutual solidarity as they listen together afresh and more faithfully to the Bible. Can this eventually happen? Now we need to move on to Jenson's Christian post-supersessionistic response to this Jewish theology.

4

The Two in the One Israelite Body
Jenson's Response to Wyschogrod

THE CONVERSATIONS BETWEEN CHRISTIANITY and Judaism in recent decades give us an opportunity not only to listen to the Jewish voices on their own identity and its relation to Christianity but also to rethink the Christian view of Judaism and its own identity. In this chapter, following Jenson's lead, we will see how Christianity can understand afresh God of Israel and its own Christian identity in relation to the Jewish existence through conversations with them and listening to their reading of the Bible. As seen in the previous chapter, Jenson's theology is already found to be alignable with the theology of Michael Wyschogrod, especially as both emphasize the ontological significances of election (chapter 1) and the body (chapter 2) in their doctrines of God. Affirming Wyschogrod's view of Israel as the dilute-incarnation of God and its significance in the divine being, Jenson offers a fresh articulation of the identity of the church. He agrees with Wyschogrod that Christians are the gathering of the nations around the Jewish people with whom God made his covenant irrevocably, while Jenson stresses that the gentile gathering is for the worship of God of Israel and for the mission of Israel. Also transposing Wyschogrod's thought into Christian ecumenical rubrics, Jenson maintains that the church is the people of God, the body of Christ, and the temple of the Holy Spirit, *only* in its anticipated union with the Jewish people which will occur beyond this age. In short, in his conversational engagement with Wyschogrod's theology, Jenson's theology of Judaism offers a non-supersessionistic understanding of God of Israel in trinitarian terms and of Christian self-identity, without compromising the Christian faith about the messiahship and the deity of Jesus. To see this, this chapter will proceed by exploring 1) Jenson's Christian reception of Wyschogrod's theology of Israel as the dilute-incarnation of God, 2) his formulation of Christian identity in relation with Judaism, and his response to a couple of Jewish-Christian long-standing issues: 3) the deity of Jesus Christ, and 4) the Torah.

The major sources of this chapter will be the later works of Jenson: The two volumes of his *Systematic Theology* (1997 and 1999), "Toward a Christian Doctrine of Israel" (2000), "Toward a Christian Theology of Judaism" (2003), and "What Kind of God Can Make a Covenant?" (2013). His theology of Judaism started coming into view in his *Systematic Theology*, as Jenson once said that "there was slightly more than a nucleus."[1]

Jenson's Reception of Wyschogrod's Theology

Wyschogrod's conception of Israel as the diluted incarnation of God is congenially accepted by Jenson, as he sees its trinitarian implications. Alluding to Wyschogrod's idea, Jenson states, "It is precisely as flesh that the people of Israel have their Son-relation to God."[2] They are the people that "God has as the locus of his own *involvement with himself*, in the very sense of the trinitarian concept of 'the Son.'"[3] As God relates to Israel, God relates to himself. Jenson also favorably quotes an old rabbi's saying: when God redeemed Israel, he redeemed *himself*.[4] As a Christian theologian, Jenson sees a crucial conceptual nexus between the community of Israel and the trinitarian concept of the Son.

Further, affirming the significance of their *fleshly* existence as argued by Wyschogrod, Jenson states that Israel is the Son of God as "the nation identified by *biological* descent from Abraham and Sarah, or by *physically* marked adoption into that descent."[5] It is their Jewish fleshly existence in which God involves himself and finds his Son. At this very juncture, Jenson refers to Wyschogrod: "the flesh of Israel is the abode of the divine presence in the world. It is the carnal anchor that God has sunk

---

1. Robert Jenson, "Toward a Christian Doctrine of Israel," 3–4.
2. *ST*, 1:78.
3. Ibid. Emphasis mine.
4. Mekhilta Y to Exod 12:41, quoted in ibid., 76.
5. Ibid., 78.

into the soil of creation."⁶ Also, here we can see that, for the Lutheran Jenson, the Sonship is not separated from the *bodily* existence.

For Jenson, even in the Old Testament period, God is not unincarnational. Jenson says, "The concept of 'incarnation' may not appear in Israel's Scriptures, but we need only ask what a God would be like who would not incarnate himself, a God of "pure spirit," to see that it would be the precise antagonist of Israel's God."⁷ The echo of Wyschogrod is unmistakable here: the God of the Hebrew Bible is not sheerly anti-incarnational; the God of Maimonides is.⁸ Like Wyschogrod, Jenson affirms the "dilute incarnation" of God in his people Israel: "God is incarnate in the people of Israel."⁹

At this point, one may note that Jenson's notion of the incarnation is quite extensively applied in establishing the meaning of the existence of God's people (the Jews). As seen before, for Jenson, the church is the body of Christ, not figuratively but in a genuine sense. Jenson takes the Pauline ecclesiological phrase as ontological terms. There is a sense in which the church can be called a form of incarnation of God, for Jenson. Further, moving in a post-supersessionistic direction, Jenson's theology accommodates Wyschogrod's conception of Israel as the dilute form of the incarnation of God. This "incarnational" ecclesiology may seem to threaten the uniqueness of the incarnation in Jesus Christ, but Jenson affirms an "incarnational ecclesiology" as compatible with an affirmation of Christ's uniqueness and as a proper application of the Lutheran christology. For Jenson, the body of Jesus Christ is embracive and accommodative of other human beings into itself since, unlike other human bodies, his body is capable of the divine (*finitum capax infiniti*).

Jenson's adoption of the doctrine of *theosis* also comes into view here: bodily beings participate in the divine life and being as they participate in the divine body of the Son. As seen in the chapter 2, Jenson embraces the doctrine of deification within his Lutheran theological fold. The advance here is its development in a post-supersessionistic direction. Jenson states, "The *content* of Israel's fully eschatological hope is, inexorably, hope for participation in God's own reality, for what the Greek fathers

---

6. Wyschogrod, *The Body of Faith*, 256 quoted in ibid., 78n23.
7. Ibid., 78.
8. Wyschogrod, "Incarnation and God's Indwelling in Israel," 167.
9. Robert Jenson, "What Kind of God Can Make a Covenant?" 16.

of the church called 'deification.'"¹⁰ Jenson maintains that *theosis* is the human soteriological coordinate, corresponding to God's identification of himself with his people: "If God is a God identified by and with the events of Israel's history, Israel's 'deification' will be simply that the corresponding relations on our part are realized, that we come to be identified by and with events in the life of God."¹¹ This deificational understanding of Israel's hope is adduced by a famous rabbinical passage: "In the World to Come . . . the righteous sit with their crowns on their heads enjoying the effulgence of the *Shekinah*."¹²

This Jewish bodily participation in the divine life and being is an ontological event significant to God's being itself. In God's covenantal unity to his people Israel, Jenson says, citing Wyschogrod, "While God remains absolute, . . . he has made himself a partner in the fate of the Jewish people, whose vicissitudes do not leave him unaffected."¹³ God's being is not closed off from the bodily events of Israel. Even his divine oneness is inextricably related to his covenantal relationship to Israel. Jenson cites Wyschogrod again, "The estrangement of Israel from Hashem when Israel sins is a divine self-estrangement."¹⁴ Of course, her sinful attempts to detach herself from God will fail; God's faithfulness will prevail. But Hashem will be one not without Israel, but by *his reconciliation with Israel*.¹⁵

Jenson appropriates Wyschogrod's portrayal of the covenantal relation between God and Israel by way of the notion of "happy exchange." Wyschogrod remarks that God's identification with his people is so intense that "Israel's sin does not leave Hashem untouched."¹⁶ Wyschogrod sees it as a feature which sharply differs from the Christian doctrine of the incarnation: "Hashem's indwelling in Israel is not the incarnation of Christianity, which results in a sinless Christ. Hashem's indwelling in Israel is 'in the midst of their uncleanness.'"¹⁷ However, Jenson finds that this Jewish theology may be aligned with Lutheran Christology in

10. *ST*, 1:71.
11. Ibid.
12. *Bab.Barakot* 17a. See Volz, *Die Eschatologie der jüdischen Gemeinde im neutestamentlichen Zeitalter*, 334–401 quoted in ibid., 71n55.
13. Wyschogrod, *The Body of Faith*, 56 quoted in ibid., 76.
14. Ibid., 85n77.
15. Wyschogrod, *The Body of Faith*, 214, quoted in ibid., 86.
16. Wyschogrod, *The Body of Faith*, 214, quoted in ibid., 85n77.
17. Wyschogrod, *The Body of Faith*, 212, quoted in ibid., 85n76.

which Christ is construed as the greatest sinner by virtue of the "happy exchange." Jenson states, "[a]s the individual Christ, the *totus Christus* is sinless; as the community related to the one Christ, the *totus Christus* is sinful. God as the Christ *of the* community is 'the chief of sinners'; as the one before whom the *totus Christus* stands, he is the righteous judge of sin."[18] For Jenson, in the Lutheran theology as well, the sin of his people does not leave God unaffected.[19] Thus, Wyschogrod's theology of Israel well settles in Jenson's Lutheran christology and soteriology.

Christian Identity (in Relation with Judaism)

Having seen Jenson's reception of Wyschogrod's Jewish theology, which was visible in his *Systematic Theology* volume 1, now we are going to delve into Jenson's development of his articulation of the Christian identity in relation to the Jewish people, with a focus on his later essays.

A Historical Observation of the Two Communities

Prior to theological reflection on the church's relation to the Jews, Jenson starts his account with "a mere historical observation":[20] Christianity and Judaism are in parallel in their claims for the identity of Israel and in their formations of the canons. Here we have to keep it in mind that Jenson is not presenting a generic or sociological account of the two covenant communities as an a priori foundation for his theological reflection. As

---

18. Ibid., 85–86.

19. I find the following comments on Lutheran theology helpful, which see the conceptual nexus between *communicatio idiomatum* and "happy exchange": "Luther is able to talk about Christ as the 'greatest sinner' not only in the sense that sins were imputed to him, but because Christ took upon himself a real human nature. Christ participates in sinful humanity in a realistic way. In the same manner, the believer participates in Christ, thus receiving Christ's very righteousness. There is something of a *communito idiomatum* between Christ and the believer. This results in the believer and Christ becoming one person. 'In faith, the person of Christ and that of the believer are made one, and this oneness must not be divided'" (Cooper and Leithart, *The Righteousness of One*, 43–44); "Since sin is so deep in the flesh that nothing seems to belong to a sinner more than this, Christ goes deeper into the flesh than sin itself. He mediates by taking the sin. This is what we mean when we use the term 'communication of attributes" (*communication idiomatum*). Christ must enter into the flesh more deeply than sin and legally" (Paulson, *Lutheran Theology*, 92).

20. Jenson, "Toward a Christian Theology of Judaism," 5.

seen in the first section, Jenson's *theological* reflection has already been in place.

In Jenson's observation, "rabbinic Judaism and Christianity are parallel claimants to be Israel after canonical Israel."[21] Canonical Israel, in Jenson's definition, is "the national political and cultic entity that was established through Moses and David and endured, in one recognizable form or another, for something like a millennium."[22] But canonical Israel *came to an end* when the temple was destroyed and the land was taken by the Roman Empire (about B.C.E. 70). Then, two *denominations* survived "within what is often called late second-temple Judaism."[23] One denomination is the rabbinic Judaism that finds its identity "in *familial* [or carnal] descent from Abraham and Sarah and in Torah-study and obedience."[24] The other is the church, which finds its identity in their faith in a particular Jew named Jesus. Both communities claim that they are the rightful successor of the canonical Israel.

Another parallel lies in their formations of their canons. Both communities have the Tanakh or the Old Testament in common, and each added a second volume to it, the *Mishnah* or the New Testament. *Mishnah* is predominantly a legal compilation; the New Testament is mainly a historical narrative (the Gospels) with comments on it (the apostolic epistles).[25] According to Jenson, the second volume guides its own community's hermeneutics of the first volume: the rabbinic Judaism reads the Tanakh largely as the law; the church the same text mainly as a narrative in unity with that of the second volume.[26]

As he admits, Jenson has conducted observations as if he stands "outside both communities . . . deliberately abstract[ing] from each community's own conception of its continuity with Israel."[27] But he remarks in confidence, "My paralleling of the two communities is purely formal, and no one, I think, should be alarmed by it. . . . [W]hatever balance an omniscient historian might make between them, the observed parallel

---

21. Ibid., 5.
22. Ibid., 2.
23. Ibid., 3.
24. Ibid., 3. Emphasis added.
25. We will see in the next chapter Jenson's hermeneutic of the Bible, how the church reads the Bible as a narrative.
26. Ibid., 10.
27. Ibid., 5.

remains."²⁸ However, mere historical observation would not tell us about how the two communities should relate to each other, and how Christianity understands itself in relation to Judaism. Now "Christianity needs a theological interpretation of Judaism."²⁹

Jenson's Theological Reflection on the Two Communities

Jenson offers his Christian theology of Judaism, strikingly shaping it "around the *ecumenical ecclesiology's* three favorite rubrics for the church: the church is the people of God, the temple of the Spirit, and the body of Christ."³⁰ It is already obvious in his statement that Judaism is not another religion but the other covenantal community, which is to be construed in the ecumenical sweep. For Jenson takes Judaism as a legitimate and genuine counterpart to Christianity in the economy of God. Importantly, Jenson seeks to articulate the identity of Christianity through his theological reflection of the Jewish-Christian relation: "A Christian theology of Judaism will be at its center an attempt to understand Judaism's claim and in so doing to understand *its own* better."³¹

The People of God

"[A] search of the New Testament references to 'the people of God' quickly discovers something rather surprising.... It is *the nation of Israel* which ... in the New Testament continues to appear as 'the people' of God."³² Jenson appeals to Ratzinger who wrote: "I stumble on an unexpected finding: while the term 'people of God' occurred very frequently in the New Testament, only in a few passages . . . did it mean the Church, and its normal meaning indicated the people of Israel. Indeed, even where it could denote the Church the fundamental meaning of Israel was retained."³³ If we go beyond Jenson's reference in his text, we can find the cardinal Ratzinger says this:

---

28. Ibid., 5.
29. Ibid., 6.
30. Jenson, "Toward a Christian Doctrine of Israel," 14. Emphasis added.
31. Jenson, "Toward a Christian Theology of Judaism, 3. Emphasis added.
32. Jenson, "Toward a Christian Doctrine of Israel," 15. Emphasis added.
33. Ratzinger, *Church, Ecumenism, and Politics*, 18 quoted in *ST*, 2:191.

> [T]he idea of "People of God" in the Old Testament includes, first, the election of Israel by God, who chooses it for no merit of its own—despite the fact that it is not a great or significant people but one of the smallest of the peoples—who chooses it out of love and thus bestows his love upon it. Second, it includes the acceptance of this love, and concretely this means submission to the Torah. Only in this submission, which places Israel in relation to God, is it the people of God. In the New Testament, the concept "People of God" (with perhaps one or two exceptions) refers only to Israel, that is, to the people of the Old Covenant. It is not a concept that applies directly to the church.[34]

This striking discovery is not presented with detailed exegesis by Jenson or by Ratzinger in the immediate context. But an important biblical passage is briefly commented in Jenson's *Systematic Theology*:

> Paul insists in a famous passage [Romans 11]: "Has God rejected his people? By no means!" We must be alert to what it means that Paul, whatever he may elsewhere say of *"Israel according to the flesh,"* here refers to that very entity: it is the Israel who are *not in the church* and so are not descendants of Abraham on account of christological faith who are his problem. Thus the people whom, according to Paul, God has not rejected is Israel *constituted a people in her own ancient ways* of national continuity, that is, by the unity of tribal descent with certain religious, legal, and civil institutions, most notably effected by circumcision.[35]

Here Israel even outside the church is the proper people of God.[36] "Now a people is a very particular sort of community. A people is an irreducible given for its members."[37] In a people, once a person is born to it, he cannot choose his membership of his people but belongs to that people forever regardless of the individual's will. Citizenship or nationality is

---

34. Pope Benedict XVI, Thornton, and Varenne, *The Essential Pope Benedict XVI*, 115. Cf. The cardinal continues: "However, the church is understood as the continuation of Israel, although Christians don't descend directly from Abraham and thus actually don't belong to this people. They enter into it, says the New Testament, by their descent from Christ and thereby also become children of Abraham" (Benedict XVI, *The Essential Pope Benedict XVI*, 115). Also note what he says: "'People of God' actually refers always to the Old Testament element of the church, to her continuity with Israel. But the church receives her New Testament character more distinctively in the concept of the 'body of Christ'" (ibid., 64).

35. *ST*, 2:191. Emphasis added.

36. Jenson, "Toward a Christian Doctrine of Israel," 19.

37. Ibid., 14.

changeable; membership of a people is not. With regard to the church, there *might* be a sense in which the church can be considered a people, especially when a church member realizes that her membership is not from her choice but that God's will is mysteriously antecedent to hers. Nevertheless, "there is . . . something *willed* about the church,"[38] in that one *decides* whether she will join, remain in the church, or leave the church. So construed, the church is not a proper or genuine people. She cannot provide a people for God as the familial descendants of Abraham, Isaac, and Jacob can.

In order to have his proper and genuine people even after the canonical era, Jenson suggests, God would have to will the continuing existence of the Jews and Judaism. The Jews are the genuine people, "with Rabbinic Judaism somehow at their center, and despite all assimilation and secularism."[39] "[I]f God is to have a people identified by descent from Abraham and Sarah, the church as it is will not provide it. . . . God wills the Judaism . . . [that is,] the lineage of Abraham and Sarah . . . ."[40]

But it seems that the Jews and Christians should have existed as *one* community early on. Why were they separated from one another? Jenson indicates: the apostle Paul, in fact, expected the two communities to be one. "Had Israel believed, something like what we now know as Judaism would have been the matrix of the ecclesia's life, the community into which baptism brought gentiles; and this is what Paul had to think was in some sense how it should have been—which was his torment."[41] However, history unfolded against Paul's original expectation. Nevertheless, Paul still maintains that God's covenant with Abraham cannot fail and accordingly that the election of Israel is irrevocable (Rom 11:28-29). Jenson states, "With Paul I will insist that there is somehow God's reason, also from the church's point of view, for Israel's separate existence . . . ."[42]

Jenson continues his theological reflection: "given what the church *in fact* quickly became and is,"[43] and for God to have his proper people, the Jews had to stay outside the church, keeping their own practice and study of the Torah, and thus having the rabbinic Judaism at their cen-

---

38. Ibid., 14. Emphasis original.
39. Ibid., 15.
40. Jenson, "Toward a Christian Theology of Judaism," 9.
41. Jenson, "Toward a Christian Doctrine of Israel," 13.
42. Ibid.
43. Jenson, "Toward a Christian Theology of Judaism," 8.

ter.⁴⁴ In the early church's history, within a few generations, the church quickly became gentile in its demography, and it was almost impossible for them to persist as the Jews (the Torah observant) within the gentile gathering. The clash between Peter and Paul is *suggestive* here,⁴⁵ even if the text of Galatians 2 is not exactly about the cultic law or the kosher requirement. The issues might be whether the Jews can eat with gentile believers. For instance, when dining with gentile believers, must Jewish believers still follow dietary laws, eating Kosher food? What about the gentile believers? Should they eat non-Kosher food even when dining with the Jewish believers or are they allowed to follow dietary laws and eat Kosher food like their fellow Jews? Their relation could become more complicated with baptism issues. If a Jew had been baptized by John's baptism, should he be baptized again in the triune name? Or he should not? Further, marriage with other gentile believers would make it even harder for the Jewish believers to keep their Jewish identity. It seems the case that the gentile Christian did not encourage the Jews to stick to the Torah and discourage their marriage with a gentile believer. For various reasons, "identifiable Jewishness does not long survive within the gentile-dominated church."⁴⁶ Then, for the Jews to keep their Jewish identity—and if the God's covenant has not been made obsolete, they had and still have to keep a distance from the church for their survival and to provide God his proper people.

In this account, while Jenson does not explicitly mention Michael Wyschogrod, it is not difficult to perceive parallels between them. To recall the previous chapter, Wyschogrod is concerned about Christian missional approach to the Jews, as it poses a threat to the Jewish existence: it was hard for Jewish believers to keep themselves from intermarrying with other gentile believers in the early church. Jenson shares this Jewish concern, based on the conviction that the biological descendants of Israel should be kept distinctive from the gentiles, since they have a unique role to play in the economy of God, and since God's covenant with Israel is still valid. Jenson develops this line of argument, of course, seeing it compatible with Paul's teaching on God's fidelity to his covenant with Abraham and with Israel (Rom 9–11). Wyschogrod's voice also resonates when Jenson holds that the Torah is not made obsolete by the coming

---

44. Ibid., 5.

45. Cf. Ibid., 9. I am adding some words here which I take implicit in Jenson's account. Cf. Bockmuehl, *The Remembered Peter*, 46.

46. Jenson, "Toward a Christian Theology of Judaism," 9.

of Jesus, but still binding on the Jews. This last issue will be discussed further in a later section.

In what sense, then, is the church the people of God? Jenson states, "That the church is the people of God can be an exclusive proposition *only eschatologically*."[47] He indicates: "The . . . New Testament references to the church as the people of God are overwhelmingly eschatological."[48] In the book of Revelation, when the new Jerusalem comes down from heaven, it is proclaimed: "He will dwell with him as their God; they *will* be his people and God himself will be with them."[49] In the book of Hebrews, "'the Sabbath rest' of 'the people of God' is still future."[50] Paul's reference to the church as "God's people" is also eschatological: "the people of God are those whom God has 'prepared beforehand *for glory*—to whom then he has called us, not from the Jews only but also from the gentiles.'"[51] Jenson also notes that Paul supports his claim with a citation from Hosea: "Those who were not my people I *will* call 'my people.'"[52] For the church to be the people of God is to anticipate the promised future.

Having affirmed that the Jews—the familial descendants of Abraham, Isaac, and Jacob—are the proper people of God and that the church is the people of God only in the eschatological sense, Jenson proposes that the church is the people of God *only in union with* the Jewish people. The church will be the people of God "when Israel and the church will be one."[53] To construe the church as the people of God is to cultivate an apocalyptic vision of the church, anticipating the church to enter into the household of Israel. But this future is not simply a distant reality to the church; as we will see, the future breaks into the present of the church so that the church can taste the reality of the glorious future even in the present.

The Body of Christ

Jenson proceeds his account under another ecumenical rubric, the body of Christ, by indicating that the church is the body of Christ. But she is

---

47. *ST*, 2:192. Emphasis added.
48. Ibid.
49. Rev 21:1–3 in *ST*, 2:192.
50. Heb 4:9 in ibid.
51. Rom 9:23–26 in ibid.
52. Hos 2:23.
53. Jenson, "Toward a Christian Doctrine of Israel," 17.

his body as the gathering is around his (sacramental) body and so at a distance from his body. The church is the body of Christ "only in that within her that same Christ is present as *an other than* she, as a Word she must hear and sacraments she must see and taste and touch."[54] For this reason, "[t]he church is not now simply identical with Christ."[55] In other words, the church is still an association.[56]

Why is there still otherness between the church and Jesus? Jenson says, "The suggestion may be surprising, but I commend it to you: in that he is a Jew, in that his proper people is Israel, and in that the continuing community of Israel is an other community than the church."[57] The church is not identical with Christ yet but only approaches him sacramentally. She "does not now see her Lord *in the flesh* because he is a Jew according to the flesh and the church is separated from Judaism according to the flesh."[58] This entails that the otherness between the church and Christ will be made obsolete in the End only when the union between Christians and the Jews is accomplished and so when *totus Christus* is realized and God is all in all. Until then, he is other than she. "[T]he risen Jew, Jesus the Christ, must not only be embodied as the church, but embodied in the flesh of Israel—until these two are one."[59] Thus, as Jenson argued under the rubric of "the people of God," "[t]he church and the synagogue are together and only together the present availability to the world of the risen Jesus Christ."[60]

The Temple of the Holy Spirit

The last ecumenical rubric that Jenson employs for his account of Judaism is the temple of the Holy Spirit. "The church is *to be* the temple of the Holy Spirit."[61] But which spirit is it? "The world is full of, as we now say, 'spiritualities,' each luxuriating in some spirit or other. And through-

---

54. Ibid., 20. Emphasis added.
55. Ibid., 19.
56. As discussed in a previous chapter.
57. Ibid.
58. *ST*, 2:335.
59. Jenson, "Toward a Christian Doctrine of Israel," 19.
60. Jenson, "Toward a Christian Theology of Judaism," 13. Under this ecumenical rubric, the body of Christ, Jenson affirms again the salvific (divine) value of the carnal existence of the Jews.
61. Jenson, "Toward a Christian Doctrine of Israel," 17. Emphasis added.

out her history, the church has again and again misidentified the spirit, offering at least a side-chapel or two for accommodation of some spirit of the age or of a nation or of a gender or of whatever."[62] According to Jenson, a couple of phrases from the creeds, especially the Nicene Creed, are essential for the church to identify the Spirit: "who proceeds from the Father" and "who spoke by the prophets."[63] The Spirit is the one who proceeds from the Father, the God of Israel,[64] and who came upon the prophets of Israel and made them utter the Word of God. Thus, the Spirit is identified "by Old Testament exegesis."[65]

For Jenson, to be a community of the Spirit who proceeds from the God of Israel and came upon the prophets of Israel means to be a hermeneutical community.[66] When the Spirit came upon a person or a group of people, prophetic words relentlessly uttered from their mouths. And in their prophecies, interpretation occurred: interpretation of the old events occurs in anticipation of the new salvific events in the future.[67] In the New Testament period, when the Spirit was outpoured on the gathering of the people in the Pentecost (Acts 2), the same phenomenon occurred: the group of people began to prophesy and interpret the old events in light of the new salvific events. Thus, the church came into being as the prophetic and hermeneutical community, which "knows how the Bible should be read." It means that the church is "the same community of interpretation [as the Old Testament Israel]"[68] by the power of the same Spirit given to the old Israel. For Jenson, the Spirit is the agent who secures the hermeneutical continuity between the Old Testament Israel and the church.

---

62. Ibid.

63. Ibid.

64. Hunsinger argues that in Jenson "only God the Father is the God of Israel" while the Son is not (Hunsinger, "Robert Jenson's Systematic Theology," 171). But I take Jenson's view consistent with the dominant usage of *theos* as a referent to God the Father in the New Testament. For example, see Rahner, "*Theos* in the New Testament," 79–148. And Jenson does not deny that the Son is God as we can see his account and endorsement of Barth's view of the Trinity as the threefold repetition of God (chapter 1).

65. Jenson, "Toward a Christian Doctrine of Israel," 17.

66. Ibid.

67. This will be explored in the next chapter. This is not apparent on the surface of the texts of his essays on Judaism, "Toward a Christian Doctrine of Israel" and "Toward a Christian Theology of Judaism." But the idea is lurking when it is suggested that the Spirit enables a community to be a community of interpretation (ibid.).

68. Ibid., 18.

Given that the covenants of each community are valid in its own right in God's salvation history, and that the two covenant communities have their own second volumes added to the first by their own hermeneutical activities, it follows that the Spirit's work of interpretation of the old Israel has occurred in both communities. In Christianity, the New Testament is the work of the Spirit.[69] And if the Spirit has been working on the other paralleling community as Jenson argues, this requires Christians not to ignore but to eavesdrop the Jewish rabbinic interpretation of the Tanakh. Jenson avers, "Christian exegetes have no reason either to defer to Rabbinic exegesis or to regard it as a priori wrong."[70] Further, the church may hope for the day when the interpretations of both communities are complemented and enhanced by the power of the Spirit and, beyond this age, when the church will be "taught exegesis by the 144,000 [of the Jews] in the assembly around the throne."[71]

Two Paralleling Detours to the Kingdom of God

In addition to the above ecumenical motifs, Jenson employs another ecclesiological concept, "detour," for his theology of Judaism: the church and the Jews are the paralleling *detours* to the kingdom of God, and in her detour, the church is called to conduct the mission of Israel to gather the nations around the proper people of God, the Jews, for the worship of God of Israel.

Even before his explicit outworking of a theology of Judaism which comes into view in his later essays, Jenson has already had this ecclesiological concept of the church as a detour to the kingdom. In the second volume of his *Systematic Theology*, Jenson indicates, "Jesus announced the Kingdom, but it was the church that came."[72] This is originally what Alfred Loisy said with sarcasm—as the high expectation of the kingdom has not been fulfilled by the coming of Jesus Christ, but only the church came into being. Jenson still sees a kernel of truth in Loisy's remark on the church. The kingdom is still to come, and the church is a detour to the kingdom. "[T]he church is neither a realization of the new age nor

---

69. Jenson, *On the Inspiration of Scripture*.

70. Jenson, "Toward a Christian Doctrine of Israel," 18.

71. Ibid. This hermeneutical and pneumatological aspect of Jenson's theology of Judaism will be expanded later.

72. Loisy, *L'Évangile et l'Église*, 153 in *ST*, 2:170.

an item of the old age."⁷³ In other words, "[t]he straight line route to the Kingdom is broken, and a side trip through the church ... is ordained."⁷⁴

During this time of the detour, the church is given a mission, the mission of Israel. When the disciples asked Jesus before his ascension, "Lord, is this the time when you restore the kingdom to Israel?"⁷⁵ Jesus promised the gift of the Spirit "as the power to conduct a mission to Jews and gentiles,"⁷⁶ instead of answering, "Well, it really isn't that kind of kingdom, it's more spiritual."⁷⁷

Israel's mission conducted by the church will be completed only at the End. Israel was called to be a blessing to all the nations since God made the covenant with Abraham. But this call will be fulfilled not in this age but in the age to come. The prophets interpreted the Israel's calling as the calling to gather "the nations to fellowship with her in worship of the true God"⁷⁸ and to be fulfilled as the eschatological event at the very end of history, accompanying the apocalyptic signs. Here only two biblical verses may be noted from Jenson's account: "It shall come to pass in the latter days that the mountain of the house of the Lord shall be established as the highest of the mountains ... ; and peoples shall flow to it ... , and say, 'Come, let us go up to the mountain of the Lord ... , that he may teach us his ways. . . . [N]ation shall not lift up sword against nation, neither shall they learn war any more . . . ."⁷⁹ "Darkness shall cover the ... peoples; but the Lord will arise upon you, and his glory will appear over you [Israel]."⁸⁰ As the Israel's mission will be completed at the End, when those apocalyptic signs are present, the church exists as a detour, until then, conducting the mission of Israel to gather the nations around the people, the biological descendants of Abraham.

Jenson notes that Judaism has a similar theological understanding of this age. In Jenson's term, Judaism is also on a "detour" to the kingdom of God. "Judaism emerged to enable this Israel's continued coherence in the absence of the Temple. . . . [It] consciously exists in a *pause* of history,

---

73. Ibid., 171.
74. Jenson, "Toward a Christian Doctrine of Israel," 11.
75. *ST*, 2:170.
76. Ibid.
77. Jenson, "Toward a Christian Doctrine of Israel," 11.
78. *ST*, 2:170.
79. Micah 4:1–3 quoted in *ST*, 1:70.
80. Isa 60:2, quoted in ibid.

between the destruction of the Temple—contemporaneous with the first flourishing of the gospel's mission!—and the advent of Messiah."[81] Judaism lives its life in the time between the destruction of the temple and reconstruction of the temple. Here Jenson depends on the work of Jacob Neusner. In his treatment of the Jewish concept of history, Neusner indicates that the Jewish sages "did not believe the Temple would be rebuilt and destroyed again, rebuilt and destroyed, and so on into endless time. They stated the very opposite: the Temple would be rebuilt but never against destroyed."[82] The Jewish understanding of history, not allowing a cyclical pattern of history, is rather a "paradigmatic" conception in which the old event serves as a paradigm for a new event, and the later event recapitulates the earlier: for instance, Eden and the Land, Adam and Israel, the first destruction of the temple in 586 B.C.E. and the second destruction in 70 C.E, and the first rebuilding of the temple and the second rebuilding of the imperishable and glorious temple. In the rabbinic Jewish understanding, their life is situated in the time between times. Thus, Judaism emerged in the absence of the temple and will be concluded in the reconstruction of the final temple. Until then, Judaism lives "a pause of history" or, as Jenson suggests, is on a detour along with Christianity to the kingdom.

In sum, in Jenson's theology of Judaism, the identity of the church is articulated: the church will be and so is the people of God, the body of Christ, and the temple of the Holy Spirit, only with the Jewish people, the carnal descendants of Abraham, Isaac, and Jacob, with whom God's covenant is irrevocably made and to whom God is faithful even in their unfaithfulness and so even in their no to Jesus Christ. As the Jews are called to be a blessing to the nations and as they are going to be one with the church, when the church becomes supersessionistic, she can do so only at the risk of her life. For the church is called to the missionary community, carrying out the mission of Israel, calling the nations around Israel to Zion for the worship of God of Israel.

The Deity of Jesus Christ

As seen in the last chapter, Wyschogrod, appealing to Maimonides, says that Christianity certainly plays a significant role in God's redemptive

---

81. *ST*, 2:335. Emphasis added.
82. Neusner, *Rabbinic Judaism*, 185.

The Two in the One Israelite Body

history to judaize or "purify" the gentile languages and concepts through their understanding of Jesus of Nazareth. But the rabbis never endorse the deity of Jesus or his Messiahship. For Wyschogrod, Christian faith in the deity of a man constitutes the gulf between Judaism and Christianity, even though he believes it is not unbridgeable. The works of Jesus and the church are, for Wyschogrod and Maimonides, only a preparation for the coming of the true Messiah.[83] One of the reasons for their rejection of Jesus as the Messiah is that "as the rabbis have always insisted, had the Messiah simply arrived, were Jesus' Resurrection and Ascension his advent as such, things would have to look rather different than they do."[84] The works of Jesus are still short of such signs of the kingdom as the restoration of Israel, God's judgment of the nations, and the general resurrection.[85]

To this, how could Christian theology respond without relapsing into supersessionism or diluting Christian faith in Jesus of Nazareth? Jenson upholds the deity and the messiahship of Jesus, arguing that the Christian confession of the deity of Jesus Christ (and also the doctrine of the Trinity) is "wholly Jewish"[86] and so can be explicated by exegesis of the Old Testament even before the Jewish audience,[87] even though Jenson does not attempts to "convert" them by this.[88] Jenson explains only 1) *what* Christian means when they affirm the deity of Jesus and his messiahship and 2) *why* they would do it,[89] without undermining the irrevocability of the Abrahamic covenants.

83. Maimonides, *The Code of Maimonides*, Book 14, xxiii, quoted in Wyschogrod, "Why Was and Is the Theology of Karl Barth of Interest to a Jewish Theologian?" 213.

84. Jenson, "Toward the Doctrine of Israel," 9.

85. Cf. According to Levenson's reading of Ezekiel 37, "the Jewish expectation of a resurrection of the dead is always and inextricably associated with the restoration of the people Israel" (Levenson, *Resurrection and the Restoration of Israel*, 165).

86. Jenson, "Toward a Christian Doctrine of Israel," 4. Cf. For this trinitarian explication of Israel's faith, see *ST*, 1:63–89. Also see Rottenberg, "'Comparative Theology' vs. 'Reactive Theology,'" 411–18. Rottenberg points out: "Even a cursory reading of the *Targumim* will show that almost all divine appearances in the Hebrew Bible and virtually every act of God are attributed to the *Memra* [Word] and the Holy Spirit" (Rottenberg, "'Comparative Theology' vs. 'Reactive Theology,'" 416).

87. "[I]t seems to me that if the two communions make an effort to think within each other's language, they may decide that we have not yet reached a point of mutual dissent" (Jenson, "What Kind of God", 15).

88. "I certainly do not hope with such explanations to make the Trinity doctrine convincing in this gathering, only to make it less puzzling" (ibid., 16).

89. "That point, of course, is reached when Christians identify Jesus of Nazareth

What then do Christians mean when they confess that Jesus of Nazareth is the Son of God and the Lord? Jenson starts his account, saying:

> According to the Prologue of John's Gospel, the Logos/Son "became flesh and dwelt among us." That is, the content—the Son—or plot—the Logos—of the Lord's history with Israel came, at the beginning of the End of Days, to dwell in Israel as the teaching and suffering and action of one Israelite. What the Lord and Israel are together as a joint reality, appeared as one concrete person, and so as one personal and simultaneous participant in God's life and in the life of his people. At a session of this colloquium, I was asked whether I would be willing to say that God is incarnate in the people of Israel. I answer that he is, if we read the whole history of Israel as the coming of the Son/Logos, as the church does—or did before she lost her exegetical nerve.[90]

In Jenson's exegesis, Jesus is the Word of God whose content is Israel's history. Jesus is the person who has the whole history of Israel in and as himself. He is the concentration of the whole life of Israel. This Word as the person of Jesus is the Word *of God*. The whole story of Israel that Jesus has within himself is God's Word. Conversely, the Word of God that, according to Christian theology, is one being with God himself, is the whole history of Israel. God's reality, life, and his words are so intertwined with those of Israel that one cannot be separated from the other, precisely even at the ontological level. God's story is his story *with* his people. This *divine and human* life and being are inextricably integrated and concentrated into the person of Jesus of Nazareth. "God is incarnate in the people of Israel"[91] in a diluted manner; God is incarnate in Jesus in a concentrated manner. As the concentration of Israel, Jesus is divine and human.

At this point, we see again that Jenson's theology of incarnation affirms and accommodates Wyschogrod's theology of Israel (the Jews) as the dilute incarnation of God. Yet, in his exegetical account of the Johannine prologue, another layer of Jenson's understanding of God is observable: a hermeneutical understanding of the Word and the being of God. This will be explored in the next chapter.

---

as the Son/Logos. Here we must first ask what is involved in that, and then why Christians would do it" (ibid., 15).

90. Ibid., 16.
91. Ibid.

Also, it may be noted that in Jenson the incarnation of Jesus and his deity are accounted for only at the historical (and just so ontological) level since Jenson has jettisoned any pretemporal reality from the beginning of his theological career, as seen in the first chapter. There is no such thing as the pretemporal Logos or the pretemporal Jesus in Jenson's thinking. Therefore, the incarnation is not a movement of the Logos from pretemporal eternity into the human time or into the human flesh. The Son is always in time and in flesh.[92] Moreover, Jenson does not try to prove "the deity of Jesus" by demonstrating that he has atemporal omni-divine natures. He only says at this point that Jesus is the concentration of what Israel is, supposing that what Israel is is somehow divine or that Israel will be deified by the one Israelite who has the whole Israel in himself.

Now why ever would a Christian make such an extravagant claim about the man Jesus of Nazareth? Jenson answers: the Christian claim about Jesus is justified by the event of the resurrection. Jenson states that the Christian understanding of Jesus Christ "under the rubric of incarnation and by the doctrine of Trinity"[93] has been considered the major divisive issue between Judaism and Christianity over the last couple of millennia. Yet, Jenson indicates the issue at the root of this division is the Christian claim about the resurrection: Christian "belief in Jesus' Resurrection is the true division between Judaism and Christianity."[94]

Jenson turns to Peter's paradigmatic preaching (Acts 2): his "sermon is very simple: in ignorance you gave Jesus up, but God has raised him."[95] Many Jews believed this, without "much other alteration in their theology."[96] Moreover, those who believed in the resurrection of Jesus continued to worship in the temple with the other Jews.

For Jenson, the resurrection of Jesus of Nazareth prior to the general resurrection justifies the deity of Jesus Christ: "Christ is risen into God."[97] But how does the priority of his resurrection to the general resurrection justify the deity of Jesus? Jenson looks to the Old Testament and indicates the *dramatic necessity* of the resurrection of one Israelite, also noting the dialectic relation between the one Israelite and the whole Israel commu-

---

92. Some Christian theologians would worry about Jenson's rejection of the pretemporal eternity, as seen in chapter 1.
93. Ibid., 14.
94. Ibid.
95. Ibid.
96. Ibid.
97. *ST*, 1:201.

nity. While Jenson considers a series of phenomena in which a certain figure displays the dialectic relationship with Israel—the Son, the Servant, and the Word, here we will focus on the Servant of YHWH who not only displays such a relation but also invigorates the hope of resurrection in the Old Testament period. In the Isaianic "Servant Songs," *Israel* appears as the servant of YHWH. Yet, suddenly the servant is an individual Israelite *within* Israel.[98] Who then is this servant? Jenson avers, "The Servant is Israel *and* one within Israel who, for Israel, is what Israel is."[99] There is an individual Israelite servant of YHWH who is distinguished from and identified with the communal servant of YHWH.[100]

Further, Jenson notes: "Servant Israel sings of the individual Servant that in being sent to 'a grave with the wicked,' 'he has borne *our* griefs and carried *our* sorrows,'"[101] when the Servant Israel faces her communal death in her history. Now the Servant Israel has heavily loaded her eschatological hope upon the one individual servant, who will die for the community. Yet, it is said: "After he has suffered, he will see the light of life and be satisfied; by his knowledge my righteous servant will justify many."[102] If this individual servant of YHWH is raised from the dead, his resurrection will be for Israel's eschatological hope.

This is what Christianity sees in the resurrection of Jesus of Nazareth: God's raising of the Isaianic individual servant for the hope of Israel. God raised Jesus from the dead "in anticipation of the general resurrection[;] the Lord fulfilled on this one Israelite the great and encompassing promise to *all Israel*, that she will live with death behind her and even bring gentiles into this new life."[103] Many Jews would complain that if Jesus is the Messiah or if the resurrection had happened, then things must have looked better than now. But what Christians see is rather the dramatic necessity that the one individual Israelites had to be risen *first* for Israel.

Now, for Jenson, the resurrection of Jesus justifies his deity. His resurrection prior to the general resurrection demonstrates his ontological

---

98. Ibid., 80. Discussion of this Servant has been done already in previous section in connection of the role of the Spirit in prophecy.

99. Ibid., 81. Emphasis added.

100. Ibid. For Jenson, it is nothing but the relation between the risen Lord and his community.

101. Ibid., 82.

102. Isa 53:11 referred in ibid., 83.

103. Jenson, "What Kind of God," 16. Emphasis added.

superiority over all the other creatures and so his full divinity. Jenson argue, "Jesus is risen into God."[104] His divine sonship comes from the resurrection; also he is the Word of God *by* the resurrection: "the Jesus of history must . . . be what God says *by raising him.*"[105] In short, for Jenson, the resurrection *constitutes* the divinity of Jesus of Nazareth. Thus, he is the second person of the Trinity.

At this point, we have to note Jenson's theological conviction deeply rooted in his exegetical and narratival account of the Trinity. For Jenson, it is not the antecedently possessed divine qualities that make Jesus divine and then are made manifest in the resurrection. It is the other way around: *because* he is risen (prior to the general resurrection), he is fully divine, ontologically one with the Father, and the Lord over all the creation. As discussed before, Jenson has jettisoned the very possibility of the pretemporal eternity and of any pretemporal existence from the start of his theology. Now the *futurity* is the constitutional element for the being of God in Jenson's theology. And the resurrection is the very point when Jesus entered into the (eschatological) futurity, and just so he is divine. "Jesus is risen into the future."[106] Just so, he is risen into God. Anything else is not essential in establishing the deity of Jesus, for Jenson, but his resurrection prior to the general resurrection.

In the fifth chapter of *Systematic Theology*, "Persons of God's Identity," which we have been focusing on in this section as a prime source, Jenson corrals the phenomena of the figures who display the double identity—differentiated from the Lord and identified with and as the Lord—such as the Angel of God, the Word of God, the Glory of God, in order to argue that these are the appearances of the second person of the Trinity. Seeing his trinitarian hermeneutic of such divine figures in the Old Testament congruous with the old rabbinic perceptions of the "Shekinah," Jenson suggests that some Shekinah phenomena are the theophanies of the God who participates in Israel's drama. He is the one of the *dramatis dei persona*,[107] for Jenson, the second person of the Trinity.

In fact, in Jenson's account, it is the preexistence of the Son in the Old Testament narrative. It may appear that such a preexistence of the

---

104. *ST*, 1:201.

105. Ibid., 165. Emphasis added. Cf. "[T]he doctrine of Trinity only explicates Israel's faith in a situation in which it is believed that the God of Israel has prior to the general resurrection raised one of his servants from the dead" (ibid., 63)

106. Ibid., 198.

107. Ibid., 75.

Son is the *ontological* basis for the resurrection of Jesus which happened later in the New Testament. For Jenson, however, it is actually the other way round: *his resurrection* is the ontological basis for the "Shekinah phenomena" in the Old Testament. Because he is risen, he is preexistent. This ontological weight and priority of the resurrection of Jesus, preceding the general resurrection, is the theological subterranean stream running under his exegetical and narratival account of *dramatis dei personae* in the Israel's Bible. And this is the theological foundation on which Jenson can confidently argue, displaying his premodern exegetical nerve, that the "Shekinah" phenomena were the appearances of the Son, the *risen* one.[108] The ontological priority of the resurrection and the future will be discussed in chapter 6 in more detail.

We may wonder to what extent Jenson's rejection of any possibility of pretemporal being and his robust notion of the futurity, lurking in his exegetical account, will be accepted among the Jews, or even Christians. However they or we respond to Jenson's tacit ontological thinking, we may still appreciate Jenson's indication of the convergences between the old rabbis' perception of the Shekinah and Christian theologians' perception of the second person of the Trinity in the Israel's Bible, without diluting Christian faith in Jesus Christ the Lord.

Further, Jenson demonstrates how one Israelite's resurrection prior to the general resurrection can "resolves an antinomy at the heart of Israel's hope."[109] As indicated above, the Jews did not expect the resurrection of the one Israelite prior to the national or general resurrection. They did not expect that when Messiah is enthroned, "his people are still on the way [to the kingdom] and . . . people continue to die."[110] This is, "to be sure, unexpected by previous versions of Israel's hope."[111] However, Jenson argues, the temporal gap between the resurrection of the one particular Israelite and the general resurrection not only confirms the dialectical relation between the one peculiar Israelite and his community as displayed in Israel's narrative, but also resolves the antinomy of hope of Israel. Israel is called to be a blessing to all the nations from the time of their first patriarch Abraham. And the fulfillment of that calling is interpreted by prophets "as the gathering of the nations to fellowship

---

108. Jenson, "What Kind of God," 16.
109. *ST*, 2:170.
110. *ST*, 1:85.
111. Ibid.

with [Israel] in worship of the true God."[112] Also, it is eventually seen that "Israel's destiny can be fulfilled only in a new creation beyond this age."[113] Then, if the resurrection of the Messiah had brought about the restoration and the resurrection of Israel and so the End of this age, there would have been "no historical space . . . left in which the ingathering [of the nations to Zion] can occur."[114] "Had Jesus' Resurrection been immediately the End, Israel's mission would have been aborted,"[115] as there could have been *no time left for the gentiles* to come together to worship God of Israel. The church could have not existed, as she is the gathering of the nations.[116] So the historical opening between the first and the general resurrection, namely, the detour to the kingdom, resolves the antinomy of the hope of Israel, the hope to be the blessing for the nations. And this is another dramatic necessity of the resurrection of the one Israelite prior to the general resurrection, which—at least—demonstrates the deity of Jesus of Nazareth.

The Torah

The Torah is another crucial issue in Jewish-Christian relation. Sharing the Jewish concern about the Christian supersessionistic view and probably engaging with Wyschogrod's theology in his mind, Jenson works out his Christian theology of the Torah. Here this section will explicate Jenson's account of the Torah: the Torah is eternally and irrevocably given to the carnal descendants of Abraham, Isaac, and Jacob; Jesus is the Torah in flesh; and the church and the Jews are the two Torah-communities in parallel.

Torah Given to the People of God

Jenson shares with the Jewish conviction that the Torah is given to the carnal descendants of Abraham, Isaac, and Jacob. As seen earlier, for Jenson, the Jews are the people of God in the genuine sense, while the church is the people of God only with her anticipated union with the proper

---

112. *ST*, 2:170.
113. Ibid.
114. *ST*, 1:85.
115. Ibid., 171.
116. Jenson, "Toward a Christian Doctrine of Israel," 9.

people. That entails that, to this particular people only, God has given the Torah. Upon the Abrahamic covenantal lineage, God's bestowed the Mosaic covenant. By being born into the Jewish family, they are inevitably called to be the bearer of the Torah and so to be the holy people of God. As seen in the previous chapter on Wyschogrod's theology, the Jews bear the covenantal blessing and duty in their familial lineage and so in their carnal existence. Jenson's account of the Torah comes closely aligned with Wyschogrod's view.

While it is true that, because the people of Israel are chosen in the Abrahamic covenant, they are given the Torah, it is also true that because they keep the Torah, they remain as the chosen people of God. If a Jew does not observe the Torah's commandments, he may keep his identity as a Jew by virtue of the Abrahamic covenant, but if he marries a gentile (Christian) woman and does not observe the law, his family would lose the Jewishness in a few generations. The observance of the Torah is essential to the Jewish identity. Put it more drastically, as one may speculate, it is theoretically possible—even though impossible due to God's faithfulness and power—that God might lose his special people when they do not follow the Torah. So Jenson says, "God, in the time between the times and when there is no temple, wants a community that studies and obeys Torah as Judaism does, so that he may have an unavoidably special people also in that time."[117]

There are indeed some arbitrary commandments in the Torah, which Christians have thought to be made obsolete by the coming of Jesus Christ. But such arbitrary commandments still functions to mark out God's special people. They are chosen and called to be holy and different from other non-elect peoples. Jenson says, "[S]ome individual commands seem to have no point *except* to mark out God's people as particular."[118]

But such commandments do more than marking out. "Why, after all—as David Novak put it to [Jenson]—can't Jews eat shrimp? Just to be marked off as different? Shrimp indeed lack properly fishy fins, but then fish lack proper exoskeletons. The seeming arbitrariness is much of the point."[119] Jenson draws upon Luther's understanding of the tree of the knowledge of good and evil: the tree "is so called only after the fact,

---

117. Jenson, "Toward a Christian Theology of Judaism," 11.
118. Ibid., 10.
119. Ibid.

in view of the consequences of disobeying God's command.... [And] the arbitrary *choice* of a particular tree was part of the point."[120] The arbitrariness of such commandments seems to entail a theological truth: God's sovereign freedom exercised in his act of election of his people. God could have chosen another nation—probably the Egyptians or the Romans, but he did not. But why Israel, why shrimp, or why the particular tree in the garden? There seems to be no other reason but God's sovereign choice. This seems embedded into the Jewish dietary law.

Jesus as the Torah

Jenson offers a non-supersessionistic *christological* account of the Torah: Jesus is the Torah in flesh. Jenson looks again into his favorite text, John 1, which he calls "a foundational text of Christology":[121] "In the beginning was the Word" (John 1:1). The inter-textuality of the John's prologue with Genesis 1 reveals who the Word really is. Also, Jenson indicates that there is an ethical aspect to the Word. God *commanded* the universe to be: "Let there be . . . !" And his Word was *obeyed* in the creaturely act of coming into being. When they were spoken to by the divine Word, they responded by their existence. "[B]y this uncreated Word . . . the 'created word' is evoked, the created word of obedience and worship that every creature is."[122]

In Jenson's account, the creative Word—the moral command in the creation—is the very Word that created Israel. Jenson notes a parallelism in Romans 1 between the knowledge of God inexcusably manifest from creation and the knowledge of God given to Jews as Torah. According to Paul, Jenson observes, both the gentiles and the Jews "violate [the same entity] though differently."[123] Another parallelism or even identification of the divine Word in creation and the Torah is also noted in Psalm 147: "He sends out his command to the earth, and his word runs very swiftly. . . . He makes his wind blow, and the waters flow. . . . He declares his word to Jacob, his statutes and his judgments to Israel."[124] Jenson comments: "Israel understood the reality of the world on the pattern of her

---

120. Ibid. Emphasis added.
121. Ibid., 11.
122. *ST*, 2:8.
123. Ibid., 153.
124. Ps 147:16–20, in ibid., 8.

own reality: just as she depends on the Lord's moral utterance, so does the world."[125] Jenson continues, "Both the creation and Israel live 'by every word that comes from the mouth of the Lord.'"[126] As the world was created by God's Word, the moral command, so was Israel. When Abraham obeyed to the commanding word of the Lord, "Leave . . . ," Israel came into being. Israel was created by the word of God spoken to Abraham.[127] Jenson states, "Thus his creating of the world is agency of the same sort as the *torah* by which he creates Israel."[128]

Another strand interwoven into the Johannine prologue is that the creative Word in the beginning is Jesus. In the Christian faith, the Word of God has a particular content: the story of Jesus. "God speaks a moral command to create the world. The moral command that he speaks is the Son. And the Son is in fact Jesus of Nazareth. Therefore, the story of Jesus, as the story of this one man's moral will, is the content of the command 'Let there be . . . ,' by which the creation comes into being and perdures. The story told in the Gospels states the meaning of creation."[129] So Jenson holds, "it is the Word called the Torah."[130] In his exegetical account of the Johannine prologue, he puts it, "*Torah* 'became flesh and dwelt among us.'"[131]

Yet, to make it clearer how the God's creating command is the Torah that was given to Israel through Moses at Sinai, it would be helpful to look to a Jewish source, even though Jenson does not draw upon it. It is remarkable to note in *Genesis Rabbah* in midrash: "The Torah declares: 'I was the working tool of the Holy One, blessed be He'";[132] and "God consulted the Torah and created the world."[133] According to this midrash, God created the world by the Torah, and the Torah is depicted as a personified form or even a person, that God consulted with. It is also noteworthy what Jacob Neusner, another revered rabbi of our days, says, as he carefully engaged in conversations with Jesus in his *A Rabbi Talks with Jesus*. Neusner says that he is alarmed at the teaching of Jesus as a Jewish

125. Ibid.
126. Ibid.; Deut 8:3.
127. Ibid., 13.
128. Ibid., 8.
129. Ibid., 27.
130. Jenson, "Toward a Christian Theology of Judaism," 12.
131. Ibid., 3.
132. *Bereshit Rabbah* 1:1.
133. Ibid.

rabbi: "He who loves father or mother more than me is not worthy of me; and he who loves son or daughter more than me is not worthy of me."[134] For, in Judaism, a family is of great significance, as we can now understand from Wyschogrod's account of the Jewish carnal existence as the covenantal abode of the divine presence. In Wyschogrod, disintegration of the Jewish families would amount to jeopardize the divine abode on the earth. Further, given that God commanded to honor your father and mother in the Ten Commandments, following this first-century rabbi, Jesus of Nazareth, seems to require a Jew to violate the one of the Ten Commandments.[135]

Nevertheless, Jesus' command still makes sense to Neusner. The rabbi says, "The Torah left as a mere book dies, mere words on a page or parchment. The Torah comes to life, in particular, in attitude and action, in the way in which masters of the Torah embody it. So the demand to study the Torah at some point is going to conflict with the requirement to honor father and mother."[136] If a student wants to follow his master who "embodies" the Torah in his action and his life, he would be required to love him more than his father and mother for his study of the Torah. Prescient students will expect that his master would call them away from their home and family and to "leave their wives and children for a long period of time, so as to study the Torah."[137] Neusner tells "one of the great love stories of Judaism builds on precisely that motif: the willingness of the wife to send her husband to study the Torah, even to the neglect of herself."[138] Given that what the Torah may require the Jews, Neusner comes to understand that Jesus' command to love him more than your father and mother is not a peculiar demand: it was "no more than what the masters of the Torah asked for the Torah."[139] Neusner adds: "If *the Torah were personified—as Wisdom is personified in Scripture*—it could have said no less. All Jesus asked was that disciples place their love of him over their love of family."[140] In the rabbi's understanding, Jesus asked exactly

---

134. Matt 10:37; Neusner, *A Rabbi Talks with Jesus*, 57.
135. Ibid., 58.
136. Ibid., 59.
137. Ibid., 60.
138. Ibid.
139. Ibid.
140. Ibid., 61. Emphasis added.

what the Torah embodied could and must ask. As the Pope Benedict XVI also said, "In the Christian faith, Jesus is the Torah in person."[141]

Neusner continues, noting that for Israel, honoring and loving your parents is analogous to honoring and loving God. Neusner refers to a halakhic midrash, *Mekhilta Attributed to Rabbi Ishmael Bahodesh* 8, where a list of biblical texts are present with parallelism between honoring parents and honoring God.[142] Then, if a master of the Torah requires disciples to love him more than their parents, when it is obvious that love for parents is analogous to love for God, the disciples of the master are likely to be asked by other fellow Jews: "And is your master God? For, I now realize, only God can demand of me what Jesus is asking."[143] It is indeed striking to the rabbis to note that the first-century master requested the highest honor that is only due to God.[144]

The Torah to be Observed and Believed

Now we turn to Jenson's ecclesial proposal in connection with the Torah: the church and the synagogue are the Torah communities, for the Torah is not only to be believed, but also to be observed. Given that Jesus is construed as the Torah and that the Torah is not made obsolete, as seen

---

141. "In the Christian faith, Jesus is the Torah in person" (Pope Benedict XVI, *Jesus of Nazareth*, 90).

142. "It is written: 'Honor your father and your mother,' and as a counterpart: 'Honor the Lord with your substance' (Prov 3:9). Scripture thus has declared equal the honor owing to them and the honor owing to him. 'You shall fear every man his mother and his father' (Lev 19:3), and, as a counterpart: 'You shall fear the Lord your God' (Deut 6:13). Scripture thus has declared equal the fear owing to them and the fear owing to him. 'And he who curses his father or his mother shall surely be put to death' (Exod 21:17), and correspondingly: 'Whoever curses his God' (Lev 24:15). Scripture thus has declared equal the cursing them and cursing him . . . ." (Mekhilta Attributed to Rabbi Ishmael Bahodesh 8, quoted in Neusner, *A Rabbi Talks with Jesus*, 67).

143. Neusner, *A Rabbi Talks with Jesus*, 68.

144. For another account on how Jesus is the very personification of the Torah, see Johnson, *The Writings of the New Testament*, 189–90. Jesus takes up the place of the Torah when he says "If you want to be perfect, . . . sell all you possess . . . and come, follow me," (Matt 19:21) as an answer to the rich man who wanted eternal life, and when he says, "Heaven and earth will pass away, but my words will not pass away" (Matt 24:35). Above all, Matt 11:28–30 suggests unmistakably that Jesus is the personification of the Torah: "as Torah revealed God's will, so Jesus reveals the Father. . . . His 'yoke' corresponds exactly to the symbol of Torah as 'yoke of the kingdom of God.'" . . . [A]s the Pharisees looked to Torah to learn God's ways, so those whom Jesus calls are to 'learn from me'" (Johnson, *The Writings of the New Testament*, 190).

earlier, the Torah is not only to be believed, but also to be practiced. The synagogue obeys and practices the Torah; the church believes the Torah-in-flesh.[145] Jenson argues, "[T]his Judaism must continue lest God's torah be forgotten"[146] and fail to be obeyed fully. God has willed the Judaism in separation from the gentile gathering, the church, for his Torah to be observed and performed. On the other hand, the nations have their own way to relate to the Torah, even though Paul dissuaded the gentiles from their observance of the Torah. The nations relate to the Torah by faith, believing that the Torah is an embodied person, made himself available to the nations and invited them into the household of Israel. This leads Jenson to suggest that, in the last judgment, the Lord will find "*both* those who 'have believed' in his coming in the flesh and those who hang on every syllable of that Word that he is."[147] Jesus the Torah will need both communities, the Torah-believing community and the Torah-practicing community, to complete *his Torah-body* on earth. In the last day, then, the Lord will "dismiss . . . the generic ungodliness of the church's dominating gentiles and continuing Judaism's disbelief."[148] And finally he "will terminate the separation between the church and Israel according to the flesh,"[149] when the church will be the people of God in union with Israel, the otherness of Christ to the church will be brought to an end, and the two communities will be presented as the one body of Christ, the one Torah-body in glory.

Conclusion

In his congenial engagement with Wyschogrod's theology, Jenson recognizes afresh the irrevocability and its unsurpassability of the Israelite covenants that the church cannot supersede, taking these themes into his own christological/trinitarian reflection by way of his Lutheran christological and soteriological commitments. For Jenson, the "*finitum capax infiniti*" accommodates the doctrine of *theosis*, and his theology proper

---

145. If the Torah is to be obeyed fully and completely, then this might entail a political meaning for the contemporary world. If that means that full obedience to the Torah requires the land and the temple in the specific area *in this age*, then it would involve with sensitive political issues.

146. *ST*, 2:336.

147. Jenson, "Toward a Christian Theology of Judaism," 12.

148. *ST*, 2:335.

149. Ibid.

is construed in close relation to the covenanted bodily existence. And Jenson comes to develop his conception of the church in relation to the Jewish covenantal existence: the church is the people of God, the body of Christ, and the temple of the Spirit only in her anticipated union with the biological descendants of Abraham, Isaac, and Jacob. In this construal, the church can attempt to replace or supersede them only by ignoring the original branch that she is engrafted into and so by putting herself at risk.

Jenson also attends to a couple of long-standing issues between the two covenant communities. In Jenson's account, the deity of Jesus Christ is not impugned. Perceiving in Israel's narrative the dramatic necessity of the resurrection of the one Israelite prior to the general resurrection, Jenson argues that the resurrection of Jesus Christ entails his divinity and his messiahship. He argues this, having the ontological significances of the resurrection (chapter 1) and the ontological priority of the future at work in his account. With regard to the Jewish observance of the Torah, Jenson argues that the Torah must be kept by God's chosen people forever and that Jesus himself is the Torah after all, which the Jews and the church are called to obey in different ways—whether by observance or by faith. Each community is called to embody the Torah on earth in their own way—one community keeps the Torah; the other takes the bread and wine at the eucharistic table. Having said all these, Jenson's theology of Judaism must be construed on the trajectory of his body ontology (chapter 2) that God is embodied in Jesus of Nazareth, and that his risen body is available within and as the church in this present age. In this regard, it has been envisaged in Jenson that as the church and the Jewish community now in parallel will end their detours and be one in the eschatological future, and thus the one body of Jesus-Torah will be available on earth in the End.

5

God's Being in the Word-Torah
Hermeneutical Ontology

IN JENSON'S THEOLOGY, WORD and reality are inextricably related. Reality is always the bespoken reality. Even the reality of God and his word are intrinsically related and so inseparable. For Jenson, the event of Word is the event of God's being. But the being of God does not occur in a generic event of words but in the event of the particular Word, that is, in the hermeneutical tradition of God's chosen people. God has chosen Israel so that they may speak the special words in which God's being occurs. Israel speaks the particular Word in their history as recorded in the Old Testament. This Word is spoken in and by Israel across her history, as her hermeneutical tradition keeps recapitulating her past in anticipation of the future in her present hermeneutical activity. This unity of the past and the future in their present hermeneutical activity is achieved as "a narrative unity." In the middle of history, the ontological basis of that narrative unity—the Word—became flesh in the community of Israel and was named Jesus. He recapitulated the narrative and hermeneutical thread of Israel and played them out in his life, death, and resurrection. Now the church recognizes the narrative thread of Israel's life which is woven climactically into the events of Jesus, and the church continues to narrate it.

Jenson's hermeneutical theo-ontology comes to recognize, moving in a post-supersessionistic direction, that the presence of Jesus cannot be embodied by the gentile gathering (the church) alone, and claims that Jesus is the Torah (in both narrative and codified ways) which is to be embodied by both covenant communities—the Jews and the Christians in their own distinctive ways, as seen in chapter 4. This leads Jenson to recognize the other hermeneutical counterpart in the Jewish community. For Jenson, one community's hermeneutical practice cannot supersede the other's; rather they must be in parallel to each other. In effect, the antinomian and supersessionistic sentiments are to be purged out of Christian hermeneutics of the Bible.

In order properly to grasp the relation between Jenson's hermeneutical ontology and his later theology of continuing Judaism, we need to begin far back, by examining the early development of what we may call his "hermeneutical theology," that is, by observing Jenson's synthesis of some key themes in the works of Rudolf Bultmann (and his pupils) and Gehard von Rad. For Bultmannian ontological understanding of the Word in close relation to the being of God is visible in Jenson's theology of the Word, and as we will see, this theo-ontology of the Word accommodates von Rad's notion of Israel's tradition. This line of thinking develops in a post-supersessionistic direction later, as Jenson recognizes the theological perils of Christian antinomian and supersessionistic hermeneutics of the Bible. In other words, Jenson's doctrine of the Word advances in a particularistic, hermeneutical, and post-supersessionistic way. Now to see this, the present chapter will proceed in three sections: 1) Jenson's appropriation of the Bultmann school's hermeneutical ontology, 2) Jenson's appropriation of von Rad's theology of Israel's tradition history, and 3) his rejection of antinomianism in Christian hermeneutics.

Jenson's Appropriation of the Bultmann School's Hermeneutical Ontology

Traveling on the trajectory of the so-called Bultmann school, Jenson comes to affirm a crucial ontological insight on the being of God: *God happens in human speech.* The human speech is the very locus of the event of God's being. Precisely, God *is* the speech-Word.

This section will see how Jenson employs Bultmannian insights into historicity, existence, and language. And while I have some developmental scheme in view, I will not be interested in offering a strict chronologically ordered exposition but are drawing freely from earlier and later works.

Bultmann's Notion of the Event of God in Word

Rudolf Bultmann is rightly characterized as an existentialist. Regarding existentialism, Bultmann says, "we should learn from existentialist philosophy, because in this philosophical school human existence is directly the object of attention. . . . Existentialist philosophy does not say to me 'in such and such a way you must exist'; it says only 'you must exist.'"[1] While other beings are "extant" (*vorhanden*), humans *exist* "because they are historical beings."[2] As a historical being, in each moment of "now," a human being makes a decision on whether he is going to be an authentic self or not, that is, whether he will be free from his past self and embrace his new genuine self.

In Bultmann's existentialist theology, a crucial ontological insight on the *inextricable* relation between God's being and human speech is nascent, as Jenson notes. Bultmann says, "God meets us in . . . the *preaching* instituted in Jesus Christ."[3] "The idea of the omnipresent and almighty God becomes real . . . only by His Word spoken here and now."[4] That is, God happens in his Word. Jenson approvingly rephrases Bultmann's idea: "indeed God himself *happens* to me. *The gospel proclamation* challenges me to stop understanding my life from the past; it does this as it is a word of forgiveness, that addresses me *as* one free from my past."[5] Again, the human (proclamatory) speech is the locus of God's being and of his coming to us. This ontological implication must be drawn out for a constructive theological proposal: for Jenson, God's being is (in) an *event* of speech. God's *coming* to us in his Word and his *being* are identical.

The Bultmann School's Linguistic Turn: Being in the Future Language

Continuing in the Bultmannian line of thinking, Jenson notes the thoughts of Bultmann's students, Ernst Fuchs and Gerhard Ebeling: the relation between reality (created or uncreated) and language is *intrinsically mutual*, and language and reality proceed together into the future.

---

1. Bultmann, *Jesus Christ and Mythology*, 55.
2. Ibid., 56.
3. Ibid., 78.
4. Ibid., 79.
5. *ST*, 1:167.

In so doing, language and reality seek the new and final language which will illuminate the reality in light of the ultimate truth. For the Bultmann school, the final and new language is the language of Jesus in which God happens or comes to "appear." This line of argument is adopted and developed in Jenson as he conceives that the Word of God—the person—is the final and eschatological interpretive Word, which will shed light on the whole reality and the whole of history and in which God happens.

(Our Understanding of) the Reality in Language

The Bultmann school emphasizes the intrinsic relation of reality and language: reality is presented to us in language. Human understanding does not depart from language but only makes "a deeper penetration into the linguistic realm."[6] Language does not hinder a clear understanding of the reality. Rather, "the removing of hindrances to understanding can usually likewise take place only by word."[7] Language is not a disposable device for human understanding, but true understanding is achieved only through language. Accordingly, the reality is presented to us as *interpreted reality*.[8] Language, which is given by the community to one individual, is the precondition of his or her understanding of reality, by which one relates to other persons and to objects. Precisely in this communal-linguistic structure, understanding is possible. As Hans-Georg Gadamer puts it (and as Jenson approvingly quotes it), "the world is there for us as the world only in that we meet reality as *bespoken reality*."[9]

The Flow of Language to the Future Language

Language develops or flows from the past to the future. From the past, language is given and inherited. "Languages are . . . structures of tradition grown up through centuries, in which the whole many-leveled reality of historical life has stored itself. . . . All speech depends on this previous givenness of language . . . ."[10] Language is given to us from our com-

---

6. Ebeling, "Word of God and Hermeneutics," 94.

7. Ibid.

8. "[T]he world is not merely presented to us but present as interpreted in signs and symbols" (*ChrD*, 1:175).

9. Gadamer, *Wahrheit und Methode*, 415–17 quoted in *KTHF*, 178.

10. Ebeling, *The Nature of Faith*, 124; *KTHF*, 180.

munity, spoken and handed down to us from the past. As we acquire a language, we inherit this communal structure of understanding of reality from our antecedent community. This received structure of the community's understanding and interpretation shapes and preconditions our construal of and our relation to the reality.

As a member of a community continues to use language given from the past and encounter new situations in their present, she becomes aware of the limits of the current structure of understanding for a new understanding of reality and for a new relation to reality. New understanding requires a new language. Then, "new possibilities of bespeaking and understanding" struggle to emerge.[11] In their emergence, a new horizon opens up for the community's understanding of reality. Thus, language becomes and will "become the source of light which can *again and again* lighten up the darkness of existence"[12] as language phylogenetically (in the history of one's people) develops through history.

Ebeling calls this emergence of a new possibility of interpreting of reality a "word-event": in the historical change of language, when a community encounters a new and extraordinary event, a new word emerges, or an old word comes to have a new meaning. Such "an extraordinary word-event creates language, i.e., it creates new possibilities of bespeaking and understanding the reality."[13] In history, as "something 'comes to word' that was not before amenable to language, [and so] 'new possibilities of bespeaking and understanding' emerge,"[14] the word-event opens the future, by opening up a new possibility of interpretation and understanding of the reality *and* a new possibility for the language community's *new relation* to reality and for mutual personal relations in the community.

It is also true of one individual's situation and of her understanding of herself. As one's personal self is also understood in and through language, for true self-understanding, she would also need a new language by which not only her community will understand the reality and itself and but also she will understand herself. To seek myself is then "to seek new agreement, to participate in the birth of the *new language*. Thus only new language can be the language of self-understanding, where it is the

---

11. Ebeling, *Das Wesen des christlichen Glaubens*, 252 quoted in *ST*, 1:166.
12. Ebeling, *The Nature of Faith*, 188.
13. Ebeling, *Das Wesen des Glaubens*, 252 quoted in *KTHF*, 180.
14. *ST*, 1:166.

clarity of my existence that determines when and if I speak."¹⁵ For one's self-understanding, one has to wait for a linguistic breakthrough—one cannot stay in the old matrix. "The language in which I can understand myself is, therefore, always new language, the language which is my 'unique possibility.'"¹⁶

But would it be possible that the phylogenetical development of language reaches its final destination or the resting place, without being caught up in an endless cyclical eternity or in endless linear linguistic tradition? Can one speak of *the* new language, the *telos* of our all languages which will shed the ultimate light on the reality and our existence? If there is such a new and final language, that would be our resting place "in which we are free from our past history for our future history,"¹⁷ and in which we could understand the whole reality and ourselves.

The New Language Already in which We Love and Understand

According to Fuchs and Ebeling, *the* ultimate new language has been given and spoken in the middle of history. The human predicament is that humans cannot speak the new language on their own even though they are in profound need of it. Humans can only receive the new language from the outside, waiting for it to come to be spoken at some point of history. But the good news is that *the* new and final language has been given already in history, the language in which the whole reality is understood finally and in which we are called to be and can be the new self.

On Fuchs's account, the new and final language is the language that Jesus has brought into history, the language of love. That language calls us to liberation from ourselves, from our self-dependence (*Selbstbegründung*).¹⁸ In Fuchs's exposition of John's Gospel, love comes to us in our concrete historical situation as liberating address, freeing us from the past self for the future self of love. In Jesus' address to us, love becomes possible as our existence and so as our true existence.¹⁹ This

---

15. *KTHF*, 197. Emphasis added. Jenson here quotes Fuchs, *Hermeneutik*, 143.
16. *GAG*, 185.
17. *KTHF*, 198; Fuchs, "Was wird in der Exegese . . . ?" 47–48.
18. Fuchs, *Hermeneutik*, 246.
19. "Die Liebe will also als Wort zu uns kommen, als die Anrede in einer uns treffenden, historisch festgelegten Situation (Joh. 1,14)" (ibid.).

language of love is the eschatological and final language, as Jenson puts it, "in which the '*inner tendency* of language itself' is fulfilled."[20]

Another eschatological word that fulfills the inner tendency of language itself and illumines all the other reality is "God," according to Fuchs. Jesus brought "God" to speech. In Jesus' proclamation, especially in his parables, his hearers are challenged and called to a new selfhood—called to consider themselves, for example, as the prodigal son who returned to his father's house, not as his brother, and as the laborer who "actually came too late to the generous lord of the vineyard."[21] In such callings and challenges, one is called to "receive himself from *God* as a new creature, who is able to love even his enemy (Luke 6:27b f.; Matt. 5:44f.)."[22] God happens as God calls and enables the hearers to be authentic futural self. "Thus Jesus intends to 'bring God to speech.'"[23] When God comes to us through language in that way, Ebeling says, "the reality of man is shown in its true light."[24] When the divine word-event "lighten[s] up the darkness of existence,"[25] the existence of the futural self becomes possible. One is enabled to act upon the vision and the reality of the futural self.

When the light of God shines through words, the whole world also comes under the new light of his Word.[26] "When God speaks, the whole of reality as it concerns us enters language anew. . . . If God's countenance shines upon us, the world has for us another look. The Word, as the reality which concerns us, in whatever language it has hitherto been expressed, is the call and question of God to us, even though we do not understand."[27] When God occurs in word or when God is brought into speech, the reality is interpreted in a new light and word and called to be anew. After all, the whole reality becomes new when it is called anew by his creative and powerful Word.

---

20. *GAG*, 187. Emphasis added; Fuchs, *Hermeneutik*, 139, 265–66.
21. Fuchs, "Proclamation and Speech-Event," 348.
22. Ibid.
23. Ibid.
24. Ebeling, *Theology and Proclamation*, 29.
25. Ebeling, *The Nature of Faith*, 188.
26. Ibid., 190.
27. Ibid.

Heidegger's "Word-Event" of Being: Language Enowns Us in Our Speech.

At this point, it would be helpful to turn briefly to the philosophical source of this hermeneutical ontology, in order to understand better the concept of the word-event (*Sprachereignis*). Even though Heidegger is hardly visible in Jenson's account of hermeneutical ontology, as is well known, the *later* Heidegger's influence upon the students of Bultmann is unmistakable in their conception of the word-event. As Braaten and Jenson put it:

> [I]n the hermeneutical writings of Ebeling and Fuchs, the catchword is not "existential understanding" [as in the writings of Bultmann] but "linguistic event." Fuchs used the term "Sprachereignis" (language event); Ebeling preferred the term "Wortgeschehen" (word event). The difference between Bultmann, on the one hand, and Ebeling and Fuchs, on the other hand, parallels the shift in Martin Heidegger's thinking from earlier to his later period.[28]

So it is appropriate here to briefly look at the ontological thought lurking in Jenson's appropriation of the Bultmann school's concept of word-event.

Heidegger's later historical-ontological (*seynsgeschichtlich*) approach is less anthropocentric than his existentialism in *Being and Time*.[29] It is not an existing human being (Dasein) that approaches and grasps Being. However, it is "Being [that] claims human being for grounding its truth in beings, [and] man is drawn into the history of Being."[30] Dasein is conceived rather as an acquiescent agent, "'called' to the task of the 'safekeeping' of being."[31] Humans are thrown into "an event that is always already under way, an event in which [they] can only let [themselves] be carried along. This event is one that 'throws' to [humans] a task and a calling: it calls on [them] . . . to let [themselves] be the *site* or clearing in which beings can show up . . . and, in doing so, to *be* what [they] are meant to be . . . ."[32] Humans do not appropriate being for themselves, but being appropriates humans.[33]

---

28. Braaten and Jenson, *A Map of Twentieth-Century Theology*, 117.
29. Mulhall, *The Routledge Guidebook to Heidegger's Being and Time*, 29.
30. Heidegger, *The End of Philosophy*, 82.
31. Guinon, *The Cambridge Companion to Heidegger*, 15.
32. Guinon, "The History of Being," 403.
33. Denker, *Historical Dictionary of Heidegger's Philosophy*, 67.

God's Being in the Word-Torah

For the later Heidegger, "[t]he essential being of language is Saying as Showing [Das Wesende der Sprache ist die Sage als die Zeige]:"[34] "Language speaks."[35] Here humans are primordially hearers rather than speakers. Humans listen to speaking of language "not *while* but *before* we are speaking."[36] Then, when humans speak in turn, the saying and showing of Being (a saying as showing) comes into view. Thus, "we let it say its Saying to us."[37] For this Saying to *show*, "[i]t allows us to attain the ability to speak."[38]

How does the Saying come into Showing? There is "the moving force in Showing of Saying,"[39] which Heidegger calls *Ereignis*—here the key word of this hermeneutical ontology emerges. This term is commonly translated as "appropriation," "enowing" or "event." But in *The Way to Language* Heidegger carefully qualifies his own use of the term: "Appropriation [*Ereignis*] . . . cannot be represented either as an occurrence or a happening."[40] "Appropriation [*Ereignis*], needing and using man's appropriations, allows Saying to reach speech. . . . The way [to language] is *appropriating*."[41] Appropriation (*Ereignis*) is the way for Saying to be spoken in human speaking. In line of this reading, the "*Ereignis*" in Fuchs and Ebeling's writing is to be understood as "appropriation" if they are borrowing Heidegger's concept.

How does Being happen? Heidegger answers, "Be-ing essentially happens as Ereignis [*Das Seyn west als das Ereignis*]."[42] "Being *enowns* [*ereignet*] Dasein and only in this way holds sway as *enowing* [*Ereignis*]."[43] So "man as Da-sein is *en-owned* [or appropriated] by Be-ing as enowning and thus belongs to enowning itself."[44] For the advent of Being, humans need to surrender and "become the en-owned and to belong to be-ing."[45] In its enowning, Being shelters itself "in art, thinking, poetizing, deed—

---

34. Heidegger, *On the Way to Language*, 123.
35. Ibid., 124.
36. Ibid., 123.
37. Ibid., 124.
38. Ibid.
39. Ibid., 127.
40. Ibid.
41. Ibid., 129. Emphasis added.
42. Heidegger, *Contributions to Philosophy*, 183 (GA 65: 260).
43. Ibid., 180 (GA 65: 265).
44. Ibid. (GA 65: 265). Emphasis added.
45. Ibid., 177 (GA 65: 251).

and therefore requires the inabiding of Da-sein."⁴⁶ Thus, Being enowns or appropriates (*ereignet*) human speaking agents, as it hides and emerges in and through human language—often poetry language.

In this hermeneutical ontology, a revisionary step has been taken. Being is primarily construed in linguistic and auditory terms, rather than conceived as a visual image. Regarding this ontological paradigm shift, Jenson says, citing Franz Mayr: "'Being' has been interpreted in western thought . . . on the model of the particular being as this 'appears' to a 'seeing.' But there is another starting point . . . by which being is understood from *hearing* what is *said* about it by someone, whether by gods or men."⁴⁷ Jenson welcomes this shift. On these lines, in Christian hermeneutical ontology, God is understood to happen in and even as *Sprach-ereignis*.⁴⁸ Jenson states, "being is coming to word, is the coming-on of things to us by what God or others speak to us."⁴⁹ Put differently, "[God] occurs *between* us."⁵⁰ In Jenson's theology, we may put it, God "enowns" us for his coming to speech and hearing.

Jenson's Divergence from the Bultmann School

Jenson does not, of course, slavishly adopt the various positions developed by those thinkers of the Bultmann school. Rather, he exercises considerable exegetical and speculative freedom in appropriating some central elements of their works. While Jenson appreciates the school's emphasis on the intrinsic mutuality of being and language (and understanding), he diverges from them when they fail to press their linguistic thought consistently into their ontological reflection.

In his ontological reflection, Fuchs argues that being is "the possibility of letting oneself he called into question."⁵¹ Jenson agrees with Fuchs:

---

46. Ibid., 180–81 (GA 65: 265).

47. *KTHF*, 206. Emphasis added.

48. "For appropriating Saying brings to light all present beings in terms of their properties—it lauds, that is, allows them into their own, their nature" (Heidegger, *On the Way to Language*, 135); "Language has been called 'the house of Being.' It is the keeper of being present, in that its coming to light remains entrusted to the appropriating show of Saying" (ibid.).

49. *ST*, 1:210.

50. *GAG*, 190.

51. Fuchs, *Hermeneutik*, 56 quoted in *GAG*, 183.

"Being . . . occurs only in 'call' and 'address,' in the event of speech,"[52] as God happens and challenges us to be the new self in his proclamation, that is, in his call and address. Jenson demurs, however, when Fuchs gives more weight to something other than word: "if being is the possibility of being called into question," Fuchs states, "time is being. Time is the 'ground' of our questioned and questioning existence."[53] However, Jenson runs counter to it: "Instead of saying that time is the possibility of the true word, we must say that the word is the possibility of true time."[54] On Jenson's account, *utterance creates time*. In utterance, we are called to temporally transcend our past selves and become new selves. Because we are addressed, that is, because we live in communication, we move beyond and for the future. Thus we live in time as the future opens to us by word and in communication. To put it differently, "the promise creates the future, not the future the promise."[55] Jenson concludes, "Therefore the word is prior to time, if indeed time is historical time."[56]

In this line of argument, we may affirm a theological axiom that because the Word is spoken in the beginning, time "came into being." Time is creation; the Word is creative and divine in Christian theology. Here the Word is not a mute idea, but can be and has been uttered and spoken to us and among us. As we speak of Jesus Christ, the Word is spoken among us. For the Word is Jesus Christ. Just so, word is prior to time and the ground of time.

For Jenson, word is ontologically weightier than time. To put it in theological terms again, God's being *is* Word, as the title of the concluding chapter of one of Jenson's books suggests: "God as Word."[57] Jenson avers, "God *is* his word."[58] "[God] not only has a word for us . . . but *is*

---

52. Fuchs, *Hermeneutik*, 130–33, quoted in ibid., 184.

53. Ibid.

54. Ibid., 188.

55. Ibid., 189.

56. Ibid.

57. Ibid., 180. Cf. "God as Discourse" in *ChrD*, 1:175; "God as conversation" in *ST*, 1:223.

58. *VW*, 31. Jenson's treating the Word as the essence of God seems to come from his Lutheran conviction, which can be found in Luther's Christmas sermon: "Since there is but one God, it must be true that God himself is the Word, which was in the beginning before all creation. Some change the order of the words and read, And the Word was God, in order to explain that this Word not only is with God and is a different person, but that it is also in its essence the one true God with the Father. But we shall leave the words in the order in which they now stand: And *God was the Word*;

his word for us: The Word is 'of one being with the Father.'"⁵⁹ Here the Word is not a timeless idea as the Greeks once conceived, but Utterance or *Speech*. The divine being is verbal.

Jenson diverges from the Bultmann school also when he argues that the Word that is one being with God has a *particular content*. The *material* aspect of the God's Word has been considerably overlooked, Jenson diagnoses, in Fuchs's hermeneutical account. Fuchs rightly pointed out that language calls human beings forward and so to the future. However, if human beings are just called forward in time, without a promise of any material content of the future, then the formal structure of the event of communication would only directs us to the future in which "we confront nothingness."⁶⁰ In Fuch's eschatology, the eschaton is merely envisaged but not narrated, so that his eschatology "remains bound within the abstract opposition of 'eschatological' and 'historical'"⁶¹—the limitation Jenson finds already in Bultmann.⁶²

On the contrary, for Jenson, the truly liberating language is not just the language that happened in Jesus' preaching but the language that has Jesus as its particular content and so is Jesus himself. "The essential language is the language of Jesus, not just in its formality, but *materially* as the language which *narrates* the last future."⁶³ The reality and the human beings are called and liberated for the future by the promissory and narrative language. The final promised future has the particular man Jesus and his story in its center. Put differently, Jesus is the *last Word* in the final

---

and this is also what it means; there is no other God than the one only God, and this same God must also essentially be the Word, of which the evangelist speaks; so *there is nothing in the divine nature which is not in the Word*. It is clearly stated that this Word is truly God, so that it is not only true that the Word is God, but also that *God is the Word*" (Luther, *Sermons of Martin Luther*, 182). Emphasis added.

59. *ChrD*, 1:175. Cf. "[T]he being of God is always conceived of as *verbum*, and the fundamental relation of man to him as *audire*" (Heidegger, *Supplements*, 110).

60. *GAG*, 189.

61. *ST*, 1:170. This is also the symptom of their master that, according to Jenson, his students finally cannot remedy.

62. To see more of Jenson's criticism of Bultmann, see ibid., 169–70. Cf. "The principal error of Rudolf Bultmann's students was to deny this—the case of Bultmann himself is complicated by his denial that any story at all needs to be told. Neither Ebeling nor Fuchs denied that Jesus is risen. What they taught was that 'Jesus is risen' is our necessary true *response* to the Gospel narrative, not part of the narrative itself. In this, they intended to carry on the tradition of Wilhelm Herrmann" (Jenson, "Identity, Jesus, and Exegesis," 82).

63. *GAG*, 189. Emphasis added.

future as well as the first in the beginning of the creation. Jesus is the last word in which the "*inner tendency* of language itself"[64] is fulfilled and which will illuminates all the beings and all the events.[65] Jenson writes, "Jesus the Christ, in his full historical reality of birth, life, death, and resurrection, is the Word of God in that he is the identity of the future opened by the Word of God. He is the Word of God in that he is the narrative content of the proclamation that, because it poses eschatological possibility, is the Word of God. He is the Word of God because he is the narrative content of the word-event that is the Word of God."[66]

Jenson's Appropriation of Gerhard von Rad's Idea of the Tradition History of Israel: God's Being in Israel's Tradition History and the Church's Hermeneutic

Now to understand the *material* aspect of Jenson's hermeneutical ontology, we need to examine Jenson's engagement with the works of Gerhard von Rad. In so doing, we will see how Jenson portrays the way in which the divine Word "happens" with a particular content across the history of Israel; that is, how Jenson narrates the history of Israel as the history of the being of God. To bring up the material content of his hermeneutical ontology, Jenson draws particular inspiration from von Rad's description of Israel's tradition history, posing a question in his earlier essay: what would the doctrine of God look like if von Rad's idea of tradition history is true?[67] In the following, we will explore Jenson's answer to this question. But now let us begin with a brief account of von Rad's own narration of Israel's history.

64. Ibid., 187. Emphasis added.

65. Here thus earlier hermeneutical idea that the future has the particular content, Jesus, is congruous with Jenson's later thought that Jesus is risen into the future.

66. *ST*, 1:171.

67. "Ist die Aufnahme des Alten Testaments in das neutestamentliche Wort, in der zeitlichen Struktur des Tuns betrachtet, nur ein neues Glied dieser Reihe, wie von Rad z. B. manchmal zu meinen scheint? Wir wollen sehen, wie unsere Hoffnung und ünser Bekenntnis zu Gott aussehen würden, wäre dies der Fall" (Jenson, "Die Kontinuität von Altem und Neuem Testament als Problem für Theologie Heute," 92). Cf. Jenson recalls his earlier days in Heidelberg: "All [faculty members of Heidelberg] but Schlink influenced me importantly; but I was especially shaped by Brunner [Jenson's *Doktorvater*]'s theological care and precision, and . . . by von Rad's construal of the Bible's unity as an historical unity . . ." (Jenson, "A Theological Autobiography, to Date," 49).

Von Rad's Tradition History: from the Confession to the Canon

In von Rad's account, the tradition history of Israel is construed as the complex tradition process through which the Old Testament came into the present form, as other literary and historical materials were added to and around the nucleus "creed," especially when their authors and redactors encountered momentous events, whether salvific or catastrophic.[68] According to von Rad, the confession "Jahweh, 'who brought Israel out of Egypt,' is probably the earliest and the same time the most widely used."[69] Among this kind of confessional formulae, Deuteronomy 26:5–9 is considered as the chief *Credo*:

> And you shall make response before the LORD your God, "A wandering Aramean was my father. And he went down into Egypt and sojourned there, few in number, and there he became a nation, great, mighty, and populous. And the Egyptians treated us harshly and humiliated us and laid on us hard labor. Then we cried to the LORD, the God of our fathers, and the LORD heard our voice and saw our affliction, our toil, and our oppression. And the LORD brought us out of Egypt with a mighty hand and an outstretched arm, with great deeds of terror, with signs and wonders. And he brought us into this place and gave us this land, a land flowing with milk and honey."[70]

From this nucleus *Credo*, the account of their salvation history expanded, as it takes in and adopts the narratives which explicated the elements of the primal creed, from the history of the patriarchs and to the conquest of the promised land. After this narrative expansion of the ancient creed, there was "the prefixing to it of an account of the creation and the primeval history, and the insertion of the Sinai pericope, which as a block of *tradition* has a completely different derivation."[71] These were

---

68. Cf. For example, regarding the case of the Hexateuch—which includes the book of Joshua, von Rad says, "the Hexateuch itself may, and indeed must, be understood as representative of a type of literature of which we may expect to be able to recognize the early stages, the circumstances of composition, and the subsequent development until it reached the greatly extended form in which it now lies before us" (von Rad, "The Form-Critical Problem of Hexateuch," 2).

69. Von Rad, *Old Testament Theology* vol. 1, 121.

70. Deut 26:5–9 (ESV).

71. Von Rad, *Old Testament Theology* vol. 1, 124.

done mostly by Jahwist and the Elohist, and thus the Hexateuch[72] took its current shape.

But even before the content and the form of the Hexateuch settled down, "when the theological elaboration of the old Credo was still at its beginnings,"[73] the God of Israel started a new phase of salvation in the history of Israel. YHWH raised up military leaders to protect Israel, later established a monarchy in Israel, entrusted it to the Davidic house, and also allowed the temple to be constructed in Israel. However, when Israel or its kings became disobedient, the kingdom was divided and the judgments were enacted upon Israel, finally by the rods of Assyria and Babylonia. These events were captured in the writing of Deuteronomist, and so the canonical traditional Israel's history carried on, as the Deuteronomist picked up the thread of Israel's tradition history.[74]

Once again, before the tradition settled into Israel's historical consciousness, soon after the fall of Babylon, another phase of the salvation history unfolded: the temple in Jerusalem was rebuilt and a large number of the exiles returned to their land. Witnessing God's new salvific act, one (group) of the writers had to carry once again "the thread of history with God which had been so abruptly snapped."[75] In the hands of the Chronicler, the pre-exilic history continued, legitimating "the cultic restoration in the post-exilic period on the basis of a legacy of David's which had not been brought into effect until this time."[76] In addition, the post-exilic prophets "Jeremiah, Ezekiel, Zechariah, and, more than anyone else, Deutero-Isaiah"[77] exhorted to forget the former things and proclaimed that God was going to do totally new things: new exodus, new covenant, new temple, and so on. Thus, the tradition history of Israel on the whole took literary shape through successive editions and was canonized in the form now familiar to us.

Here it must be noted that, as the Bible takes form through the process of tradition history, the Bible comes into shape as a *unified* whole. But it is not their theology, according to von Rad, that unifies the

---

72. This term is von Rad's proposal, referring to the first six books of the Old Testament, from Genesis to Joshua, viewing them as one literary unit. Jenson does not use this term.

73. Von Rad, *Old Testament Theology* vol. 1, 125.

74. Ibid., 126.

75. Ibid., 127.

76. Ibid.

77. Ibid.

different biblical literary forms and genres; the Bible has different theologies within it. As von Rad's student Hartmut Gese succinctly puts it, the unity of the Bible "exists already because of tradition history."[78] It is the process of the tradition history that maintains the unity of the Bible, as the hermeneutical process occurs, recapitulating the old events in the present language in anticipation of the future of salvation. The unity of the Bible is constituted through the successive hermeneutical process.

Now we turn to Jenson's account which follows the basic tenet of von Rad's description of Israel's tradition history, with a focus on its hermeneutical aspect. Jenson notes that Israel's acceptance of the ancient "confession" is already a hermeneutical activity. The creed from the old tradition narrated the works of God that were enacted among their patriarchs, and it was received in the hope for God's salvation, at that time, in the hope for preservation of the saving status quo, especially, the land. In their reception of the old tradition, Israel was aware that even the saving status quo was given and realized through God's promise and so through the patriarchs' hope for the future that God promised. So "[t]hey put Israel in the position that the tradition described for the patriarchs; but now it was no longer a matter of the reconstructed situation of half-legendary ancestors, now the actual historical people, with all its fears and responsibilities, by what was promised rather than by what already was, by hearing rather than by sight."[79] As Abraham believed the divine promise in hope for its realization in the future, Israel was to believe and live by the every word from the mouth of God. Thus, the old traditions were received and recapitulated in their present hermeneutical activity with their new hope for the future.[80]

However, Israel's saving status quo was taken away later: the land, the kings, the temple, and the people. The catastrophe was the result of Israel's sin, as prophets indicated. It was also God's will: in Jenson's theological reading, after all, God's will is not to preserve what was established in the past but to move beyond the present. Israel's salvation and their destiny do not lie in the past or in their restoration of the old glory but in the future. For this reason, even in Israel's collapse, the old events and the old promises were recounted again and again in prophetic words of new

---

78. Gese, "Tradition and Biblical Theology," 322.

79. *SP*, 25.

80. Cf. "The historical memory of a people or of an individual is built up and reshaped as time goes by" (Jenson, *A Theology in Outline*, 13).

hope.⁸¹ Israel's prophets interpreted the old salvific events in the hope for the new salvation, and it was portrayed to transcend the glory of the old saving status quo.⁸² Thus, the tradition history carried on, through their reading and re-reading of the past in the hope for the future. Recalling the old exodus, the old kings, and their old international relations, Israel envisages that "there will be a new Exodus (this time from Babylon), a new king, who will really do what the kings were supposed to do ('the Messiah'), and all nations will at last turn to Israel and find their peace and righteousness in the liberating will of Jahve (the 'nation of priests' will achieve its purpose)."⁸³ As von Rad puts it, "the ceaseless process of the handing on of tradition that is so typical of ancient Israel, . . . it takes seriously this openness to the future which again and again directs the reader's eyes to divine fulfillment."⁸⁴

At this point we are in a position to note the way in which the two theological strands of Bultmann and von Rad are interwoven in Jenson's thought. Jenson's reception of von Rad's tradition history of Israel operates on the Bultmann school's hermeneutical-ontological claim that God happens in and as Word-event. The being of God primally occurs in a particular Word-event, that is, the Word-event of Israel's tradition history. God happens through Israel's hermeneutical activity, that is, as Israel recaptures the old tradition in their present, hoping for the new and final salvation in the future. As the *unity* of the Israel's history is constituted through this hermeneutical activity across their time, so the being of God coheres across time. "Indem es die alte Verheißung immer wieder in der neuen Verheißung wiederfand, glaubte Israel an die Treue Gottes. *In seinem neuen Wort blieb Gott bei seinem alten [Wort]* . . . ."⁸⁵ And "dieser Gott *ist* das Geschehen dieser Differenz [von Vergangenheit und Zukunft]"⁸⁶

The unity of Israel's history across her time is something that can be called "drama", "coherence," or "rhyming" of time. So it follows that

---

81. "Die alte Verheißung wurde also immer wieder in ihrer Fraglichkeit erkannt und ihr Inhalt in eine neue, sie überbietende Verheißung hineingenommen" (Jenson, "Kontinuität," 92).

82. "[D]ie Propheten ihre Hoffnung in der früheren Tradition Israels gelesen haben" (ibid.).

83. *SP*, 25.

84. Von Rad, *Old Testament Theology*, 2:428.

85. Jenson, "Die Kontinuität," 92. Emphasis added.

86. Ibid., 101.

God happens in the dramatic coherence of Israel's history or the rhyming of her time. "Gott so glauben hieße für uns, die wir uns des Auslegungsprozesses selber bewußt geworden sind, die Struktur des Dramas, die Struktur vom anfänglichen Wort und neuen Wort in der Einheit ihrer sich immer neu öffnenden Zukunft; *als das Sein Gottes* glauben."[87] Jenson states it succinctly, "the one God is an event; [the biblical] history occurs not only in him but *as* his being."[88]

Jenson puts this theological idea in more generic terms, having his theological and particular hermeneutical ontology at work in his account of God and eternity. So Jenson defines eternity in hermeneutical terms: "*eternity* is the real possibility—if indeed there is one—of the rhyme of the old language and the new word"[89] given that any hermeneutical activity is "an act of confidence that old and new can rhyme."[90] For Jenson, this concept of eternity may be transposed into the doctrine of God: "[God] is the person present to every moment, *as* the rhyme and bracket of future and past in which that moment can be real."[91] This is also a hermeneutical construal of God. For after all God is one being with his word.

Put differently, as God makes promises and fulfills them over and across time, and as Israel's tradition history captures and recaptures it through prophetic words by the power of the Spirit,[92] God's words cohere across time. Just so there are rhyming and coherence of the old and the new words across time and thereby the past and the future. Because of this *hermeneutical* coherence, there is coherence *of time and history* since word is ontologically prior to time, not the way around.[93] And the words uttered from prophets' mouths are the word of God, which are not different from but one being with God. Thus, as the words of Israel unfold, God's being occurs through her time.

---

87. Ibid., 95. Emphasis added.
88. *ST*, 1:221. Emphasis added.
89. *SP*, 105. Emphasis added.
90. Ibid.
91. Ibid., 163. Emphasis added.
92. It is not that God takes his own the words uttered by the human agency on their own. But it is God himself that puts his words into the prophets' mouths. And by the power of the Spirit, they utter the prophetic and interpretive words, which cohere with the old words.
93. In Christian theology, because God *spoke* in the beginning, so time "came into being." Contra Fuchs, time is not the possibility of speech, but speech is the possibility of time.

In my reading of Jenson, at this juncture, we should find Jenson's chief attack on the Hellenic conception of God in which God is ineffable and atemporal. His commitment to "Word theology" or hermeneutical ontology that God is one being with his Word brings forth a relentless attack on the traditional concept of atemporality *and* ineffability of God. For God occurs and so he is when the Word is spoken among us, when there is the rhyme of the old and the new, and when the coherence of words is narrated among us. God comes into speech and hearing.

A major criticism often leveled against Jenson's theology is that Jenson conflates the being of God into the creaturely history. I believe that there are some elements of truth in such criticisms.[94] However, prior to riding roughshod over Jenson's temporal conception of God, we should attend to Jenson's emphasis on the conceptual nexus between the Word (with particular content) and the being of God, which runs below the surface of his temporal account of God.[95] For Jenson, as mentioned above, word is the ground of time; not the other way around. Jenson's reflection on the relation between God and time is a consequent apprehension of the relation between God and his Word—Jesus, which comes into speech and hearing among his people.

In my judgment, even if von Rad's account of Israel's tradition history turns out to be problematic, one may be able to follow the basic tenet of Jenson's hermeneutical ontology, as long as one could accept the following: 1) The Word captures the reality of God. 2) The reality of God and the Word are intrinsically and mutually related since God is one being with the Word (the second person of the Trinity). 3) And the Word has become and so *is* Jesus eternally. Thereby, the eternal Word has a particular content—the life of Jesus. 4) The life of Old Testament Israel overall points to the person of Jesus Christ, and this entails that the Word was enacted and performed at some fundamental level of Israel's life in the Old Testament period. 5) Thus, (the being of) God occurred in Israel's life when the Word was spoken through its prophetic activities.

---

94. I believe that the Trinity is eternal apart from creation. I find it difficult to embrace Jenson's proposal that the Sonship comes from the resurrection and so the Trinity is constituted in the resurrection. See chapter 1.

95. E.g., See McCall, *Which Trinity? Whose Monotheism?* Chapter 4; Murphy, *God Is Not a Story*, 16–22.

God as the Word-Event in Church's Canonical Hermeneutic

Christian theology does not stop with the Old Testament but must move into the New Testament. As von Rad writes, "the ceaseless process of the handing on of tradition . . . [leads to] this openness to the future which again and again directs the readers' eyes to divine fulfillment" and so "lead us beyond the Old Testament."[96]

Jenson suggests that the tradition history of Israel has not ceased with the Old Testament by maintaining that Jesus interprets the old events of Israel for the new saving event. To understand this, let us start from where the line of the Old Testament narrative broke off. Jenson places a particular emphasis on Ezekiel's prophetic vision of Israel.

Israel's saving status quo is completely undone. Israel was exiled. It was their national death. Israel was found as dry bones in a valley, as depicted in Ezekiel's vision. However, would this be the end of Israel? Is Israel's salvation now to be construed as "life after death," a disembodied life in "heaven"? To put this in theological terms: with this death of Israel's hermeneutical life, would the occurrence of God's being be deceased in history? Would God lose the locus for his Word to be spoken and heard, through which his being comes into speech and hearing? Or alternatively his Word be spoken and heard again? "Can these bones live again?"

In the New Testament, the thread of Israel's tradition history once snapped off is carried on by Jesus of Nazareth. Continuing the *traditio*, Jesus interprets the history of Israel in his words and acts, that is, in his person. Jesus interprets and makes the life of Israel as his own, also making the death of Israel depicted in Ezekiel's vision as his own on the cross.[97] Jesus has identified Israel with himself, binding the life and destiny of Israel with his own. And now on his interpretation, the divine verdict is to be made: would God approve Jesus' interpretation and identification of Israel in his life and death? If Jesus is raised from the dead, that would mean God's Yes to Jesus' hermeneutical activities and his identification with Israel. Then, Jesus will be Israel. His resurrection will be regarded as (the guarantee of) the resurrection of the whole of Israel.

Now "can these bones live again?" Christianity answers: he is risen. "Christians are those who believe Jesus' Resurrection was the Lord's answer

---

96. Von Rad, *Old Testament Theology*, 2:428.

97. "Jesus spielte das Sterben Israels aus, um gerade so die Zukunft zu erreichen" (Jenson, "Die Kontinuität," 94).

to his own question [in Ezekiel 37]."[98] God has taken this one Israelite as the whole Israel and has raised Israel in this person. By the resurrection, "*Israel concentrates to this one.*"[99] So Jesus is in Israel and Israel is in Jesus by God's authorization of Jesus' hermeneutics of Israel's life.

Thus, the old history of Israel is once again recaptured in Jesus' hermeneutical act for the new salving event. The being of God carries onward with this continuation of the hermeneutical life of Israel. So God occurs as the word-event, the word-event of Israel's tradition history, by which everything and every previous event in history will be illuminated, interpreted, and understood in the Bultmannian sense. The whole history of creation will cohere when it is related to this Word(-event), that is captured in and in fact *is* the person of Jesus.

In theological terms, God has taken the tradition history of Israel—or simply, the narrative of the Old Testament—into his very own being by the resurrection of Jesus. Jesus is the one Israelite, as said above, who has the whole Israel's life in his person by the divine authorization, that is, by the resurrection. At this point, we have to recall the concept of the resurrection in Jenson's theology: as seen in earlier chapters, the resurrection is the act of God that takes this Jesus into his very being by the Spirit. As Jesus is risen, he is risen into the very inner being of God: "Christ is risen into God."[100] Now, if Jesus is the one who has the whole Israel in himself and he is taken up into the very being of God and if God constitutes his being by this act of resurrection, it follows that God has taken the whole Israel and so the whole hermeneutical life of Israel into his inner being, and thereby God constitutes himself and understands himself. The hermeneutical life of Israel is deeply internalized into God's being in the resurrection of Jesus. By this, the covenant with Israel is ontologically weighty.[101] Then, as Ochs puts it in his exposition of Jenson, "God's identity is as inseparable from the story of Israel as it is from the story of Jesus."[102]

---

98. *ST*, 1:12.

99. Jenson, "The Bible and the Trinity," 335. Emphasis added. Cf. Regarding the suffering Servant in Israel, Jenson says, "Is the Servant Israel or an Israelite? Again the only answer that can be fitted to the texts without Procrustes' methods, is that he is both at once. He is a prophet within and to Israel who just so is Israel as prophet to the nations. Or vice versa: he is Israel, as Israel appears also within Israel for Israel" (Jenson, "The Bible and the Trinity," 334).

100. *ST*, 1:201.

101. One may call it a "covenantal ontology."

102. Ochs, *Another Reformation*, 88. Cf. As seen in the first chapter, in Jenson's theology, God's eternal election of the Son, or even eternal generation, happens on the

Jenson's Rejection of Antinomianism in Christian Hermeneutics

Having looked at the being of God happening as the Word spoken in the old Israel and the church and so in the coherence of the Old Testament and the New Testaments, we move on to see how Jenson's hermeneutical ontology works in his later post-supersessionistic development. As we have seen in the previous chapter, Jenson comes to conceive Jesus as the Torah in his later post-supersessionistic account. Here, having his Torah-Christology in view, we will consider how in Jenson the being of God occurs as the (hermeneutical) coherence of the time of Judaism and Christianity. For Jenson, construing the being of God in and as the hermeneutical unity over the time of Israel requires purging Christian biblical hermeneutics of antinomian and anti-Semitic sentiments.

Jon Levenson, a leading Jewish scholar of Israel's Bible, has astutely indicated supersessionistic and antinomian elements lurking in Christian hermeneutics of the Old Testament. In his historiographical analysis of Christian historical criticism,[103] Levenson has drawn attention to the statement of Julius Wellhausen (1844–1918), a pioneer of historical criticism: "When it is recognized that the canon is what distinguishes Judaism from ancient Israel, it is recognized at the same time that what distinguishes Judaism from ancient Israel is the written Torah."[104] Driving a wedge between Judaism and the canonical ancient Israel's history, Wellhausen describes the Torah as the Jewish book—"a ghost that makes a noise indeed, but is not visible and really effects nothing."[105] In Levenson's judgment, von Rad's theology is not far from this error, marked as it is by an antinomian Pauline-Lutheran hermeneutics. To take one example: according to von Rad, in the course of Israel's history as early as the post-exilic period, "[the Law] ceased to be understood as the saving

---

horizon of time, not in the pretemporal eternity. *Thus* God is triune: "The resurrection is God's ousia" (*TI*, 168); "to attend theologically to the Resurrection of Jesus is to attend to the triune God" (ibid., 13). And as seen in the second chapter, in the resurrection, Jesus is taken as the body of God, as he is as the Son. In the resurrection, Jesus is the objective self not only available to us but also to God himself, to his consciousness. "Jesus is the object and his resurrection is the grant" (ibid., 146); "Christ's Sonship comes from his Resurrection" (*ST*, 1:143).

103. For this, see Levenson, *The Hebrew Bible, the Old Testament, and Historical Criticism*, 1–61.

104. Wellhausen, *Prolegomena to the History of Ancient Israel*, 410.

105. Ibid., 3–4.

ordinance of a special racial group (the cultic community of Israel) linked to it by the facts of history, and when it stepped out of its function of service and became a dictate which imperiously called into being its own community."[106] One may legitimately question here whether Christian hermeneutics can maintain the unity of the canon without undermining the Law in the Old Testament. If Christian hermeneutics are to find the unity in the Bible, Levenson says, it may be done with a supersessionistic view of the Law, but the Bible as a whole will fall into shards.

Jenson voices a similar concern in his brief historiographical sketch: Christian hermeneutics has often undermined the value of the Old Testament in its supersessionistic and antinomian tendency. Antinomianism, supersessionism, and even anti-Semitism are clustered issues, for antinomianism often leads to supersessionism and a contemptuous view of the Law-observants, the Jews; and anti-Semitism to supersessionism and antinomianism. These also hamper Christian hermeneutics of the Old Testament. For instance, as Jenson indicates, Schleiermacher contended that it would be better if "the Old Testament followed the New as an appendix,"[107] considering Judaism not different from heathenism.[108] In a similar vein, Harnack remarked that to conserve the Old Testament since the nineteenth century as a canonical document is "the result of religious and ecclesial paralysis."[109] Harnack regarded Marcion's dichotomy of the law and the gospel alignable with Pauline theology, being sympathetic toward Marcion.[110] Also Bultmann argued that "[f]or the Christian faith, the Old Testament is no longer revelation as it had been, and still is, for the Jews. . . . [T]he history of

---

106. Von Rad, *Old Testament Theology* vol. 1, 201.

107. Schleiermacher, *The Christian Faith*, 611.

108. "Christianity does indeed stand in a special historical connexion with Judaism; but as far as concerns its historical existence and its aim, its relations to Judaism and Heathenism are the same" (Schleiermacher, *The Christian Faith*, 60).

109. "[D]as A[lten] T[estament] im 2. Jahrhundert zu verwerfen, war ein Fehler, den die große Kirche mit Recht abgelehnt hat; es im 16. Jahrhundert beizubehalten, war ein Schicksal, dem sich die Reformation noch nicht zu entziehen vermochte; es aber seit dem 19. Jahrhundert als kanonische Urkunde im Protestantismus noch zu konservieren, ist die Folge einer religiösen und kirchlichen Lähmung" (Harnack, *Marcion*, 217).

110. "[E]r war in dem paulinischen Gegensatz von Gesetz und Evangelium, übelwollender, kleinlicher und grausamer Strafgerechtigkeit einerseits und barmherziger Liebe andrerseits gegeben." (Ibid., 30).

Israel is not the history of revelation for us. . . . To Christian faith the Old Testament is not in the true sense God's Word."[111]

For Jenson, supersessionism and antinomianism are not only hermeneutical issues but also theological issues resulting in serious distortion of the doctrine of God. When Christian theology prosecutes antinomian tasks, its doctrine of God becomes foreign to the gospel. On Jenson's account, such a prosecution was made in the very early church's history, in the form of Marcionism, even though that was rightly and promptly refuted in the church.[112] But the Marcionism revisited the church from time to time. "When the church has fallen to it, even partially or ambiguously," says Jenson, "the result has been mere replacement of her God by some numen of the momentarily surrounding religious culture."[113] In the case of Marcion, the whole Old Testament was sheared off in his own theology; his god was not God of Israel anymore or the creator of the entire universe, but a god available from their neighboring cultural numen.

In the twentieth century, the spirit of Marcionism was conjured up by von Harnack, who claimed that Christianity is a new religion in sheer contrast to the Old Testament religion. For Harnack, the old religion was characterized "with the backwardness that is unable to free itself from the Old Testament."[114] Unfortunately, "such views were common in German academic theology of the time," says Jenson, "in which the pastors and teachers were educated who in their generation would indeed overcome this 'backwardness.'"[115] In this tendency, many of the early twentieth-century German theologians put a great deal of their energy to de-judaize the God of Christianity, and predictably they attempted to discover their god from their neighboring ideologies. Jenson finds the Marcionism entered into the bloodstream of Nazi's ideology. Their god which overcomes the backwardness demanded the *Blut* of the descendents of the Old Testament people in the concentration camps. So they "find God in *Blut und Boden*. . . . [And] the victims then offered to this particular idol were the Jews."[116]

---

111. Bultmann, "Die Bedeutung des Alten Testaments für den christlichen Glauben," 333.
112. *ST*, 1:42.
113. *ST*, 1:42-43.
114. Harnack, *Marcion*, 33 in ibid., 43.
115. Ibid., 43 n4.
116. Ibid.

In Jenson's view, Marcionism has not been entirely expunged from Christian theologoumena today: churches often depict the God of the Old Testament in contrast to the God of the New Testament. Jenson remarks, "[In their depiction,] the God of the gospel is pacific, nonjudgmental, and in general a really nice person. In much of the liberal church, in many Evangelical groups, and indeed among many 'progressive' Catholics, theology has thus been replaced by sentimentality: God is not so much fatherly as grandfatherly, endlessly 'accepting' and 'inclusive.'"[117] As soon as such a theology freely floats away from the Old Testament, any ready-made cultural ideologies may provide the framework for their theologoumena. "[T]he function of the Old Testament's depiction of God is taken over by an alternative depiction ready and waiting in the tradition."[118] Alternative frameworks can be Platonic, Aristotelian, or Aryan, etc.

Jenson's response is not only historiographical but also theological, as we have already seen in chapter 4: Jesus is the Torah.[119] To recapitulate: the Torah is composed of narratives *and* codified laws. Given that God's covenant with Abraham and Moses and with their descendants has not been revoked, the law is not made obsolete but should be kept and obeyed as the Word of God. The codified aspect of the Word is still authoritative to his covenant people, the Jews. The legal aspect of the Old Testament flows into the Jewish hermeneutical stream; the narrative aspect into the church's. The church reads the Torah in a narrative way while the synagogue reads it in a codified way. So construed, the two different hermeneutics are not contradictory to or superseding each other, but they can and should be in companion, yet without interfusion. Jenson says the church can and should "strive to overhear that other reading of the same documents, conducted over there by other folk [the Jewish people], some of whom even dress and act in particular ways as they do it."[120] Each covenant community makes a hermeneutical contrapuntal in their own way, even though they sometimes or often seem on wrong notes, hitting off-beats: the two will be in the perfect harmony in the End.

Lastly, we can see that the hermeneutical ontology and body-ontology are intertwined in Jenson's theology. The two communities make a

---

117. *CC*, 31.
118. Ibid.
119. This is discussed in chapter 5.
120. Jenson, "Toward a Christian Theology of Judaism," 11.

contrapuntal in their hermeneutics after all *because* the church and the Jewish people are one body of Christ. The two are the Torah communities which involve not only hermeneutical tasks in each community but also the availability of the enfleshed Torah to the world. For the church is the body of Christ; the Jews are the incarnation of the Torah in a "diluted" manner in their continuing fleshly existence.[121] Jenson states, "Israel according to the flesh, as Paul put it, and the church are *one* body of the *totus Christus*."[122] Thus, Jesus the enfleshed Torah—the narrative and the law—would not be available completely to the world if one of the communities attempts to supersede the other's hermeneutical task. Put it differently, as God "enowns" his people—the church and the Jews together—for his coming to speaking and hearing and to practice as the Torah, his people in some ways must and does embody the Torah by their faith and practice. After all, the voice of the Word-Torah may be heard through the two hermeneutical covenant communities.

Conclusion

We may summarize by starting with protology: in the beginning was the Word-Torah. The Word-Torah was with God. And the Word-Torah was God. And so God is one being with the Word-Torah. God and his Word-Torah are intrinsically mutual and even mutually indwelling. Just so God has defined himself by having the Word-Torah at the center of his being.

When the Word-Torah was uttered, space-time bursted into being, with all the particles and galaxies in the gravity field and in harmony. And human beings came into being, linguistically and ethically able and ready for the revelation of the Torah—the narrative and the law. By language, humans understand the reality and others. To put precisely, it is language that illumines the meanings of the reality and others beings, as it comes through human speech. The Word has gathered people into a linguistic community and will finally interpret and illumine the reality and its history as well as the meaning of human existences. It will shine forth its eschatological light upon all the creation, and by its power the whole creation will become new.

---

121. Wyschogrod speaks of "the more diluted form of incarnation that was true in God's relationship with the whole people of Israel" (Wyschogrod, "Incarnation," 215).

122. Jenson, "Hermeneutics and the Life of the Church," 102.

The Word, which has a particular content, ventured into *Israel*. When the Word came to Israel, the community spoke forth the Word, and a series of comings of the Word across her history occurred and secured a narrative coherence of Israel's life. The Word is the very ontological basis for the integrity and coherence of Israel's history and life. Further, by the Word which came to humans through Israel, the meaning of the whole world and universe will be illuminated. Now, inheriting the narrative tradition of Israel's life, the church continues to carry the narrative thread of the Word.

The Word-Torah is also a set of moral commands, by which all beings came into being. That was given to Israel only, and she is called to observe it and just so embody it. This divine Torah will not leave Israel but adhere to the very (fleshly) existence of Israel as they are fatefully and irrevocably chosen. Now the biological descendants still bear the fate to embody the law by their observance.

Lastly, two points will be noted: first, Jenson's hermeneutical ontology is an operation of the Lutheran christological notion that God is Word: God who is one with the Word and who comes to us in Word is not a mute being but can be spoken among us. Being *is* the *speech* through which being comes to us. Second, Jenson works out his hermeneutical ontology in close connection with his body ontology (chapter 2). After all, the Word is the bodily figure, Jesus of Nazareth. He is the visible Word of God. To transpose it into the non-supersessionistic ecclesiological register, the Word-Torah communities—the Jews and the church—are not only to speak the Word but also to *embody* the Word-Torah in the world. And the two communities will be the one body of Christ in the End. In short, Jenson's theology of Judaism has a layer of hermeneutical ontology, which is a revisionary outworking of the christological notion that God is the Word, and which is inextricably related to his body ontology.

6

God's Spirit

Eschato-pneumatological Ontology

In this last chapter, we will explore Jenson's eschato-pneumatological ontology that moves in the post-supersessionistic direction. Having the previous discussions in mind, we will see how the divine becoming is made possible *by the power of the Spirit*, that is, how the third hypostasis enables the being of God to open for the future. For Jenson, by the Holy Spirit, Jesus as the second person of the Trinity embraces others into himself, and so the divine being is (in) becoming. Moreover, for Jenson, God is not only open for the future but also possesses the future in himself and therefore engages with his creation *recursively from* the future, by the Spirit. Especially, the risen Jesus is enabled to be retroactively present to the Old Testament people from the eschaton by the Spirit. In short, the Spirit is the eschatological power and hypostasis of God that frees his being *to* the future and enables him to engage with his creation *from* the future.

Following the trajectory of his eschato-pneumatological thinking, we will see the post-supersessionistic development: how the Spirit works in the people of Israel and their post-canonical descendants (the Jews) as well as in the church. On the whole, the point of the chapter is that Jenson presses the eschatological and futural role of the Spirit into his onto-theological thinking, developing the post-supersessionistic aspect.

To see this, this chapter will unfold in three steps: 1) Jenson critically engages with prominent theologians of eschatology; 2) in Jenson's theology, the Spirit is the eschatological power of God, which frees God's being for the Future; and 3) the Spirit is the recursive power from the future by which God, especially the Son, retroactively engages with his creation.

The Sources upon which Jenson Draws

First, we begin by looking at the theological sources that Jenson draws upon and critically engages with for his eschato-pneumatology: Karl Barth, Rudolf Bultmann, and Wolfhart Pannenberg.

Karl Barth

Barth's notion of eternity is one of the primary inspirations for Jenson's eschatological thinking. Jenson genuinely agrees with Barth: "Barth is right that the *resurrection* is the temporal event of God, that the post-crucifixion appearances of Jesus to his disciples are the center of God's self-revelation, their time the time taken from our time to be God's eternity."[1] The time of the resurrection is to be deeply seated at the core of God's eternity. The resurrection is construed as the decisive element in God's eternity.

In line with this understanding of the resurrection and God's eternity, Jenson offers his account of the risen Jesus. For Jenson, the resurrection of Jesus is the event of eschatological future that occurred in the middle of history, ahead of time. Jenson notes and emphasizes that the post-resurrection appearance of Jesus is *elusive*. While the risen Jesus is a physical being, his bodily presence is not restricted by the temporal-spatial conditions of this age. "The risen Jesus is elusive because he is not present but future: his appearances are appearances of what is not yet."[2] In my reading, Jenson's emphasis on the eschatological character of the post-resurrection appearances is aligned with Barth's account of the resurrection of Jesus. For Barth, the resurrection-time is the futural and eschatological one as it is closely related to the time of *parousia*.[3] Similarly, in Jenson's construction, the eschatological and futural character of Jesus's resurrection is acknowledged, and it is integrated into the doctrines of God's eternity and the divine transcendence.

1. *GAG*, 157.
2. Ibid., 158.
3. *CD* III/2, 499–502.

However, Jenson diverges from Barth. For Barth's conception of God's eternity still holds onto the notion of *analogy*, despite the telling nexus between the resurrection and the eternity: God's eternity is merely *analogous* to the human time of the risen Jesus. In Jenson's diagnosis, Barth's commitment to the analogous notion of eternity hampers his thinking from moving beyond "the shadow of religious direction to the past."[4] If God's eternity is only analogous to the time of Jesus, the gap between the eternal being of God and the temporal life of Jesus must be haunting to the Lutheran. For, in Jenson, the eternal and timeless Son cannot be the Jesus of Nazareth. The ontological gap between the eternal Son and Jesus of Nazareth cannot be closed in the framework of analogy after all. For Jenson, this dualism, which entails the notion of God's eternal being as immune to time or history-proof, must be jettisoned along with Arianism, which conceives Jesus as a semi-deity because he is temporal.[5]

Rudolf Bultmann

Bultmann is another important informant of Jenson's eschatological conception of God's being and his eternity. Jenson is drawn to Bultmann's idea that God comes to us as "constant futurity": "The transcendence of God in the Bible is not conceived as the transcendent otherness of Spirit over against the material and sensory sphere, or as timelessness over against becoming and passing away, but as the absolute authority, the unavailability and constant futurity of God."[6] This entails the non-objectifiability of God's being: "God's being [is] removed in principle from the domain of objectifying thinking. . . . God always remains beyond what has once been grasped, which means that the decision of faith is genuine only as actualized ever anew . . . this constant futurity of God is God's transcendence."[7] And yet, more importantly, this suggests that God relates to us from the future as futurity. In Bultmann, God encounters

---

4. *GAG*, 173.

5. *ST*, 1:100.

6. "Die Transzendenz Gottes ist in der Bibel nicht gedacht als die Jenseitigkeit des Geistes gegenüber der Sphäre des Materiellen, Sinnlichen, als die Zeitlosigkeit gegenüber dem Werden und Vergehen, sondern als die schlechthinnige Autorität, die Unverfügbarkeit und ständige Zukünftigkeit Gottes" (Bultmann, *Geschichte und Eschatologie*, 107).

7. Bultmann, "Science and Existence," 144.

humans in preaching, addresses us and demands us to venture into the future and to be the new and genuine self. God offers freedom from our past and for the divine future. God who calls us to the future is the one who has the future in himself. "[A]s the one who demands my decision ever anew, God ever stands before me as one who is *coming*, and this constant futurity of God is God's transcendence."[8]

However, Jenson registers an objection that Bultmann's notion of futurity does not allow its actualization in time, as the eschaton always stands *beyond* the human history. Consequently, according to Jenson, the concrete aspect of Bultmann's eschaton is put into danger: Bultmann's eschatological theology does "empty the gospel's eschatological promise of describable content."[9] In Jenson's diagnosis, Bultmann displays the same kind of symptom, as Barth does, which lurks and determines his eschatological thinking: the dualism of God's timeless eternity and the creaturely time. God's eternity only touches the human historical time, as a circle touches a tangent line, but there is "no segment that is a segment of the line."[10]

Wolfhart Pannenberg

Jenson underscores his own intellectual debt to Pannenberg as "doubtless considerable."[11] That said, Jenson does not offer a fine-grained analysis of Pannenberg's treatment of the relation of time and eternity but sketches Pannenberg's teaching only with broad brush strokes. In Jenson's observation, unlike other eschatological theologies, "a passion for the future as such does not seem to be Pannenberg's original concern. Rather, his thinking starts with a concern for wholeness [of reality]."[12] For Pannenberg, reality is not abstract or changeless entity but history. And the wholeness of historical reality is achieved only when history arrives at its end, namely, the final future.[13] In Pannenberg's argument, another axiomatic conviction is that God of the Bible is God of history: "It is specific

8. Ibid.
9. *ST*, 2:321.
10. *ST*, 1:170.
11. "Exactly how directly indebted my reflections are to [Wolfhart Pannenberg], I am not sure. The indebtedness is doubtless considerable" (*GAG*, 175).
12. Ibid.
13. "History is whole only from its end. Thus the God of history is his own truth only as the End of history—and so Pannenberg arrives at the futurity of God" (Ibid.).

for Israel, that she did not experience the reality of her God in reflections of a mythic primal event, but rather, and ever more decisively, in historical change itself."[14] So to await the completion of history means to await the whole of God's revelation. For the full revelation of God, humans must wait until the history unfolds to the End.[15]

The good news is that Jesus Christ is "the end of history, which has occurred ahead of time in history."[16] "Just and only so, he is the revelation of the God of history, of the meaning of history as a whole."[17] Particularly, the resurrection is of paramount importance as the revelation of God's history that occurred ahead of time. "[T]he resurrection of Jesus is the proleptic manifestation of the reality."[18] It is "the inbreaking of the future of God."[19] And this has a crucial implication for the doctrine of God: since "[t]his revelation in Christ['s resurrection] defines who and what God is,"[20] God is the one who makes possible the inbreaking of the future. Pagan deities are "turned toward primeval time, and closed against the future."[21] The God of Israel, on the contrary, is "the power of the future."[22] This does not mean, in Jenson's reading of Pannenberg, that God is not yet and only will be, but that, by virtue of the incursive power of the future, God will be and *therefore* God *is*.[23] Or, as the futural power, God *is* present.

14. Pannenberg, *Grundfragen Systematischer Theologie*, 24, quoted in ibid.

15. In Jenson's analysis, Pannenberg's argument may be regarded an attempt to reconcile between universality and particularity—one of the longstanding traditional philosophical problems. Pannenberg combines these two into one: the particular universality, namely, the historical wholeness. Put differently, the issue here is "the contradiction between the necessity that God, as the meaning of all reality, be infinite, and the idea, seemingly contained in the very notion of God, that he is a particular being" (ibid). The particular and the universal have been thought as irreconcilable over a couple of millennia in the Western thought. But in Pannenberg's theological thinking—even though he is probably not the first thinker in such historical thinking of the being—"a 'God' who lacked universality, or who lacked individual personality, would not be God. Only if we can find a new way to think of God as at once universal and individually personal can the crisis of western religion be overcome" (ibid.). Here Jenson cites Pannenberg's *Grundfragen Systematischer Theologie*, 387–89.

16. Ibid., 176.

17. Ibid; Pannenberg, *Grundfragen Systematischer Theologie*, 42–44.

18. Pannenberg, *Systematic Theology* vol. 3, 627.

19. Ibid.

20. *GAG*, 177.

21. Pannenberg, *Grundfragen Systematischer Theologie*, 286–88, cited in ibid.

22. Pannenberg, *Grundfragen Systematischer Theologie*, 393, cited in ibid.

23. Pannenberg, *Grundfragen Systematischer Theologie*, 393, cited in ibid.

This understanding of the resurrection as the incursion of the eschatological future into history requires a revisionary thinking of time as well, which gives more weight to the power of the future than that of the past. In Pannenberg's theology, the procession of history is not the actualization of the possibility latent in the past but the future's interruption to status quo. Accordingly, the future, not the past, is the genuine "origin" of the procession of history. The future agitates and incites the inert and passive history to move forward and transcend its past conditions. "The Power of the Future is this root (of history)" and "origin of the contingency of events."[24] Here, importantly, the power and the primacy of the future is not ground in something else but the future in itself,[25] as the future is fully charged with the divine power and energy.[26] In the direction of Pannenberg's futuristic theo-ontology, Jenson aligns his thinking, simply saying, "the whole of what is here outlined of Pannenberg's position is affirmed."[27]

However, Jenson raises a question whether "Pannenberg's fundamental and overriding concern for wholeness and universality does not pull him in a direction opposed to the direction we have been going."[28] As noticed earlier, Pannenberg's thinking "is guided by the postulate of a totality of history."[29] Does the very notion of totality not entail a notion of "close-down"? Does it not suggest that history will be closed when it arrives at the End and so it becomes an entity of the past? "[I]f God is God in that history stops and becomes a completed entity, this God is the God of past history after all."[30] In Jenson's view, Pannenberg's guiding principle eventually hampers his theological thinking from being genuinely eschatological.

Seeing the limitation of Pannenberg's thinking, alternatively Jenson emphasizes the contradictory tension between the past and the future. These two poles of time are hardly reconcilable. As *historical* time, time is not abstract: the past is deficient in salvation; the future is charged with

---

24. Pannenberg, *Grundfragen Systematischer Theologie*, 73–74, cited in ibid., 178.

25. Pannenberg, *Grundfragen Systematischer Theologie*, 391, cited in ibid., 177.

26. For a recent account of Pannenberg's conception of time, particularly, the concept of *Rückbindung*, see Lakkis, *A New Hope: Wolfhart Pannenberg and the Natural Sciences on Time*, 136–49.

27. *GAG*, 178.

28. Ibid.

29. Ibid.

30. Ibid.

the divine energy, glory, and salvation. Mere infinite prolongation of the past would not lead to the glorious future. No procession that only deploys the energy of what is already given from the past cannot lead to the future of the new heaven and new earth. "A true future is thus no mere possible rectification of one or another shortcoming of the present."[31] For this reason, the future is not derived from the past but "must subsist in its futurity of itself."[32] For Jenson, the guiding principle for our thinking must be the divine and salvific future's stark *contradiction* to the past and the future's ontological *priority* over status quo.

For Jenson, the contradictory tension between the past and the future reaches its climax at the crucifixion. And the victory of the future over the past is achieved in the resurrection of Jesus Christ. "[I]n historical time, the unity of the transcendence of the future with that of the past . . . occurs as contradiction, suffering and overcoming. It occurs as the cross."[33] And the futural power of God *triumph* over the power of the past occurs in and as the resurrection. What this entails about the whole of history is that the process and the plot of history is made possible by the incursive interruption of the future into the present. Here Jenson's underlying understanding of God—along with Pannenberg's—is that God's being is eschatological and futural. "God is not a presence possessing his past and future in himself; he is a future possessing his past in himself and therefore always present."[34] The transcendence of God is the inexhaustible renewing power which transcends every antecedent and deterministic conditions.

In his theological account, Jenson also offers a solution to "the antinomy of hope." The eschatological future must remain as the *future*, never to be actualized *exhaustively*. Otherwise, history will be complete and become a past entity in the end. This is what Jenson worries about Pannenberg's notion of the historical wholeness. On the contrary, the promised future must be fulfilled and realized in history and so must have the material and historical content within it. This is the material aspect of the future which Jenson sees lacks in Bultmann's eschatology. Then, questions may arise: when the promised future is fulfilled concretely at some point of time, how can the promised future be still transcendent

---

31. *GAG*, 165. Cf. "Every hope is a contradiction of the present" (ibid.).
32. Ibid.
33. Ibid., 170.
34. Ibid., 171.

and open to the future? How can the promised future be at once concrete *and* transcendental reality? To this quandary of hope, Jenson suggests, love is the answer. For Jenson, love is a particular reality with material content *and* the constant transcendental reality. "Love is a describable state of affairs, a particular relation among specific persons. . . . Yet when love arrives, neither does life thereby become static nor do we need to move on from love to maintain liveliness. . . . For love is itself openness to unbounded possibility."[35] In the gospel, the ultimate love has a particular content and so is a describable reality because the particular man, Jesus of Nazareth, is love itself. This person of love does and will surpass any and every present moment inexhaustively and so subsists in the final eschatological future as the overturning futural power. He is the inexhaustible transcendental love, which will renew us day by day. The risen one is the "love that the Spirit brings as the End and as himself."[36]

The Spirit as the Divine Freedom for the Future

Now we are in a position to see how this notion of the futurity as the transcending power of God is worked into Jenson's pneumatology. In Jenson's construction, the futurity of God is attributed to the Spirit. In our next exploration, we will see that the Spirit is the futural and eschatological power/hypostasis of God by whom God is transcendent.

In God Himself

The Holy Spirit works as the power of transcendence "*first* in God himself."[37] In his bold speculative thought-experiment, Jenson poses a question: what would be God like, without the Spirit?[38] His answer is that, without the Spirit, God or the Father would be merely an actualization of the past possibilities, "an immovable fixed Beginning, a Something-or-Other that already is everything it could possibly be, a lifeless eternity."[39]

In terms of phenomenology, given that in Jenson's account God is a person who find his objective self in the Son, it is can be said that God's

35. *ST*, 1:220.
36. Ibid.
37. Jenson, *On the Inspiration of Scripture*, 33. Emphasis added.
38. Ibid.
39. Ibid.

finding himself in the Son is made possible by the Spirit. The Consciousness's finding of this objective self occurs in the resurrection by the Spirit. Without the Spirit, God could have been mere consciousness which has no objective self. By the Spirit, "the true God avoids—so to speak—the timelessness of mere form or mere consciousness."[40] One of the postmodern tendencies is disintegration of the self, that is, the breakdown of the unity between the apperceptive consciousness and the objective self. "Paul Sartres' *Transcendence of the Ego* perhaps best marks the break. . . . But Christian theology may greet it as liberation from a conceptual straitjacket."[41] In Jenson's diagnosis, the *third* factor is necessary to hold in unity the consciousness and the objective self. By freedom, the consciousness and the objective self "I" come into unity. To put this in theological terms, Consciousness finds his "I" by the Spirit: the Father finds himself in Jesus by the Spirit.

As God is not only a person but also the one who posits "you" within himself and so is communion, we also need to consider this matter in terms of relation or communion: without the Spirit, the communion of love would be impossible. In Jenson's account, the Spirit is not the result from the love between the Father and the Son. But the Spirit plays an active role in that love of the divine communion. The Spirit makes the Father and the Son transcend for the other and thus for the future, the future of love and unity. To highlight this point, Jenson employs Hegel's master-slave analogy, maintaining that, without the Spirit, the Father and the Son would fall into the master and slave relation. In Hegel's observation, one tries to uphold his subjectivity by making the other his object. So does the other, in turn, by objectifying the one who first objectifies him. But mutual objectification eventually reaches a breaking point, and thus a power struggle begins between the two subjects. Only one of the two will assert and maintain his sole subjectivity over the other, making him his "slave." In Jenson's observation, such power struggles are common phenomena in Greek myth: "a sibling kills a sibling, or a child kills a parent, or a husband kills a wife."[42] Inevitably their theology is polytheistic, without resolving the tension of the two subjects, and the unity is unachievable between plural deities. Then, Jenson turns to the gospel with a question: "Now—why are not the Father and God the

---

40. *ST*, 1:217.
41. Ibid., 121.
42. Jenson, *On Thinking the Human*, 83.

Son locked in mutual struggle for domination?"[43] The Greek doctrine of emanation is a possible solution. However, the problem is that once the other proceeds from the One by emanation, the one cannot be on the same ontological plane or cannot be a genuine Other distinguished from and *within* the One. In stark contrast to such pagan theologies, Christian theology maintains that God is one, having the otherness in himself due to the role of the Spirit: "The Father begets the Son, but it is the Spirit who presents this Son to his Father as an object of the love that begot him, that is, to be actively loved. The Son adores the Father, but it is the Spirit who shows the Father to the Son not merely as ineffable Source but as the available and lovable Father."[44] By the Spirit, the dialectic of the subjectivity and the objectivity may be kept without falling into mutual struggle for dominion. In the mutual objectification of the two persons, "[t]he Spirit is both the one who intends the Father and the Son to love one another *and* in classical doctrine is himself the love between them: within God the Spirit exhausts himself in the gift he give—here is the moment of truth in Eastern doctrines of self-emptying."[45]

But why does Jenson employ the Hegelian analogy? First, Jenson wants to emphasize that the mutual objectification is the precondition of love. One-way objectification cannot be love but only end up in the master-slave relation. In Jenson's trinitarian theology, within the Godhead, there must be the mutual objectification since God is love. Within God, one hypostasis is *both* the object before the other hypostasis, who is standing before him as the subject, *and* the subject who objectifies the other in turn. God's love upholds the subjectivity of the other object, by the Spirit. Secondly, Jenson wants to emphasize the role of the Spirit, apart from whom such communion of love would be impossible. Without the Spirit, the relation of the two would not be transcended for the other or for the love but stuck in some impasse. Obviously, Jenson moves beyond—or counter to—the tradition in which the Spirit has been considered rightly as "the bond of love between the Father and the Son," but "as if the Father and the Son loved each other in any case, and 'the Spirit' was a *subsequent* name for that love."[46] The Spirit is depicted as *resultant* from the relation between the Father and the Son. However,

---

43. Ibid.
44. *ST*, 1:156.
45. Jenson, *On Thinking the Human*, 84–85.
46. Jenson, "Second Thoughts about Theologies of Hope," 342.

Jenson regards the Spirit as an active agent who plays a constitutive and essential role in the love of the Father and the Son.

Now in accordance with his eschatological construal of the Spirit's transcendence, Jenson formulates the trinitarian relations. In classical trinitarian theology, "[t]he Father is the Source of Godhead. The Spirit and the Son receive their Godhead from the Father, they owe their Godhead to the Father. There is traditional language: God 'Begets,' and 'is Begotten,' and . . . 'Proceeds from' this relation. In God there is an Origin and two Goings-forth."[47] For Jenson, that is too origin-oriented, and the Spirit is construed only a hypostasis resultant from the antecedent reality. Moving beyond this, Jenson underlines the futural and liberating role of the Spirit in God himself: "Indeed the Father is the fount of the Trinity, but the Spirit is the *finis* of the Trinity and this must now become systematic center. Instead that there are one ground and two different processions in God, [it must be stated] that there are one goal and two different *anticipations*. The hypostases in God should be subsistent personal relations, but the personal relations are relations *to the future*."[48] In Jenson's theology, within the Godhead, there are not only two processions from the Origin, the Father, but also two *openings* to the Goal, by the Spirit.[49] By the power of the Spirit, the Father and the Son are open up for each other and so for the future.

In the Relation between Jesus and Israel

The Spirit is the liberating futural power not only within God himself but also in the relation between Jesus and the Old Testament Israel. But this is after all about God's becoming, as Jesus is not a closed self, but rather opens himself up for the others and embraces them into himself by the power of the Spirit.

Yet, before discussing how Jesus embraces the *Old Testament Israel* into himself, this section will first see that, on Jenson's account, there was Jesus in the Old Testament period: the Word that appeared to the Old Testament prophets was a *man*. Drawing upon von Rad, Jenson holds that the Word of YHWH is always *the same reality*. According to von Rad: "The phrase, 'the word of Jahweh came to so and so' . . . represents

---

47. *SP*, 126.
48. Jenson, "Kontinuität," 101. Emphasis added.
49. *SP*, 126.

the apperception of the divine word as event, a unique happening in history.... It is very significant that *the phrase always appears with the definite article, 'the word of Jahweh,' and never in the indefinite form, 'a word of Jahweh.'*... The word that came on each occasion is not to be set alongside the rest of the words of Jahweh.... [I]t is the complete word of God, and has no need of tacit supplementation by the other words which the prophet had already spoken on other occasions."[50] Noting that it is the *same* word of God and taking one step further, Jenson takes the word of YHWH as a *consistent* reality, dwelling among the people of God in the Old Testament period. So construed, "the formula of prophetic inspiration 'The word of the Lord came to ...' does not merely mean 'The Lord said....'"[51] Jenson says, "The Word of the Lord is not a set of words provided to the prophets on one occasion and a different set provided on another occasion. The Word of the Lord is a *single reality*, that *comes* to and *addresses* the prophet. That is, this Word is *a person*."[52] So when the Word came to Abraham, the Word could take a walk with him and have a conversation with him (Gen 15:1–6).[53]

Jenson also indicates that the Word was (identified with) God. "'When the word of the Lord came to Solomon' about his temple, what the Lord promised was the permanence there of 'my word,' which was equivalent to 'I will settle among the children of Israel.'"[54] And when the word of YHWH came to Abraham, he said, "I am your shield." To this, Abraham replied, "O Lord God...."[55] Also when the Word of YHWH came to a prophet, the prophet cannot but say, "Thus says the Lord."[56] In Jenson's theological reflection, the Word is the appearance of God who dwells among his people. It is the Logos that God identifies himself with. In this identification of God with the Word, what happens to the Word is taken to be happenings to God; what is spoken to the Word is regarded to be speech to God; what is speaking from the Word is a speech from God himself. In short, the Word is the Word *of* God, and the Word *is* God.

---

50. Von Rad, *Old Testament Theology*, 2:88–89.
51. *ST*, 1:78.
52. Jenson, *On the Inspiration of Scripture*, 28. Emphasis added.
53. *ST*, 1:79.
54. Ibid., 78.
55. Ibid., 79.
56. Jenson, *On the Inspiration of Scripture*, 28.

Who is this Word? Jenson answers that before the modernism taints Christian exegesis, "[t]he [church] Fathers . . . knew this all along . . . : This Word, the singular and constant reality that comes to the prophets, is none other than Jesus the Christ, whom the church knows to be the second triune person, the singular Logos of God."[57] Here Jenson is not being rhetorical, but literally means and argues that the Word was Jesus Christ, the *man* of Nazareth. At this point, it should be noted, Jenson's thinking operates on the Lutheran assumption that the Logos or the Son is never abstracted from the flesh but that the Logos is always Jesus. And this issue about the presence of the man Jesus of Nazareth in the Old Testament has to do with the revisionary metaphysics of time in Jenson's theology and will occupy us later on.

How does the Spirit work in the relationship between Jesus the Word and the prophets of Israel? Jenson's answer is: when the Word of God comes to someone, the Spirit comes upon and enables him or her to receive the Word so that "the Word can speak not only to the prophet but *from* him."[58] Just so the Word speaks through a human being in the Spirit. For instance, when we hear the prayers of the Psalter, we hear the voice of the Christ himself.[59] "[W]hen the church sings the psalms, this is simply the members of Christ chiming in with their head."[60] "Thus Augustine said it was the *totus Christus*, the whole Christ, head and body, who prayed the psalms, and that it always had been."[61] In the Spirit, prophets or the prophetic community utter the Word in union with the Word as their head.

The work of the Spirit who comes upon people and makes them inevitably utter the Word can be called *inspiration*. Jenson himself works out this idea in his account of the inspiration of the Scriptures.[62] The doctrine of inspiration is a linguistic and hermeneutical aspect of the doctrine of the union with Christ. The Son of God embraces others into himself as they speak the Word by the Spirit.

We may think this matter in terms of hermeneutical ontology as it is also the Spirit that enables the word-event in which God happens. As

---

57. Ibid., 29.
58. Ibid., 28–29.
59. Ibid., 25.
60. Ibid.
61. Ibid.
62. Jenson, *On the Inspiration of Scripture*.

discussed in chapter 5, the word-event within Israel is the locus of the happening of God's being. God enowns (*ereignet*) his people so that he may "appear" and comes into word in Israel's tradition in which Israel recapitulates the past and anticipates the future in her present hermeneutical activities. This hermeneutical flow and connection between the past, the present, and the future constitute to be a narrative after all. That is the narrative of *the Word* that the people of Israel were enabled to speak *by the Spirit* when they encountered the Word. Israel's hermeneutical tradition has the narrative of the Word—the story of Jesus—at some ontological level, and therein God's being occurs and comes to us. On a larger historical scale or phylogenetically, the words uttered by the prophets in their encounter with the Word become coherent and a story after all, the story of the Word. On the whole, the history of Israel communicates the Word-Jesus, through and in which God happens. "[God's] hypostatic being, his self-identity, is constituted in dramatic coherence."[63]

This means that Israel's hermeneutical tradition runs in *anticipation* of the End to complete the portrait of the Word-Jesus in her life and history. And along with this flow of the hermeneutical tradition, God's being moves forward and to the Future. Israel's history moves, having within it "*God's inner-historical anticipation of that outcome.*"[64] Thus, "the Lord's self-identity is constituted in dramatic coherence . . . [and] established . . . in *anticipation.*"[65]

This means that the Spirit must come upon the people of Israel again and again in the course of their history so that God's being along with Israel's history may be open up again and again *to the End* and *to its completion.* The Spirit opens and frees Israel for the future and also *God's being* for the future. This entails "confessing God trinitarian . . . differently than the tradition theology did."[66] As the role of the Spirit is stressed, according to Jenson, it should be stated that there are the two processions from the Father *and* the two going-forth to the future by the Spirit.

---

63. *ST*, 1:64. For Jenson, the concept of dramatic coherence is not the first cart of his train of thought. Rather it is one of the consequent notions from his hermeneutical thinking, which, in my view, draws upon or appropriates the Bultmannian school and von Rad's theology, as shown in chapter 5.

64. Jenson, "A Theological Autobiograhpy, to Date," 48. Emphasis added.

65. *ST*, 1:66. Emphasis original. Here the terms "identity" would be appropriate because God's being is now construed on the historical and hermeneutical horizon. The question of *who* someone is always historical one as it involves description of his *acts.*

66. Ibid., 101.

"The Father and the Son are God only in that [they] are wholly open to their mutual and free Future in the Spirit,"[67] as the Father who identifies himself with the Son and the Son-Word whose story unfolds in Israel's tradition history are constantly open for the future by the Spirit. Thus, the Spirit makes possible the divine becoming, as the Son, the objective self of God, moves from the Origin to the Future by the power of the Future, embracing his people and their story into himself in the Spirit.

In the Relation between Jesus-Israel and the Nations

Christ's becoming to be the *totus Christ* by the Spirit is through Christ's embracing not only Israel but also *the gentile nations* into himself. The Spirit frees Jesus to open up himself further and to embrace the nations into himself. Jesus carries out *the final mission of Israel* to invite the gentile nations to the worship of God of Israel, by opening up himself to take the nations into his Israelite body, the body of the one who has the whole Israel in himself.

This entails for Jenson that the post-canonical descendents of Abraham are also the community of the Spirit. Since Jesus-Israel embraces the nations into his Israelite body by the Spirit and since the two covenant communities, the Jews and the church, will join together and be the one body of Christ in the End as seen in the chapter 4, it can be said that both are directed by the Spirit. As argued in the previous chapter, God's covenant with the carnal descendents of Abraham is irrevocable, and the two covenant communities, the Jews and the church, together build up to be the one body of Christ and so to be the *totus Christus*, joined with their head. The two communities will be one in the End. Until then, the Spirit continues to blow and liberate both communities for the future and will finally complete the eschatological body of Christ. Then, "the Spirit will no more bring and join the Son's people to him, for they will be with and joined to him."[68] Hence, Jenson's doctrines of Judaism and of the Spirit suggest that, as a Pentecostal scholar rightly indicates in his exposition of Jenson, the Jews "too are bearers of God's ruah, communities animated by the dynamic power of God's Spirit."[69]

---

67. *SP*, 126.

68. *ST*, 2:339. Cf. "The Last Judgment will be according to the law that unites the totus Christus and that is as such the torah that the Son is for the Father" (ibid., 354).

69. Chan, "Reflecting on Roots: Robert Jenson's Theology of Judaism in a

To put this in a hermeneutical perspective, as discussed in chapter 5, the hermeneutical flow of the Word-Torah of the Old Testament is divided into the two different streams in the New Testament period: the church and the Jews. If the church is the community that continues the narrative hermeneutical task of the Old Testament Israel, and the Jews is another hermeneutical community that inherits the codified aspect of Israel's tradition, and if, as argued in that chapter, the Spirit is the agent who enables the hermeneutical work of Israel, then both covenant communities are the communities of the Spirit. Thus, as the Spirit blows on the two hermeneutical communities, the eschatological body of Jesus Christ will be established and offered to the Father in the End.

The Spirit as the Power from the Future

Now we are going to look at how the Spirit is the recursive power and agent *from* the future in Jenson's theology. We have already seen in the first section that God's power is recursive from the future and in the second section that the God's futural power is the third hypostasis, the Spirit. Now we simply explicate the corollary that the Spirit is the power from the future, as we observe the *phenomenon* of the recursive eschatological power, which is displayed in the "pre"-existence of the Son: by the power of the Holy Spirit, the Son Jesus preexists retroactively, as already mentioned earlier. So this section corrals and expands what was sketched before.

Let us follow here Jenson's account of the preexistence (or the retroactive presence) of Christ. In his exposition of Johannine prologue, Jenson says:

> [I]n John's prologue we read that "In the beginning was the Word," and that the Word then "became flesh." But before we cast too simple a scheme of successive states of the Word, that he is first unincarnate and then incarnate, we should note that in the Gospel so introduced we find this Word himself testifying to the mode of his pre-existence: "Before Abraham was, I am." It is precisely the aggressively incarnate protagonist of this Gospel's narrative who says this of himself, and he puts his antecedence to Abraham in the present tense. Thus despite what may at first seem the obvious reading of the prologue, we may not, if we follow the Gospel it introduces, conceive the preexistence of the

Pentecostal Key," 33.

Son as the existence of a divine entity that has simply not yet become the created personality of the Gospels.[70]

In Jenson's account, the Word in the beginning who made the whole creation is not the Logos *asarkos*, which this Lutheran theologian has militated against, or even the Logos *incarnandus* since this concept of the Logos also does not fully embrace the bodyness of Jesus. For Jenson, the Word is always "aggressively incarnate."[71] The Word is Jesus, and vice versa. There was no time when the Word was not the man Jesus.[72] If the Word was aggressively incarnate from the beginning, then it suggests that it is the retroactive presence of Jesus by the power of the Spirit, who breaks into history *from* the future.

At this point, it would be clearer that the Spirit is the eschatological power *from* the future and so by the power of the Spirit Jesus is retroactively pre-existent before his birth to Mary, when we look at Jenson's construal of Jesus' post-resurrection appearance and his ascension.

> The appearance stories plainly do not suppose that the risen Jesus had returned to inhabit the witnesses' time and space. Although the witnesses saw something visible and tangible in their world, between appearances the risen Jesus had no such location—he was not thought to be lodging with Mary and Martha or staying at the Jerusalem caravansary. He appeared when and as he would and then "vanished from their sight" or "withdrew from them"—neither "walked away" *nor* "disappeared" would be quite the right phrase. Nor were his appearings subject to the regularities of this age: "Although the doors were shut," Jesus yet "came and stood among them . . . ." If we ask where Jesus was—so to speak—resident during the days of the appearances, the immediately available answer is that he was in the heaven of the apocalypses, that is, *in God's final future, from which he showed himself—or the Spirit showed him—to the chosen.*[73]

After the resurrection, the presence of Jesus is not restricted by space and time as we are in this age. The risen one appears in the *apocalyptic* fashion: "Paul calls what he saw a 'revelation' (*apokalypsis*)."[74] Jen-

---

70. *ST*, 1:139.

71. Ibid.

72. And this fits well with Jenson's Lutheran conception of the visible Word in which the Word must be always embodied.

73. Ibid., 197. Emphasis added.

74. Ibid., 196; Gal 1:12.

son states, "What certain persons saw after his death was a reality of *that future*."[75] So Jesus is "risen into the future that God has for his creatures."[76] Now he is in the Eschaton, and he is the Eschatos. He is coming to us by the rushing power of the Spirit. He comes by the Spirit as he comes from the future. "Thus Paul can even say, precisely in this context, 'The Lord is the Spirit.'"[77] Obviously here the heaven is construed as the eschatological future. In Jenson's account, "heaven is finally defined within apocalyptic metaphysics, where it is the created future's presence—as future!—with God...."[78]

Furthermore, in connection with the pre-existence of the risen one by the retroactive futural power of the Holy Spirit, we may recall the discussion on the relation Jesus as the Word and the words of prophets. As emphasized earlier, some people of Israel in the Old Testament encountered the Word. Now the identity of the Word is even clearer in light of Jenson's construal of the ascension and the power of the Spirit. The Word is the risen Jesus of Nazareth. What happened in the Old Testament period was, according to Jenson, that the risen one as the Word came to some people by the power of the Spirit. And in this encounter, they received the Word and uttered the words of prophecies in the Spirit, the words regarding the Word in union with it, as they themselves become one with him in the Spirit. The Word that came to the prophets was *the retroactive existence of the risen one*, from the heaven/future by the Spirit.

In line of this, we may note further Jenson's account on the prophetic vision that Ezekiel had: when Ezekiel saw the Glory of the Lord, he saw it on the throne that looked like a man. In his exposition, Jenson inquires the identity of the "figure with the appearance of a man."[79] And he says, "the man on the throne who shines with God's own glory, who indeed is God's Glory, must either be *Jesus* the Christ or something highly problematic."[80] If the figure is not a man but only an anthropomorphic theophany, then it would be some sort of the Logos *asarkos* or *incarnandus* or even some hidden deity behind the man Jesus. Following the exegetical insight of the sixth-century pope Gregory the Great, Jenson

75. Ibid., 198. Emphasis added.
76. Ibid.
77. Ibid., 175.
78. *ST*, 2:121.
79. Ezek 1:26.
80. *CC*, 85. Emphasis added.

states, "[The] fathers of the church supposed that the Glory appearing to Ezekiel looked like a man because He is one. For they knew of an actual identifiable man, with His personal story and personal name, who shines like the figure on the throne: *Jesus on the mountain of Transfiguration.* Who could the man on the throne be but He?"[81]

In other words, what Ezekiel and other Old Testament prophets saw was the one who the apostle Paul encountered on the road to Damascus. Jenson writes, "It thus seems to have been Paul's understanding that what he and the other witnesses saw was of the same ontological character as what Zechariah or Daniel or the postcanonical apocalypticists saw, that is, the fulfilling future of creation as it already now comes to the Father in the Spirit and as God therefore can, if he will, show it to us."[82] So construed, God could engage with Israel in a *fleshly* manner and precisely in the eschatological power. That was "the Lord's fleshly involvement with Israel."[83] God could "indulge in a little wrestling match with Jacob, or sit down to Abraham and Sarah's cooking, or converse with humans as his own 'angel;' . . . [and] establish an earthly address at Number One Temple Avenue."[84] For he is risen.

If the individual Son can reaches back by the power of the future, then why not his Bride from the final future? Jenson draws upon again von Rad and theologically exegetes Proverbs 8. Jenson makes some observations on this wisdom: "In this passage, . . . wisdom suddenly appears in a seemingly very different role: she is a personal voice somehow speaking from the creation and proclaiming herself as the wisdom by which God orders it."[85] Even though the voice of the Wisdom seems divine, "the voice that speaks from the experienced world is nevertheless not God's voice."[86] In Jenson's exposition, she is a creature while it is also true that she is "the architect at the Builder's side"[87] and to be desired more than silver and gold. Another wisdom literature, the book of Job, says, "Mortals do not know the way to [the wisdom]. . . . It is hidden from the eyes of all the

---

81. Jenson, "The Trinity in Ezekiel," 9. The appearance of Jesus in the transfiguration prefigures his appearance after the resurrection.

82. *ST*, 1:196.

83. Jenson, "Toward a Christian Doctrine of Israel," 6.

84. Ibid.

85. *ST*, 2:157.

86. Ibid., 158.

87. Ibid., 157.

living. ... [Only] God understands the way to it."[88] The most astonishing thing, in Jenson's observation, is that the wisdom "turns to humanity appealing and commanding, in direct address, as personality."[89] Who then is this speaker? Is the wisdom the Logos? But Jenson notes: "throughout the poems wisdom is obtrusively and consistently 'she.'"[90] Jenson's intriguing conclusion is that "it is the preexistent reality of the *totus Christus* that is the creature among the creatures who makes sense of the rest of them and whom Israel's teachers heard when the creation made sense to them. That is, *Israel herself*... spoke to her teachers."[91] At this point it should be noted where she speaks *from*: "Israel spoke to them from heaven, spoke to them from that created presence of the End within which she was already in full possession of her destiny."[92] Here again the future reaches back: by the wind of the future, the *totus Christus*, Israel together with the church, speaks to her old self who was in the Old Testament period. The resurrected Israel who enjoys the divine glory and has become one with Jesus in the End, by the power of the future, is pre-existent *retroactively*.

In Jenson's theology, this eschatological retroactive transcendence of the risen Jesus and the Spirit requires a revisionary conception of time. The implication of the recursive and retroactive presence of the risen one by the Spirit is that historical time proceeds as it is interrupted by the retroactive presence of the eschatological figure and so by the recursive power of the eschatological future. So, historical time is liberated by and for the future. As earlier said, the procession of history is not unrolling of the past, but it unfolds as the disruptive eschatological grace breaks into its status quo. Accordingly, for Jenson, time is not purely linear, but it is *recursive*. "The temporal infinity that leads all things does not stretch forward on and on, nor yet circle round and round; ... it has the recursive shape"[93] by the incursive eschatological power of the resurrection of Jesus Christ. Nevertheless, to say that time has recursive shape is probably not enough, if it must be acknowledged somehow that the risen Jesus is the

88. Job 28:1-28 in ibid., 158.
89. Von Rad, *Weisheit in Israel*, 204.
90. *ST*, 2:159.
91. Ibid.
92. Ibid. For Jenson, heaven is the final and glorious future.
93. *ST*, 1:219.

center of the universe. To put it more appropriately, "[t]ime is more like a helix, and what it spirals around is the risen Christ."[94]

At this juncture, in my view, Jenson's revisionary metaphysics of time is distanced from Hegel's philosophy in a crucial way. Acknowledging and upholding the recursive nature of the futural and transcendental power of the resurrection prevents Jenson's theology from lapsing into a Hegelian error. For Jenson, the event of the resurrection that occurred in the middle of history determines the content of the future, and it recursively breaks into any or some points of time of history, as the futural and liberating power. Again, for Jenson, procession of time is not linear, but more like a helix around the resurrection. On the other hand, in Jenson's reading, Hegel's "error is but the conceptualization of pervasive theological error. . . . The problem with Hegel is that, despite his grandiloquent talk of *Geist*, . . . [Hegel's] God, despite all his rhetoric and the insight behind it, is timeless reason, it lacks life, and therefore the sublation of history into his God is after all a return to the beginning and very much like death."[95] After all, Hegel's deity is only an actualization of the past possibility. It cannot be the God of the resurrection. More crucially, Hegel's thinking neither revolves around the redemptive and cosmological significance of the resurrection of Jesus and its impact on time, nor allows the recursive nature of the futural power.

Now before we proceed to the next section, let us briefly attend to major criticisms leveled against Jenson's doctrine of preexistence of the Son. Oliver Crisp, George Hunsinger, and Simon Gathercole raised concerns about Jenson's Christology. While it is understandable that they bring charges against Jenson from the stance of the classical doctrine of the preexistence of the Son, Jenson's doctrine is largely misunderstood in their works. The critics altogether believe that Jenson would not endorse the preexistence of the personal and individual Son. However, Jenson does not actually argue what the critics think he argues.

Hunsinger claims that Jenson's theology does not allow for the "antecedent reality"[96] of the Son, especially prior to his birth. According to Hunsinger's reading of Jenson, therefore, his Christology inevitably lapses into a kind of Arian error.[97] Gathercole makes a similar judgment,

---

94. Jenson, "Scripture's Authority in the Church," 35.
95. Jenson, "Second Thoughts about Theologies of Hope," 342.
96. Hunsinger, "Robert Jenson's *Systematic Theology*," 172.
97. Ibid.

saying, "The plain sense of Jenson's language might imply that he is falling into Arianism."[98] Gathercole offers a New Testament Christology, emphasizing that "the Logos, who is also Son of Man and Son of God, is 'in the beginning with God,'"[99] and assumes that his exegetical Christology opposes Jenson's in that regard. Thus, Gathercole's understanding of Jenson is not a far cry from Hunsinger's. Crisp astutely notes that Jenson holds onto a doctrine of the preexistence of the Son and takes it to mean that "Christ pre-exists as *Israel*."[100] Having attempted some expositional and analytic understanding, however, Crisp concludes that "[s]uch a claim is so theologically exotic"[101] since "this raises all sorts of theological problems."[102] Jenson's idiosyncratic Christology entails, according to Crisp, that all Israelites such as "Abraham, Jacob, Moses, David and Malachi are all God Incarnate."[103]

However, what must be noted here is that Jenson does argue for the doctrine of the preexistence of the individual and personal Son. In his theological exegesis of the Johannine prologue, as seen above, Jenson holds that the Word in the beginning of the creation is "precisely the aggressively incarnate protagonist of this Gospel's narrative."[104] What is baffling here is that the *preexistent* Word (the Son) in the beginning is not the *Logos asarkos* or even the *Logos incarnandus*, but the fully divine and fully *human* Jesus of Nazareth. Also as mentioned above, Jenson also claims that the Glory of the Lord, the Angel of the Lord, and the Word of the Lord, who appeared to some Israelites such as Abraham, Moses, and Ezekiel, are precisely *christo*-phanic phenomena. The glory of the Lord that some Israelites witness in the Old Testament period and especially that looked like a man (Ezek 37) was that of the Son, who was preexistent and present to Ezekiel and whose name is Jesus, the risen one. Then, the critics' charges against Jenson's christology are considerably enfeebled, first in their expositions.

98. "The plain sense of Jenson's language might imply that he is falling into Arianism, and admitting that 'there was when He was not,' but this is a charge which Jenson denies" (Gathercole, "Pre-existence and the Freedom of the Son in Creation and Redemption," 45).

99. Ibid., 39.

100. Crisp, *God Incarnate*, 72. Emphasis added.

101. Ibid., 73.

102. Ibid.

103. Ibid.

104. *ST*, 1:139.

Hunsinger argues that Jenson is playing "a fast-talking shell game,"[105] in which one is to call black white and white black. In Hunsinger's reading, Jenson regards the future as the past and the past as the future. In fact, however, Jenson's theology is not that extravagant. Gathercole maintains that the protological dimension of Christology is ridden roughshod over.[106] However, what thrust of Jenson's argument is is that the eschatos—Jesus Christ as the incarnate and risen one—has existed also as the *protos* from the beginning of the creation. The antecedent reality in the Old Testament period is the risen Jesus, the eschatological figure. As Crisp properly captures it, "it is the futurity of the Son that is somehow 'prior' to [his birth to Mary],"[107] even though he soon complains: "it is very difficult indeed to know what to make of this. . . . What can this mean?"[108]

Now all these hinge upon the question on how Jesus the man (*eschatos*) can be present even from the beginning of the creation. And this is what we have already discussed: the divine transcendence is constituted by the person of Jesus Christ, who is now risen from the dead. The risen one is the material constituent of God's transcendence of time and space.[109]

Having said all these, I understand the critics' discomfort about Jenson's audacious rejection of the pretemporal and pretemporal existence of the Son. Jenson's disavowal of the notion of the *Logos asarkos* even in the pretemporal eternity and the notion of pretemporal eternity itself causes some anxiety to many readers. At this juncture, we may diverge from Jenson, considering it doctrinally sound to admit the existence of the *Logos asarkos* at least some point in the *pretemporal* eternity. Yet, I suggest, we may still agree with Jenson that there is the ontological priority of the future and that Jesus, the risen one, constitutes the divine transcendence of time and space. In my judgment, acknowledging the pretemporal existence of the Son does *not* preclude the logical possibility of the ontological priority of the eschatological future over the past and the present. Here I am simply acknowledging the changes the Son underwent: the *Logos asarkos* at some point in

---

105. Hunsinger, "Robert Jenson's *Systematic Theology*," 172.
106. Gathercole, "Pre-existence and the Freedom of the Son," 50.
107. Crisp, *God Incarnate*, 74.
108. Ibid.
109. *ST*, 2:254.

pretemporal eternity; the *Logos incarnandus*, the Logos in flesh (Jesus) in time; and Jesus as the risen one and so as the transcendental figure over space and time. Now the incarnate and risen one must be considered as the true reality of the Son and so of God, for the past is past. He is now not the *Logos asarkos* but the *eschatos*. As seen in Jenson's theology, this requires revision of our conception of time, as the eschatological presence of the risen one is *not* restricted by temporal distance and as the resurrection certainly has the soteriological impact on time recursively.[110] So the recursive view of time may be accepted without rejecting the state of the Son in his pretemporal eternity.

The Holy Spirit, the Power of the Resurrection of Israel

Having considered all these, now we are in a position to draw out the post-supersessionistic implication of Jenson's Christian notion of the Holy Spirit, as Jenson's account of the Holy Spirit in his post-supersessionistic essays remain quite condensed.[111] We will do so first by recalling the earlier discussion on the irrevocability of God's covenant with Israel.

God is the God of Israel. He is the God of the biological descendents of Abraham, Isaac, and Jacob. God's covenant with the familial lineage still stands in full force, as discussed in chapter 3 and 4—this does not need further explication. Having secured this point of the irrevocability of God's covenant and his covenantal identity as God of Israel, we need to turn to another axis of Jenson's thinking: the God of Israel is the God *of the living*. Jenson puts it, "From first to last of biblical faith, God is death's opponent."[112] This is the substance of Israel's faith and of Christian faith.[113]

Yet, even though the God of Israel is the God of the living, Israel faced death in her history. She is portrayed as dry bones in the valley, as in Ezekiel's vision (Ezek 37). She was exiled and not fully restored, even though she returned to Jerusalem later in her history. Nevertheless, if God is the God of Israel *and* if the God is the God of the living who

---

110. Note here I distinguish between the preexistence of the Son (before his birth to Mary) and the pretemporal existence of the Son (before the creation).

111. Jenson, "Toward a Christian Doctrine of Israel"; "Toward a Christian Theology of Judaism."

112. *ST*, 1:66.

113. *ST*, 2:329.

cannot ally with the power of death, Israel must be raised from the dead. The familial descendents of Abraham, Isaac, and Jacob, whose fleshly existence secured within the eternal covenant of God, even if they try to denigrate and pry it from their fleshly existence, must await the resurrection of Israel. That will occur in the age to come. A prominent Jewish scholar, Levenson, says, "[T]he Jewish expectation of a resurrection of the dead is always and inextricably associated with the restoration of the people Israel. . . . 'Has God given up on his promises to his people?' Ezekiel's answer to the latter question is a resounding 'No!' Even a history of the most hideous disobedience and the most obscene idolatry shall not prevent the dry bones that are the whole House of Israel from living again."[114]

In fact, Christians believe that the resurrection has occurred: the one Israelite who has Israel within himself is now risen. For Jenson, as said earlier, this entails that the liberating eschatological power is not an abstract power but the power *of the resurrection*. The eschatological power is at work to agitate history and lead it to its end. The power of the resurrection is most conspicuous in the mission of the church. The church is called to carry out the mission of Israel. The mission of Israel is to be the blessing to all the nations; "and the prophets interpreted the fulfillment of that calling as the gathering of the nations to fellowship with her in worship of the true God."[115] Put differently, because the one Israelite is risen, and so ascended into heaven and seated as the right hand of the Father, as his royal Son Messiah, as the old Israel anticipated, and because he is given now all the authority from God (Matt 28) and has poured out the Holy Spirit on the church (Acts 2), the gentiles have begun to gather from the ends of the earth to worship the God of Israel. For Christianity, the very existence of the church as the gathering of the nations and as the mission of Israel is the logical consequence, if not the proof, of the resurrection.

"Had Jesus' Resurrection been immediately the End, Israel's mission would have been aborted."[116] God did not let the resurrection of Jesus coincide with the resurrection of Israel or the general resurrection. Instead, God instituted the church to fulfill Israel's mission first. The Spirit is given

---

114. Levenson, *Resurrection and the Restoration of Israel*, 165.
115. *ST*, 2:170.
116. Ibid., 171.

to the church "to conduct a mission to Jews and gentiles."[117] "The church, which came when the [final] Kingdom should have come . . . leads to the Kingdom by way of the mission to the gentiles."[118]

Her Christian faith in the resurrection and in the eschatological power, which is operative in this age as the liberating power *of the resurrection*, should not (or even cannot) run counter to the covenantal existence of the Jews and to their hope for the resurrection of Israel. The material content of the eschatological power and that of the Jewish hope are not disparate but the same. The familial descendants of Israel's hope for the resurrection is biblically legitimate and warranted. The engrafted branch must not question it. Accordingly, Christian theology must recognize that the Jewish hope for the resurrection and the eschatological divine power operative in history are in collusion. The divine eschatological power conspicuously operative in the church's mission should not or cannot betray the Jewish hope for the resurrection of Israel. The divine energy is indefatigably active in their hope and in their carnal existence.

Now we simply note that in Jenson the eschatological power is not impersonal but person/hypostasis, the Holy Spirit. In line with Jenson's thought, probably we may say, the Holy Spirit is hidden in their hope for the resurrection, as the power from the future to fulfill it—also in their fleshly covenantal existence. The Holy Spirit will blow upon the Jewish community as well as upon the gentile faith community. And finally God will raise the Israel from the dead by the eschatological power of Holy Spirit, for Jenson, which is essentially the power of the resurrection. Then, there will be the one risen body of Jesus Christ, the *totus Christus*: the two covenant communities will be one.

Conclusion

Jenson has established himself as a theologian of hope in his own right. Critically engaging with Barth, Bultmann, and Pannenberg, Jenson emphasizes that the future does not only break into and liberate the time of this age, as a self-subsisting power, but also has a material content since a particular man, Jesus, is risen into the future. God is futural and renewing power, whose material content is Jesus of Nazareth. The divine power as the power of the risen Jesus is unimpeded by space-time restriction. The

---

117. Jenson, "Toward a Christian Doctrine of Israel," 11.
118. Ibid.

risen one can be present to the very beginning of time recursively. Thus, Jenson's eschatological ontology centers upon Jesus and his resurrection.

Jenson weaves his eschatological thinking into the fabric of his pneumatology. God's eschatological and renewing power is attributed to the third hypostasis of the Trinity. In Jenson's thinking, the Spirit plays an active role in relation with the first and the second persons of the Trinity. By the futural power of the Spirit, God is active. By the Spirit, the Father and the Son are one in love; by the Spirit, the Son Jesus is one with the old Israel in the Old Testament period, as the Spirit achieves the oneness between the Word of God and their (prophetic and inspired) words; by the Spirit, in the New Testament period, the two subsequent Israelites communities, the Jewish community and the gentile Christian community, are sustained in parallel, and in the final eschaton, the two will be one.

The Jewish community's hope for the resurrection is biblically warranted and must be encouraged by Christian gathering. Given that God's covenant with Israel is not made obsolete, Christian theology must recognize that the eschatological force is collusive with the covenantal existence of the Jewish people and flickering in their eschatological hope for the restoration and resurrection of Israel. Now, we see how Jenson's eschato-pneumatological ontology has moved in the post-supersessionistic direction. This ontology is an outworking of the implication of the eschatological role of the Spirit in God's being, with recognition of the unrevoked validity of the Israel's covenant, in which, Jenson envisages, the Spirit achieves the hypostatic oneness of the two communities so that they will be one risen *totus Christus*.

Conclusion

CHRISTIAN THEOLOGY CAN RECOGNIZE the significance of the Jewish existence, without diluting its trinitarian faith, by seeing the close conceptual nexus between the doctrine of the Trinity and the doctrine of the Jews. The Christian doctrine of the Trinity can accommodate a non-supersessionistic view of Judaism by recognizing the irrevocability of Israel's covenant and the significance of the flesh of Israel within the body of Jesus Christ. The flesh of the Son is securely placed in the being of God, and the flesh of the Jews (and the church) is in the divine body of Christ. This is the provocation of Jenson's trinitarian theology of Israel, which knows of no rigorous or dualistic demarcation of the immanent and the economic Trinity. In short, throughout this book I have sought to demonstrate how, on its own terms, Jenson's "actualistic" doctrine of the Trinity can secure non-supersessionism. I have explored some major strands of Jenson's trinitarian theology woven into the fabric of his post-supersession theology, endeavoring to portray his theology as a post-supersessionistic trinitarian theology.

Our exposition of Jenson's theology may be summarized as follows:

Chapter 1. Here Jenson's trinitarian thought is characterized as an actualistic ontology that juxtaposes the doctrine of the Trinity and the doctrine of the election of the Son. The act of God's election of the Son *as* Jesus allows for the ontological weight and significance of the flesh and time of Jesus *within* the immanent Trinity. Carrying this forward, Jenson's theology identifies Jesus as the Son and so the economic Trinity as the immanent Trinity. This paves the way for Jenson's later recognition of the ontological significance of the Jews, who are considered to be in Jesus, the Son *in* the immanent Trinity.

Chapter 2. Jenson's actualistic ontology leads to his body ontology, as it is not only the life but also the flesh of Jesus that is placed in the eternal immanent Trinity, through the Father's election of the Son Jesus. The immanent Trinity is not antithetical to the body; it embraces the flesh of the Son within it. God's being is inextricably related to the bodily existence of his Son. Accordingly, his flesh is saturated with the divine glory and being. Further, the body of Jesus is regarded to be *accommodative* of other human fleshly existences. In this regard, Christian theology affirms that the church is the body of Christ. The human bodily beings are embraced into the body of Jesus Christ, when they are baptized into Christ and partake the eucharistic bread and wine, of which the Lord says, "This is my body," and "This is my blood." Moreover, Jenson presses this notion of Christ's body in the direction of the Eastern Orthodox doctrine, *theosis*. The redeemed are divinized in the *divine* body of Christ, as they participate in it. So insofar as a community is embraced into the body of Christ, it can mediate the divine energy of the presence of the Son to the world and carry within it.

Chapters 3–4. Jenson's conversation with Jewish theologians, particularly with Michael Wyschogrod, drives him to recognize the irrevocability of Israel's covenant and to work out its ontological implications on the trajectory of his actualistic and body theo-ontology. Following Wyschogrod, Jenson affirms that God is not severed from the carnal existence of his chosen Son, the people of Israel, due to his tenacious faithfulness to the covenant with Israel. Any attempts—by Israel herself or by supersessionistic Christians—cannot undo the covenantal relation between God and his people. Israel is the carnal abode of God, anchoring into this creation. God has seared the carnal existence of Israel, the Son, into his eternal being. In line with this, the Torah is regarded as the Word of God, which still stands in full force and with the full divine authority upon Israel and its biological descendants: it is not a universal law given to the all the nations but only to the chosen people, the familial descendants of Abraham, Isaac, and Jacob.

Considering the biblical legitimacy of Wyschogrod's theology of Judaism, Jenson proposes that the church cannot be the body of Christ without her union with the Jewish community. The two covenant communities will be the one body of Christ in the final eschaton (Eph 2:14). In Jenson's view, the Jews and the gentile Christians are paired phenomena. Both communities came into being as joint heirs of the tradition of the old canonical Israel. Neither community can lay exclusive claim to the legacy of the old Israel. The familial descendants of Israel have been preserved in the eternal and irrevocable covenant, as the carnal dwelling of God of Israel; the gentile church as well functions as the carnal abode of God, since it is called the body of Christ.

Chapter 5. Jenson also works out a hermeneutical ontology, centering upon the motif of the Word, that is, Jesus Christ. The two covenant communities are considered in parallel also as hermeneutical phenomena. The Tanakh/the Old Testament is the common inheritance to both communities, while they interpret it differently, based on their subsequent canon, the *Mishina* and the New Testament. On the one hand, the Christian church inherits the *narrative* strand of the old canonical Israel (or the Old Testament), witnessing the correlation between the narrative of old Israel and the life of Jesus. On the other hand, the Jewish community interprets the Tanakh as the Law, which is still binding on the Jewish covenantal existence. Here Jenson's Torah-christology implies that the Jew's No to Jesus Christ cannot invalidate *Jesus*'s relationship with them. For Jesus is the Torah. As long as the Jews hold on to the observance of the Torah, they cannot avoid relating to Jesus. Also, it is envisaged that these two will become the one Torah hermeneutical community in the End.

Chapter 6. Jenson's eschatological ontology which centers upon the work of the Holy Spirit, is also operative in his non-supersessionism: the eschatological union between the two communities cannot be achieved without the Spirit. The Spirit blows for the future and for oneness. The Spirit realizes the oneness of the Father and the Son in his *opera ad intra*, and the oneness between the Word of God and the words of (the old canonical) Israel in their prophecy in his *opera ad extra*. Also the Spirit will enable the union between the Jews and the gentile nations as he achieves the union of the people of God (the church and the Jews together) with their head, Jesus Christ.

Furthermore, the Spirit as the power of the eschaton breaks into this age and so is recursively active. As the Spirit breaks into this present age, the *eschatos*—the risen Jesus—comes to us in that Breath. Jesus Christ is now risen and so the coming one. He is "apocalypsed" as the eschatological figure. This eschatological inbreaking presence of Jesus is not hampered by temporal restriction, and this *eschatos* could be present to the old Israel, as the risen one. This is the logic underlying Jenson's account of the preexistence of the Son in which the preexistence of the Son *is* his post-existence. Also, this is the ontological rationale, on Jenson's account, of the *bodily* descriptions of the theophany, as often recorded in Israel's Bible. This incursive presence of the Son into this present and the old ages is made possible by the eschatological power of the Spirit. Finally, the eschatological power of the resurrected one and of the Spirit tenaciously adhere to the Jewish hope for the restoration and the resurrection of Israel, and so they are in deep rapport with each other.

Along the way, I have registered objections briefly to some misreadings of Jenson and attempted a fairer evaluation. Jenson's reading of Barth is not erroneous, but closely aligned with McCormack's legitimate interpretation of Barth (chapter 1). Jenson's conception of the church is not an untethered speculation; his tacit rationale is christocentric, explicating the notion of the church as the body of Christ (chapter 2). Jenson does not reject the preexistence of the individual and eternal Son prior to his birth to Mary, even though he blatantly rejects the concept of the pretemporal existence of the Son—here the pretemporal existence and the preexistence of the Son (before his birth in history) must be distinguished. Having said that, I would raise concern with critics about Jenson's rejection of the *pre-temporal* existence of the Son, but affirm with Jenson that the risen one is unimpeded by temporal restriction. Jenson's conception of the ontological priority of the future over the past and the present does not necessarily collide with affirmation of the pretemporal existence of the Son (chapter 6). Further, I believe I have explored relatively less traveled territory in Jenson's theology: his engagement with a Jewish theologian, Wyschogrod (chapters 3 and 4), and his development of his hermeneutical ontology in German soil—Fuchs, Ebeling, and von Rad (chapter 5).

"The End is music."[119] The Word is not merely a word but a lyric to rise on melody. And "the melody is fugued."[120] For "God is a great fugue."[121] The divine triune fugue "continually transcends itself with endless variations and developments."[122] Also all creation joins and is embraced into the capacious divine polyphony. "There is nothing so capacious as a fugue."[123] The whole universe will be totally reconfigured

---

119. Ibid., 369.
120. *ST*, 1:236.
121. Ibid.
122. Rook, *Rhyming Hope and History*, 194–95.
123. Ibid.

into perfect and orchestric harmony with the divine musical reality, in endless expository variations of the major theme, Jesus Christ.

In the whole web of multi-reciprocities, electrons, photons, quarks, higgs bosons, and so on will leap and dance to the pulse and rhythm of the Word and the Breath of God. The eschatological harmonious and inter-relational moves are nothing but pure music. All things will burst into song and encompassed by the divine fugal reality. Now everything is music within Music. In that new reality, as "Isaac A. Dorner wrote, 'Matter will have exchanged its darkness, hardness, heaviness, immobility and impenetrableness for clearness, radiance, elasticity and transparency.'"[124] And the speed of the light of this age will be relativized by God's eschatological effulgence. In the eschatological universe, as "Jonathan Edwards supposed[,] the saints 'will be able to see from one side of the universe to the other,' since they will not see 'by such slow rays of light that are several years traveling.'"[125] The thematic melody of the redeemed and new musical cosmos will be the risen Lord and his risen community—the Jews and the gentiles together—the risen *total Christus*.

In this present age, the fugal power from the eschaton comes through the gate of heaven/the eschaton and captures the singing of his community, as Israel sang the songs of Psalms in one voice with the Christ. In this age, the Jews and the church together are the gates of the heaven to the world. When they sing, their singing will break the spells of the powers and authorities of the dark world and lead us into the eschatological ecstasy and to the union with the risen Lord. At last, the two covenant communities will play a great contrapuntal, encompassed by and in the triune fugue, together of the songs of Moses and of the Lamb (Rev 15:3–4).

---

124. Dorner, *A System of Christian Doctrine*, 429, quoted in *ST*, 2:351.
125. Edwards, *Miscellanies*, quoted in ibid.

Bibliography

Ayres, Lewis. *Augustine and the Trinity*. Cambridge: Cambridge University Press, 2010.
———. "Remember That You Are Catholic." *Journal of Early Christian Studies* 8 (2000) 39–82.
Barth, Karl. *Church Dogmatics* I/1. Translated by G. W. Bromiley and T. F. Torrance. Edinburgh: T. & T. Clark, 1936.
———. *Church Dogmatics* I/2. Translated by G. W. Bromiley and T. F. Torrance. Edinburgh: T. & T. Clark, 1956.
———. *Church Dogmatics* II/1. Translated by G. W. Bromiley and T. F. Torrance. Edinburgh: T. & T. Clark, 1957.
———. *Church Dogmatics* II/2. Translated by G. W. Bromiley and T. F. Torrance. Edinburgh: T. & T. Clark, 1957.
———. *Church Dogmatics* III/2. Translated by G. W. Bromiley and T. F. Torrance. Edinburgh: T. & T. Clark, 1960.
———. *Church Dogmatics* IV/1. Translated by G. W. Bromiley and T. F. Torrance. Edinburgh: T. & T. Clark, 1956.
Bockmuehl, Markus N. A. *The Remembered Peter in Ancient Reception and Modern Debate*. Tübingen: Mohr Siebeck, 2010.
Braaten, Carl E. "Eschatology and Mission in the Theology of Robert Jenson." In *Trinity, Time, and Church: A Response to the Theology of Robert W. Jenson*, edited by Colin E. Gunton, 298–311. Grand Rapids: Eerdmans, 2000.
Braaten, Carl E., and Robert W. Jenson. "Introduction: Gospel, Church, and Scripture." In *Reclaiming the Bible for the Church*, edited by Carl E. Braaten and Robert Jenson, ix–xii. Grand Rapids: Eerdmans, 1995.
———. *A Map of Twentieth-century Theology: Readings from Karl Barth to Radical Pluralism*. Minneapolis: Fortress, 1995.
Bultmann, Rudolf. "Die Bedeutung des Alten Testaments für den christlichen Glauben." In *Glauben und Verstehen*, vol. 1, 313–36. Tübingen: Mohr, 1933.
———. *Geschichte und Eschatologie*. Tübingen: Mohr, 1958.
———. *History and Eschatology*. Edinburgh: Edinburgh University Press, 1955.
———. *Jesus Christ and Mythology*. New York: Scribner, 1958.
———. *New Testament and Mythology and Other Basic Writings*. Translated and edited by Schubert M. Ogden. Philadelphia: Fortress, 1984.

Burgess, Andrew. "A Community of Love? Jesus as the Body of God and Robert Jenson's Trinitarian Thought." *International Journal of Systematic Theology* 6 (2004) 289–300.

Calvin, John. *Institutes of the Christian Religion*. Translated by John T. McNeill. Philadelphia: Westminster, 1960.

Carson, D. A., Peter T. O'Brien, and Mark A. Seifrid. *Justification and Variegated Nomism*. Grand Rapids: Baker Academic, 2001.

Cary, Jeffrey W. *Free Churches and the Body of Christ: Authority, Unity, and Truthfulness*. Eugene, OR: Cascade, 2012.

Chan, M. J. " Reflecting on Roots: Robert Jenson's Theology of Judaism in a Pentecostal Key." *Journal of Pentecostal Theology* 20 (2011) 27–37.

Congdon, David W. *The Mission of Demythologizing Rudolf Bultmann's Dialectical Theology*. Minneapolis: Fortress, 2015.

Cooper, Jordan, and Peter J. Leithart. *The Righteousness of One: An Evaluation of Early Patristic Soteriology in Light of the New Perspective on Paul*. Eugene, OR: Wipf & Stock, 2013.

Couenhoven, Jesse. "Karl Barth's Conception(s) of Human and Divine Freedom(s)." In *Commanding Grace: Studies in Barth's Ethics*, edited by Daniel Migliore, 239–55. Grand Rapids: Eerdmans, 2010.

Crisp, Oliver. *God Incarnate: Explorations in Christology*. London: T. & T. Clark, 2009.

———. "Robert Jenson on the Pre-Existence of Christ." *Modern Theology* 23 (2007). 27–45.

Denker, Alfred. *Historical Dictionary of Heidegger's Philosophy*. Lanham, MD: Scarecrow, 2000.

East, Brad. Review of Scott Swain's *The God of the Gospel: Robert Jenson's Trinitarian Theology*. *Pro Ecclesia*, 23 (2014) 471–74.

Ebeling, Gehard. *The Nature of Faith*. Philadelphia: Muhlenberg, 1962.

———. *The Problem of Historicity in the Church and Its Proclamation*. Philadelphia: Fortress, 1967.

———. *Theology and Proclamation: A Discussion with Rudolf Bultmann*. London: Collins, 1966.

———. *Das Wesen des christlichen Glaubens*. Tübingen: Mohr, 1959.

———. "Word of God and Hermeneutics." In *Word and Faith*, edited by Gerhard Ebeling, 78–110. Philadelphia: Fortress, 1963.

Fuchs, Ernst. *Hermeneutik*. Tübingen: Mohr, 1970.

———. "Proclamation and Speech-Event." *Theology Today* 19 (1962) 341–54.

———. "Was wird in der Exegese des Neuen Testaments interpretiert?" In *Zur Frage nach dem historischen Jesus. Gesammelte Aufsatze* 2, 281–303. Tübingen: Mohr (Siebeck), 1960.

Gathercole, Simon. "Pre-existence and the Freedom of the Son in Creation and Redemption: An Exposition in Dialogue with Robert Jenson." *International Journal of Systematic Theology* 7 (2005) 38–51.

Gerrish, B. A. "'To the Unknown God': Luther and Calvin on the Hiddenness of God." *The Journal of Religion* 53 (1973) 263–92.

Gese, Hartmut. "Tradition and Biblical Theology." In *Tradition and Theology in the Old Testament*, edited by D. A. Knight, 301–26. Philadelphia: Fortress, 1977.

Bibliography

Goldman, David P. "Kosher by Design: How Michael Wyschogrod Taught Me to Eat Like a Jew." http://www.tabletmag.com/jewish-life-and-religion/44901/kosher-by-design#comments.

Guinon, Charles B. "The History of Being." In *A Companion to Heidegger*, edited by Hubert L. Dreyfus and Mark A. Wrathall, 392–406. Malden, MA: Blackwell, 2005.

———. "Introduction." In *The Cambridge Companion to Heidegger*, edited by Charles B. Guignon, 1–41. New York: Cambridge University Press, 1993.

Gunton, Colin E. *Father, Son, and Holy Spirit: Essays Toward a Fully Trinitarian Theology*. London: T. & T. Clark, 2003.

———. *The One, the Three and the Many: God, Creation, and the Culture of Modernity*. Cambridge: Cambridge University Press, 1993.

Harnack, Adolf von. *Marcion, das Evangelium vom fremden Gott: eine Monographie zur Geschichte der Grundlegung der katholischen Kirche*. Darmstadt: Wissenschaftliche Buchgesellschaft, 1960.

Hart, David Bentley. *The Beauty of the Infinite: The Aesthetics of Christian Truth*. Grand Rapids: Eerdmans, 2003.

Heidegger, Martin. *Contributions to Philosophy: From Enowning*. Bloomington, IN: Indiana University Press, 1999.

———. *The End of Philosophy*. New York: Harper & Row, 1973.

———. *On the Way to Language*. New York: Harper & Row, 1971.

———. *Supplements from the Earliest Essays to Being and Time and Beyond*. Edited by John van Buren. Albany, NY: State University of New York Press, 2002.

Held, Shai. "The Promise and Peril of Jewish Barthianism: The Theology of Michael Wyschogrod." *Modern Judaism* 25 (2005) 316–26.

Hunsinger, George. *How to Read Karl Barth: The Shape of His Theology*. New York: Oxford University Press, 1993.

———. *Reading Barth with Charity: A Hermeneutical Proposal*. Grand Rapids: Baker Academic, 2015.

———. "Robert Jenson's Systematic Theology: A Review Essay." *Scottish Journal of Theology* 55 (2002) 161–200.

Jenson, Robert W. *Alpha and Omega: A Study in the Theology of Karl Barth*. New York: Nelson, 1963.

———. "An Attempt to Think about Mary." *dialog* 31 (1992) 259–64.

———. "The Bible and the Trinity." *Pro Ecclesia* 11 (2002) 329–39.

———. "The Body of God's Presence: A Trinitarian Theory." In *Creation, Christ and Culture: Festschrift for T. F. Torrance*, edited by R. W. A. McKinney, 82–91. Edinburgh: T. & T. Clark, 1976.

———. "Can We Have a Story?" *First Things* 101 (2000) 16–17.

———. *Canon and Creed*. Interpretation. Louisville: Westminster/John Knox, 2010.

———. *Christian Dogmatics* vol. 1. Edited by Carl E. Braaten and Robert W. Jenson. Philadelphia: Fortress, 1984.

———. *Christian Dogmatics* vol. 2. Edited by Carl E. Braaten and Robert W. Jenson. Philadelphia: Fortress, 1984.

———. "Christ in the Trinity: Communicatio Idiomatum." In *The Person of Christ*, edited by Stephen R. Holmes and Murray A. Rae, 61–69. London: T. & T. Clark, 2005.

———. "The Church and the Sacraments." In *The Cambridge Companion to Christian Doctrine*, edited by Colin E. Gunton, 207–25. Cambridge: Cambridge University Press, 1997.

———. "A Decision Tree of Colin Gunton's Thinking." In *The Theology of Colin Gunton*, edited by Lincoln Harvey, 8–16. London: T. & T. Clark, 2010.

———. *Ezekiel*. Brazos Theological Commentary on the Bible. Grand Rapids: Brazos, 2009.

———. *God after God: The God of the Past and the God of the Future, Seen in the Work of Karl Barth*. New York: Bobbs-Merrill, 1969.

———. "God's Time, Our Time: An Interview with Robert W. Jenson." *Christian Century* 123 (2006) 31–35.

———. "Hermeneutics and the Life of the Church." In *Reclaiming the Bible for the Church*, edited by Robert W. Jenson and Carl E. Braaten, 89–106. Grand Rapids: Eerdmans, 1995.

———. "How the World Lost Its Story." *First Things* 36 (1993) 19–24.

———. "It's the Culture." *First Things* 243 (2014) 33–36.

———. "Joining the Eternal Conversation: John's Prologue and the Language of Worship." *Touchstone* 14 (2001) 32–37.

———. "Karl Barth on the Being of God." In *Thomas Aquinas and Karl Barth: An Unofficial Catholic-Protestant Dialogue*, edited by Bruce L. McCormack, 43–51. Grand Rapids: Eerdmans, 2013.

———. *The Knowledge of Things Hoped For: The Sense of Theological Discourse*. New York: Oxford University Press, 1969.

———. "Die Kontinuitaet von Alten and Neuem Testament als Problem für Kirche und Theologie Heute." In *Hoffnung ohne Illusion*, edited by Helmutt Zeddies, 88–103. Berlin: Evangelische Verlangsanstalt Berlin, 1970.

———. *On the Inspiration of Scripture*. Delhi: ALPB, 2012.

———. *On Thinking the Human: Resolutions of Difficult Notions*. Grand Rapids: Eerdmans, 2003.

———. "On 'The Philosophy that Attends to Scripture: Commentary on 'Karl Barth on Theology and Philosophy.'" https://syndicatetheology.com/commentary/robert-w-jenson/.

———. "Response to Watson and Hunsinger." *Scottish Journal of Theology* 55 (2002) 225–32.

———. "Second Thoughts about Theologies of Hope." *Evangelical Quarterly* 72 (2000) 335–46.

———. "Scripture's Authority in the Church." In *The Art of Reading Scripture*, edited by Ellen F. Davis and Richard B. Hays, 27–37. Grand Rapids: Eerdmans, 2003.

———. *Story and Promise: A Brief Theology of the Gospel about Jesus*. Philadelphia: Fortress, 1973.

———. *Systematic Theology*, vol. 1: The Triune God. Oxford: Oxford University Press, 1997.

———. *Systematic Theology*, vol. 2: The Works of God. Oxford: Oxford University Press, 1999.

———. *Theology as Revisionary Metaphysics: Essays on God and Creation*. Eugene, OR: Cascade, 2014.

———. "A Theological Autobiography, to Date." *dialog* 46 (2007) 46–54.

———. *A Theology in Outline: Can These Bones Live?* New York: Oxford University Press, 2016.

———. "Theosis." *dialog* 32 (1993) 108–12.

———. "The Trinity in Ezekiel." *Lutheran Forum* 44 (2010) 8–10.

———. "Toward a Christian Theology of Judaism." In *Jews and Christians: People of God*, edited by Carl E. Braaten and Robert W. Jenson, 1–13. Grand Rapids: Eerdmans, 2003.

———. "Toward a Doctrine of Israel." *CTI Reflection* 3 (2000) 2–21.

———. *Triune Identity*. Philadelphia: Fortress, 1982.

———. *Unbaptized God: The Basic Flaw in Ecumenical Theology*. Minneapolis: Fortress, 1992.

———. *Visible Words: The Interpretation and Practice of Christian Sacraments*. Philadelphia: Fortress, 1978.

———. "What Kind of God Can Make a Covenant?" In *Covenant and Hope: Christian and Jewish Reflections: Essays in Constructive Theology from the Institute for Theological Inquiry*, edited by Robert W. Jenson and Eugene Korn, 3–18. Grand Rapids: Eerdmans, 2012.

Jenson, Robert W., and Eric Walter Gritsch. *Lutheranism: The Theological Movement and Its Confessional Writings*. Philadelphia: Fortress, 1976.

Johnson, Luke Timothy. *The Writings of the New Testament: An Interpretation*. Philadelphia: Fortress, 1986.

Kim, Seyoon. *Paul and the New Perspective: Second Thoughts on the Origin of Paul's Gospel*. Grand Rapids: Eerdmans, 2001.

Lakkis, Stephen. *A New Hope Wolfhart Pannenberg and the Natural Sciences on Time*. Newcastle upon Tyne, UK: Cambridge Scholars, 2014.

Levenson, Jon D. *The Hebrew Bible, the Old Testament, and Historical Criticism: Jews and Christians in Biblical Studies*. Louisville, KY: Westminster/John Knox, 1993.

———. *Resurrection and the Restoration of Israel: The Ultimate Victory of the God of Life*. New Haven: Yale University Press, 2006.

Levering, Matthew. *Jewish-Christian Dialogue and the Life of Wisdom: Engagements with the Theology of David Novak*. New York: Continuum, 2010.

———. *Scripture and Metaphysics: Aquinas and the Renewal of Trinitarian Theology*. Malden, MA: Blackwell, 2004.

Luther, Martin. *Sermons of Martin Luther*. Edited by John Nicholas Lenker. Grand Rapids: Baker, 1983.

Maimonides, Moses. *The Code of Maimonides*. Translated by Abraham M. Hershman. New Haven: Yale University Press, 1949.

Mannermaa, Toumo. "Why Is Luther So Fascinating? Modern Finnish Luther Research." In *Union with Christ: The New Finish Interpretation of Luther*, edited by Carl E. Braaten and Robert W. Jenson, 1–20. Grand Rapids: Eerdmans, 1998.

McCall, Thomas H. *Which Trinity? Whose Monotheism? Philosophical and Systematic Theologians on the Metaphysics of Trinitarian Theology*. Grand Rapids: Eerdmans, 2010.

McCormack, Bruce L. "Grace and Being: The Role of God's Gracious Election in Karl Barth's Theological Ontology." In *The Cambridge Companion to Karl Barth*, edited by John Webster, 183–200. Cambridge: Cambridge University Press, 2000.

Mowinckel, Sigmund. *He That Cometh*. Oxford: Blackwell, 1959.

Mulhall, Stephen. *The Routledge Guidebook to Heidegger's Being and Time.* London: Routledge, 2013.
Murphy, Francesca A. *God is Not a Story: Realism Revisited.* Oxford: Oxford University Press, 2007.
Neusner, Jacob. *A Rabbi Talks with Jesus.* Montreal: McGill-Queen's University Press, 2000.
———. *Rabbinic Judaism: Structure and System.* Minneapolis: Fortress, 1995.
Nicol, Andrew. "The God of Israel in Robert W. Jenson's Theology." PhD thesis, University of Otago, 2011.
Ochs, Peter. *Another Reformation: Postliberal Christianity and the Jews.* Grand Rapids: Baker Academic, 2011.
———."Christian Postliberalism and the Jews." In *Another Reformation: Postliberal Christianity and the Jews*, edited by Peter Ochs, 257–68. Grand Rapids: Baker, 2011.
———. "Judaism and Christian Theology." *The Modern Theologians*, 3rd ed., edited by David Ford and Rachel Muers, 645–62. Oxford: Blackwell, 2005.
———. "Response: Reflections on Binarism," *Modern Theology* 24 (2008) 487–97.
———. "Trinity and Judaism." *Concilium* 2003/4 II.3, "Experiences and Results of Interreligious Dialogue: The Abrahamic Traditions." Translation of: "Dreifaltigkeit und Judentum." *Concilium* 39.4 (Oct 2003) *Von anderen Religionen Lernen.* 433–41.
Pannenberg, Wolfhart. *Systematic Theology*, Vol. 1. London: T. & T. Clark, 2004.
Paulson, Steven D. *Lutheran Theology.* London: T. & T. Clark, 2011.
Plato. *Timaeus.* Translated by R. D. Archer-Hind. New York: Arno, 1973.
Pope Benedict XVI. *The Essential Pope Benedict XVI: His Central Writings and Speeches.* Edited by John F. Thornton, and Susan B. Varenne. New York: Harper, 2007.
———. *Jesus of Nazareth.* New York: Doubleday, 2007.
Powell, Samuel M. *The Trinity in German Thought.* Cambridge: Cambridge University Press, 2001.
Price, Joann F. *Pope Benedict XVI: A Biography.* Santa Barbara, CA: Greenwood, 2013.
Rahner, Karl. "Theos in the New Testament." In *Theological Investigations*, vol. 1. translated by Cornelius Ernst, 79–148. Baltimore: Helicon, 1961.
Ratzinger, Joseph. *Church, Ecumenism, and Politics: New Essays in Ecclesiology.* New York: Crossroad, 1988.
Rook, Russell. *Rhyming Hope and History: Theology and Culture in the Work of Robert Jenson.* Eugene, OR: Pickwick, 2012.
Rottenberg, Isaac C. "'Comparative Theology' vs. 'Reactive Theology.'" *Pro Ecclesia* 3 (1994) 411–18.
Schleiermacher, Friedrich. *The Christian Faith.* Translated by H. R. Mackintosh, and James S. Stewart. Edinburgh: T. & T. Clark, 1999.
Shults, F. LeRon. *Reforming the Doctrine of God.* Grand Rapids: Eerdmans, 2005.
Soloveichik, Meir Y. "God's First Love: The Theology of Michael Wyschogrod." http://www.firstthings.com/article/2009/11/gods-first-love-the-theology-of-michael-wyschogrod.
Soulen, R. Kendall. "The Achievement of Michael Wyschogrod." *Modern Theology* 22 (2006) 677–85.

———. "A Biographical Sketch of Michael Wyschogrod." In *Abraham's Promise: Judaism and Jewish-Christian Relation*, edited by R. Kendall Soulen, xi–xii. Grand Rapids: Eerdmans, 2004.

———. *The Divine Name(S) and the Holy Trinity*. Louisville, KY: Westminster/John Knox, 2011.

Swain, Scott R. *The God of the Gospel: Robert Jenson's Trinitarian Theology*. Downers Grove, IL: IVP, 2013.

Vanhoozer, Kevin J. *First Theology: God, Scripture & Hermeneutics*. Downers Grove, IL: IVP, 2002.

Von Rad, Gerhard. *Old Testament Theology*, Vol. 1. Translated by D. M. G. Stalker. London: SCM, 1975.

———. *Old Testament Theology*, Vol. 2 Edinburgh: Oliver & Boyd, 1965.

———. "The Form-Critical Problem of Hexateuch." In *The Problem of the Hexateuch and Other Essays*, 1–78. New York: McGraw-Hill, 1966.

———. *Weisheit in Israel*. Neukirchen-Vluyn: Neukirchener Verlag, 1985.

Webster, John. "'In the Society of God': Some Principles of Ecclesiology." In *Perspectives on Ecclesiology and Ethnography*, edited by Pete Ward, 200–222. Grand Rapids: Eerdmans, 2011.

———. "Systematic Theology after Barth." In *The Modern Theologians: An Introduction to Christian Theology Since 1918*, edited by David Ford and Rachel Muers, 249–64. Malden, MA: Blackwell, 2005.

Wellhausen, Julius. *Prolegomena to the history of Ancient Israel*. New York: Meridian, 1957.

Westerholm, Stephen. *Perspectives Old and New on Paul: The "Lutheran" Paul and His Critics*. Grand Rapids: Eerdmans, 2004.

Wood, Susan. "Robert Jenson's Ecclesiology from a Roman Catholic Perspective." In *Trinity, Time, and Church: A Response to the Theology of Robert W. Jenson*, edited by Colin E. Gunton, 178–87. Grand Rapids: Eerdmans, 2000.

Wright, N. T. *The Climax of the Covenant: Christ and the Law in Pauline Theology*. Minneapolis: Fortress, 1992.

Wright, Stephen. *Dogmatic Aesthetics: A Theology of Beauty in Dialogue with Robert W. Jenson*. Minneapolis: Fortress, 2014.

Wyschogrod, Michael. *The Body of Faith: Judaism as Corporeal Election*. New York: Seabury, 1983.

———. "Christianity and Mosaic Law." *Pro Ecclesia* 2 (1993) 451–59.

———. "Divine Election and Commandments." In *Abraham's Promise: Judaism and Jewish-Christian Relation*, edited by R. Kendall Soulen, 25–28. Grand Rapids: Eerdmans, 2004.

———. "The Impact of the Dialogue with Christianity and My Self-understanding as a Jew." In *Abraham's Promise: Judaism and Jewish-Christian Relation*, edited by R. Kendall Soulen, 225–36. Grand Rapids: Eerdmans, 2004.

———. "Incarnation." *Pro Ecclesia* 2 (1993) 208–15.

———. "Incarnation and God's Indwelling in Israel." In *Abraham's Promise: Judaism and Jewish-Christian Relation*, edited by R. Kendall Soulen, 165–78. Grand Rapids: Eerdmans, 2004.

———. "Israel, Church, and Election." In *Abraham's Promise: Judaism and Jewish-Christian Relation*, edited by R. Kendall Soulen, 179–87. Grand Rapids: Eerdmans, 2004.

———. "A Jewish Perspective on Incarnation." *Modern Theology* 12 (1996) 195–209.

———. "A Jewish Perspective on Karl Barth." In *How Karl Barth Changed My Mind*, edited by Donald McKim, 156–61. Grand Rapids: Eerdmans, 1986.

———. "A Jewish View of Christianity." In *Abraham's Promise: Judaism and Jewish-Christian Relation*, edited by R. Kendall Soulen, 149–64. Grand Rapids: Eerdmans, 2004.

———. "Paul, Jews, and Gentiles." In *Abraham's Promise: Judaism and Jewish-Christian Relation*, edited by R. Kendall Soulen, 188–201. Grand Rapids: Eerdmans, 2004.

———. "Resurrection." *Pro Ecclesia* 1 (1992) 104–12.

———. "Theology of Jewish Unity." In *Abraham's Promise: Judaism and Jewish-Christian Relation*, edited by R. Kendall Soulen, 43–52. Grand Rapids: Eerdmans, 2004.

———. "Why Was and Is the Theology of Karl Barth of Interest to a Jewish Theologian?" In *Abraham's Promise: Judaism and Jewish-Christian Relation*, edited by R. Kendall Soulen, 211–24. Grand Rapids: Eerdmans, 2004.

Yeago, David S. "The Presence of Mary in the Mystery of the Church." In *Mary, Mother of God*, edited by Carl E. Braaten and Robert W. Jenson, 58–79. Grand Rapids: Eerdmans, 2004.

Author Index

Aquinas, Thomas, 7–8, 80–82
Augustine (Saint), 52n79, 53–54, 158
Ayres, Lewis, 52n79, 54n86

Barth, Karl. *See* Barth, Karl, in subject index
Benedict XVI (Pope), 81n111, 95–99
Braaten, Carl, 126
Brenz, Johannes, 44
Brown, Raymond, 83–84
Bultmann, Rudolf, 11, 120–21, 135, 148–49, 171
Burgess, Andrew, 42n35

Calvin, John, 15–16, 27
Cary, Jeffrey, 4–5
Crisp, Oliver, 166–67

East, Brad, 2
Ebeling, Gerhard, 11, 121, 123–24

Fuchs, Ernst, 11, 121, 124–25, 128–30

Gadamer, Hans-Georg, 122
Gathercole, Simon, 166–68
Gese, Hartmut, 134

Harnack, Adolf von, 141–42
Hart, David, 3
Hegel, G. F. W., 3, 54–57, 154–55, 166
Heidegger, Martin, 126–28
Hiyya bar Abin (Rabbi), 65
Hunsinger, George, 2–3, 18n29, 24, 101n64, 166–68

Jenson, Robert. *See* Jenson, Robert, in subject index
Johnson, Luke Timothy, 116n144

Kant, Immanuel, 75–76

Levenson, Jon, 140, 170
Levering, Matthew, 7–8
Lindbeck, George, 6
Loisy, Alfred, 102–3
Lustiger (Cardinal), 86
Luther, Martin, 14, 36n12, 37–38, 53n80, 129n58

Maimonides, 63–67, 87, 90–93, 104–5
Marquardt, Friedrich, 6
Marshall, Bruce, 6–7
Mayr, Franz, 128
McCormack, Bruce L., 19n40, 20n45, 176
Moltmann, Jürgen, 4
Murphy, Francesca, 3

Nahman bar Isaac (Rabbi), 65
Neusner, Jacob, 104, 114–16
Nicol, Andrew, 8–9
Novak, David, 7–8, 59, 112–13

Ochs, Peter, 5–6, 8, 59, 66n36

Pannenberg, Wolfhart, 4, 11, 149–53, 171
Plato, 24–26
Preus, Herman, 44

Rahner, Karl, 101n64
Rook, Russell, 3, 5

Schleiermacher, Friedrich, 141
Shults, F. LeRon, 4
Soloveitchik, Joseph B. (Rabbi), 61
Soulen, R. Kendall, 6–7
Swain, Scott, 2

Torrance, Alan, 18n29

von der Osten Sacken, Peter, 6
von Rad, Gerhard, 11, 120, 131–39, 156–57, 164

Webster, John, 35n7
Wellhausen, Julius, 140–41
Wood, Susan, 50
Wright, N. T., 83–84
Wright, Stephen, 3, 5
Wyschogrod, Michael. *See* Wyschogrod, Michael, in subject index

Subject Index

Abrahamic covenant
    deity of Jesus and, 105–11
    gentile nations and Israel and, 160–61
    Jewish rediscovery of Christianity and, 84–86
    Torah and, 111–18
actualistic ontology, 18–19, 173–74
actualistic theology, doctrine of election and, 31–32
Alpha and Omega (Barth), 13
analogy, Barth's discussion of, 148
Anfechtung, in double decree doctrine, 14–15, 26–27
antinomianism in Christian hermeneutics
    eschatological future and, 152–53
    Jenson's rejection of, 140–44
anti-Semitism, antinomianism and, 141–44
apocalyptic/futuristic theology, Jenson's trinitarianism as, 3
autonomous reason, Torah and, 81–82
availability, of body of God, 38–40

Babylonian Talmud, Tractate Berakhot, 71–72
Barth, Karl
    Augustinian-Hegelian interpretations of, 55–57
    eschato-pneumatological ontology and, 147–48, 171
    eternal double election on horizon of time, 26–27
    Jenson's reading of, 14–16, 20–26, 176
    Logos *asarkos*, 17–18
    resurrection and eternal election/generation, 28–30
    theology of, 2, 5–6, 10–11, 13
    on *urgeschichte* and human history, 22–24
    Wyschogrod's discussion of, 60–61, 71–72, 80n105
beauty, theology of, 5
Being and Time (Heidegger), 126–28
Bible, tradition history and formation of, 133–34
body ontology
    Biblical bodily description of God and, 63–67
    Christological body, 35–40, 99–100
    Ecclesial body, 48–53
    Eucharistic body and, 40–48
    God as bodily being, 34–35
    God in Jewish flesh and, 67–72
    hermeneutical ontology and, 143–44
    Jenson's trinitarianism and, 57–58, 174
    Jewish participation in, 91–93
    post-supersessionistic theology and, 33–58
    trinitarian communion and, 53–57
"The Body of God's Presence" (Jenson), 35
Bultmann School, 11, 120
    Heidegger and, 126–28
    Jenson's divergence from, 128–31

Subject Index

Bultmann School *(cont.)*
 Jenson's hermeneutical ontology and, 120–31, 135
 linguistic turn in, 121–25

canonical Israel, Jenson's definition of, 93–104
Catholic theology
 Ecclesial body and, 49–53
 Eucharistic body and, 46–48
 Jewish identity and, 81n111
 post-supersessionism and, 7–8
Christian identity, Judaism and, 93–104
Christian theology
 acknowledgment of Judaism in, 1
 deity of Jesus Christ in, 104–11
 Greek philosophy and, 24–27
 Israel in, 89–90
 Jewish identity in relation to, 62–84, 172
 Jewish perspective on, 62, 69–72, 84–86
 Torah in, 80–84, 111–18
 Wyschogrod's engagement with, 61–62
Christological body, 35–40
 criticisms of Jenson's theology concerning, 166–71
 Jewish-Christian relations and, 99–100
 Lutheran theology and, 43–48
 Torah and, 113–18
Christology, resurrection and eternal election/generation and, 28–30
church
 canonical hermeneutic of, God as word-event in, 137
 Christian identity and, 94–104
 as Christological body, 99–100
 as community of the Holy Spirit, 100–102
 as Ecclesial body, 48–53
 incarnational view of, 91–93
 Jewish-Christian relations and, 98–99, 174–75
 paths to the kingdom of God and, 102–4

tradition history of Israel and hermeneutic of, 131–39
Church Dogmatics (Barth), 18–19, 21
communalism, personhood and, 55–57
communicatio idiomatum, Lutheran doctrine of, 52–53, 58, 93n19
communion
 Christ as Ecclesial body and, 51–53
 Spirit of God and, 154–56
confession, von Rad's discussion of, 132–37
conversation, body of God in context of, 38–40
covenantal relations
 deity of Jesus Christ and, 105–11
 between God and Israel, 92–93, 97–99, 103–4, 174
 Torah and, 111–13
Credo in Deuteronomy, von Rad's discussion of, 132
cultic law, Aquinas' definition of, 80–82
culture, theology of, 5

Dasein, Heidegger's concept of, 126–28
deification, Eastern Orthodox concept of, 51–53
 Jenson's adoption of, 91–93
destruction of the Temple, Israel and, 103–4
Deus absconditus
 Barth's concept of, 16–17
 Logos *asarkos* and, 17–18
Deuteronomy, book of, *Credo* in, 132
dilute incarnation of God, Israel as, in Wyschogrod's theology, 59–88, 90–93
divine personhood, 54–57
 Wyschogrod on Israel as, 63–67
The Divine Name(s) and the Holy Trinity (Soulen), 7n38
double decree, doctrine of, 14–15, 26–27
dramatic coherence, Jenson's concept of, 159–61

Ecclesial body, 48–53

Subject Index

ecumenical theology
  Ecclesial body and, 49–53
  Jenson's trinitarianism as, 4–5
election, Barth's doctrine of, 13
  actualistic ontology and, 18–19
  eternal double election and horizon of time, 26–27
  Jenson's interpretation of, 14–15
  Jewish identity and, 72–78
  resurrection and, 28–30
  Wyschogrod on Jewish identity and, 72–78
  Wyschogrod's theology and, 71–72
emanation, Greek doctrine of, 155
Ereiginis, Heidegger's concept of, 127–28
eschatology
  Jewish-Christian relations and, 98–99
  language and reality and, 125
eschato-pneumatological ontology
  Jenson's trinitarianism and, 11–12, 146–72, 175–76
  sources on, 147–53
  Spirit of God as future and, 162–71
eternal election, Jenson's trinitarianism and, 11–12
eternity, Barth's concept of, 24–26
Eucharistic body, 40–48
existentialist philosophy
  of Bultmann, 121–25
  Heidegger and, 126–28
Ezekiel, prophetic vision of, 163–71

fatherhood, Jewish identity and, 76–78
finitum capax infiniti, *theosis* doctrine and, 117–18
freedom, Spirit of God and, 153–56
futurity
  in Bultmann School linguistics, 121–25
  Bultmann's constant futurity concept, 148–49
  Holy Spirit and, 153–71
  in Jenson's theology, 109–11
  Pannenberg's discussion of time and, 151–53

Galatians, Epistle of, 98
Genesis Rabbah, 114
God after God (Barth), 13
The God of Israel and Christian Theology (Soulen), 6–7
"The God of Israel in Robert W. Jenson's Theology" (Nicol), 8–9
gospel, eschatological nature of, 4
Greek philosophy
  Christian theology and, 24–27, 87–88
  doctrine of emanation and, 155
  Jenson's theology and, 137
  Jewish theology and, 70–72, 87–88

Hebrew Bible
  bodily description of God in, 63–67
  incarnation in, 90–93
  Wyschogrod's interpretation of, 63–67, 77–78
Hegelian metaphysics, Jenson's trinitarian theology and, 3–4
hermeneutical ontology
  antinomianism in Christian hermeneutics, 140–44
  gentile nations and Israel and, 160–61
  of Heidegger, 126–28
  Jenson's theology and, 119–45, 175
  Jewish theology and, 11
  tradition history of Israel and, 131–39
  word-event of the Spirit and, 158–61
Hexateuch, 132n68, 133
hidden decree
  doctrine of God and, 16–17
  Reformation doctrine of, 14–16
Holy Spirit
  as divine freedom for the future, 153–71
  in God, 153–56
  Jesus as Word of God and, 158–61
  as power from the future, 161–71
  resurrection and eternal election/generation, 28–30
  resurrection of Israel and, 169–71
horizon of time, eternal double election and, 26–27

human speech, God in, 120, 125

incarnation, doctrine of, 2
    deity of Jesus and, 106–11
    Israel and, 90–93
    Jewish identity and, 62–78
    Torah as Jewish identity and, 79–84
    Word of God and, 162

Israel
    Christianity and, 93–104
    deity of Jesus and restoration of, 105–11
    as dilute-incarnation of God, in Wyschogrod's theology, 59–88, 90–93
    doctrine of election and, 31–32
    gentile nations and, 160–61
    God's covenant with, 11, 67–72
    Holy Spirit and resurrection of, 169–72
    Jenson's on Wyschgorod's view of, 90–93
    Jesus's relation to, 156–61
    observance of Torah in, 79–84
    Pannenberg's discussion of, 149–53
    paths to the Kingdom of God and, 102–4
    as people of God, 95–99
    post-supersessionistic theology and, 5–7, 9–11, 13–32
    "Servant Songs" (Isaiah) of, 108–9
    theology of election for, 72–78
    von Rad's tradition history concept of, 120, 131–39
    Word of God and creation of, 113–18

Jenson, Robert
    on actualistic ontology, 18–19
    antinomianism in Christian hermeneutics rejected by, 140–44
    Barth and, 14–17, 147–48
    body ontology and theology of, 33–58
    Bultmann School and, 120–31, 148–49
    on Christian identity, 93–104
    Christian theology of Judaism of, 95–104
    criticism of Barth on, 20–26
    on deity of Jesus Christ, 104–11
    divergence from Bultmann School by, 128–31
    on Ecclesial body, 49–53
    on eschato-pneumatological ontology, 146–72
    on eternal double election, 26–27
    on Eucharistic body, 40–48
    Heidegger and, 126–28
    hermeneutical ontology of, 119–45
    on Israel, acceptance of Wyschogrod's view of, 90–93
    on Jesus' time, 24–26
    on Logos *asarkos*, 17–18
    Pannenberg and, 149–53
    post-superseccionistic development of, 30–32
    pre-existent *vs.* temporal concepts of Jesus and, 20–22
    response to Wyschogrod by, 89–118
    scholarship on trinitarian theology of, 2–11
    on Spirit of God, 153–56
    on temple of the Holy Spirit, 100–102
    temporal actualistic ontology and, 13–32
    Torah discussed by, 111–18
    on trinitarian communion and body ontology, 53–57
    von Rad's tradition history of Israel and, 131–39
    Wyschogrod's theology of Israel and, 59–88

Jesus Christ
    Christological body and, 37–40
    church as Ecclesial body of, 48–53
    deity of, 104–11, 119
    as Ecclesial body, 49–53
    eternal double election and horizon of time and, 26–27
    Eucharistic body of, 40–48
    gentile nations and Israel and, 160–61
    post-resurrection appearance and ascension of, 162–71

Subject Index

pre-existent *vs.* temporal concepts of, 20–22, 161–71, 176
speech of God and, 125
time of, 24–26
Torah and, 112–18
Jewish-Christian Dialogue and the Life of Wisdom: Engagements with the Theology of David Novak (Levering), 7–8
Jewish theology
  carnal existence in, 67–72
  Catholic theology and, 7–8
  Christianity and identity of, 62–84
  doctrine of election and, 31–32
  hermeneutical ontology and, 119–20
  identity questions in, 72–78
  incarnation of God and identity of, 67–72
  Jenson's trinitarianism and, 10–13
  rediscovery of Christianity in, 84–86
  relation to God in, 90–93
  Shoah and, 8
  Torah in, 74, 78–84, 111–18
  Wyschogrod's theology of Israel and, 59–88
Johannine prologue, Jenson's discussion of, 161–62, 167–71
John, Gospel of, 37n16
  Fuch's exposition of, 124–25
Judaism
  antinomianism and, 141–44
  belief and practice of Torah and, 116–18
  Christian identity and, 93–104
  Christological body and, 99–100
  deity of Jesus Christ and, 104–11
  hermeneutical ontology and, 119–20
  incarnation of God and, 67–72
  Jenson's Christian theology of, 95–104, 119
  observance of Torah in, 78–84
  temple of the Holy Spirit and, 100–102
  Wyschogrod's formulation of, 61–62, 117–18

kingdom of God, Jewish and Christian paths to, 102–4

language
  in Bultmann School theology, 121–25
  Heidegger on, 126–28
  reality in, 122
linguistics, in Bultmann School, 121–25
Logos asarkos
  Barth's rejection of, 17–18
  Christological body and, 37–40, 167–69
  eternity and, 26
  Word of God and, 162
Logos incarnandus, 162, 167–69
Lutheran theology
  communicatio idiomatum in, 52–53, 93n19
  Eucharistic body in, 43–48
  international ecclesiology and, 91–93
  Jenson's interpretations of, 10, 117–18

Maimon, Moshesh ben. *See* Maimonides
Marcionism, 141–44
Mekhilta Attributed to Rabbi Ishmael Bahodesh 8, 116
Messiah, Judaism and role of, 103–5
Mishinah, 94, 175
missional doctrines, Jewish relations with Christianity and, 85–86
moral law, Aquinas' definition of, 80–82
Mosaic law, 82–84, 111–13
Moses at Sinai, 114–18
mutual objectification
  Christ as Ecclesial body and, 50–53
  Spirit of God and, 155–56

New Perspective
  parallelism of Torah with, 113–18
  Pauline theology and, 83–84
New Testament
  Christian and Jewish identification with, 94
  community of the Holy Spirit and, 101–2

New Testament *(cont.)*
  Torah and, 62, 175
  tradition history of Israel in, 138–39
  Wyschogrod's discussion of, 77–78, 82–84, 87–88
Nicene Creed, 101
Noachide law, 79–80

objectivity, God as bodily being and, 37–40
Old Testament
  Christian and Jewish identification with, 94
  deity of Jesus Christ and, 107–11
  depictions of God in, 77–78
  Jesus's relation to Israel of, 156–61
  parallelism of Torah with, 113–18, 175
  Shekinah phenomena in, 109–11
  Spirit of God in, 163–71
  tradition history of Israel and, 132–39, 141–44
ontology. *See also* eschato-pneumatological ontology; hermeneutical ontology
  body ontology, post-supersessionistic theology and, 33–58
  in Bultmann's existentialist philosophy, 121–25
  deity of Jesus and, 108–11
  Heidegger and, 126–28
  Jenson's Jewish theology and, 117–18
  Jenson's trinitarian theology and, 1, 4
  temporal actualistic ontology, 13–32
Orthodox Judaism, Jewish identity and, 75–78

parousia, Barth's discussion of, 147–48
particularity, universality and, 150n15
patristic research, trinitarian theology and, 52n79
Pauline theology
  antinomianism and, 141–44
  Jews and Christians in, 97–99
  Spirit of God in, 164–71
  Torah and, 117–18
  Wyschogrod's discussion of, 82–84, 87–88
Pentecost, community of interpretation and, 101–2
people of God
  Jews and Christians as, 95–99
  Torah given to, 111–13
personhood, Western concepts of, 53–57
Peter, sermons of, 107–8
phenomenology, Spirit of God and, 153–56
postliberal theology, 5–6
post-supersessionistic theology
  antinomianism in Christian hermeneutics and, 140–44
  body ontology and, 33–58
  dilute incarnationism and, 91–93
  eschato-pneumatological ontology and, 146–72
  historiography of, 5–7
  Holy Spirit and, 169–71
  Jenson's trinitarianism and, 8–11, 30–32
  Judaisim and, 1
  temporal actualistic ontology and, 13–32
predestination, Barth on, 14–17
pretemporal reality, Jenson's rejection of, 107–11
Protestantism
  Ecclesial body theology and, 49–53
  post-supersessionistic theology and, 5–7
"psychological" understanding of God, 55–57

A Rabbi Talks with Jesus (Neusner), 114–16
rabbinic Judaisim, 94–97
Ratzinger, Cardinal. *See* Benedict XVI (Pope)
reality in language, Bultmann school and, 122
resurrection
  deity of Jesus Christ and, 108–11
  eschato-pneumatological ontology and, 147–48

Subject Index

eternal generation and election and, 28–30
of Israel, Holy Spirit and, 169–71
Pannenberg's discussion of, 149–53
tradition history of Israel and, 138–39

salvation theology, community of the Holy Spirit and, 101–2
second hypostasis, Jenson's trinitarian theology and, 55–57
self-identity, in Judaism, 62
self-repetition of God, Barth's discussion of, 18–19
self-speech of God, 35–40, 125
"Servant Songs" (Isaiah), 108
Shekinah phenomena, 109–11
speculative theology, Jenson's concern with, 17–18
supersessionism
  antinomianism and, 141–44
  in Old Testament, 47n56
Systematic Theology (Jenson), 59, 90, 96
  deity of Jesus in, 109–11
  Jewish and Christian paths to kingdom of God in, 102–4

Tanakh, 94
  Christian consideration of, 102, 175
  Wyschogrod's discussion of, 81–82
Temple Mount, God's presence on, 67–72
temple of the Holy Spirit, 100–102
temporality
  Eucharistic body and, 45–48
  language and, 128–31
  Pannenberg's discussion of, 149–53
  recursive temporality, Jenson's discussion of, 165–71
  resurrection and eternal election/generation and, 28–30
  tradition history of Israel and, 135–37
Tetragrammaton, 7–8
theological exegesis, Christological body and, 37–40

theosis, Eastern Orthodox doctrine of, 51–53, 58
  Jenson's adoption of, 91–93, 117–18
Thomistic tradition, 7–8
Torah
  bearer of, 79–80
  belief in and practice of, 116–18
  Christian view of, 80–84, 111–18
  hermeneutical ontology and, 144–45, 174
  Jesus as, 113–19
  Jewish identity and, 74, 78–84, 87–88, 111–18
  New Testament teaching of, 62
  tradition history in Israel and, 140–43
totus Christus, doctrine of, 58, 176–77
  Augustine's discussion of, 158
  Christological body and, 100
  gentile nations and, 160–61
  hermeneutical ontology and, 144
  Israel and, 93
  Spirit of God and, 165
"Toward a Christian Doctrine of Israel" (Jenson), 90
"Toward a Christian Theology of Judaism" (Jenson), 90
tradition history of Israel, church's hermeneutic and, 131–39
transubstantiation, Eucharistic body and, 40–48
Trinitarian theology
  of Barth, 2–3
  body theology and communion in, 53–57
  deity of Jesus and, 106–11
  God as bodily being in, 35–40
  Judaism and, 1, 173–77
  ontology of, 10–12, 173
  resurrection and eternal election/generation, 28–30, 137n94
  self-repetition of God and, 18–19
  Spirit of God and, 153–56

universality, particularity and, 150n15
urgeschichte, human history and, 22–24

utterance, Jenson's discussion of, 129–31

Visible Word (Jenson), 35

The Way of Language (Heidegger), 127
"What Kind of God Can Make a Covenant?" (Jenson), 90
will, doctrine of God and, 16–17
word-event
  in church's canonical hermeneutic, God as, 138–39
  Ebeling's concept of, 123
  Heidegger's word-event of being and, 126–28
Word of God
  Bultman's concept of event in, 121
  content and material in, 129–31
  God as bodily being and, 35–40
  hermeneutical ontology and, 11–12, 119–20
  Jesus as, 105–11, 156–61
  Logos concepts and, 161
  Torah as, 113–18
The Writings of the New Testament (Johnson), 116n144
Wyschogrod, Michael
  on aspects of Jewish identity, 72–78, 115
  on Christianity, 62–78
  on Christian missional approach to Jews, 98–99
  on deity of Jesus Christ, 104–11
  incarnational doctrine and, 62–78, 144n121
  Jenson and, 9–11, 31, 59–88, 89–119, 174
  on Jewish rediscovery of Christianity, 84–86
  theology of Israel and, 59–88
  on Torah and Jewish identity, 74, 78–84

Zwinglian Christology, 43–48

www.ingramcontent.com/pod-product-compliance
Lightning Source LLC
Chambersburg PA
CBHW051740230426
43670CB00012B/2092